Medieval Academy Reprints for Teaching

Christopher Dawson

MISSION TO ASIA

Published by University of Toronto Press
Toronto Buffalo London
in association with the Medieval Academy of America

© Medieval Academy of America 1980
Printed in the United States of America
ISBN 0-8020-6436-1
Reprinted 1987, 1992

First published by Sheed and Ward Ltd, London, in 1955, as *The Mongol Mission*.
Reprinted in 1966 by Harper and Row, Publishers, Incorporated, as *Mission
to Asia: Narratives and Letters of the Franciscan Missionaries in Mongolia
and China in the Thirteenth and Fourteenth Centuries*, translated by a
nun of Stanbrook Abbey, edited and with an introduction by Christopher
Dawson.
This edition reprinted from the 1966 Harper Torchbook edition by arrangement with Harper and Row, Publishers, Incorporated, and by permission of
Sheed and Ward Ltd.

Canadian Cataloguing in Publication Data

Mission to Asia

(Medieval Academy reprints for teaching; 8)
Originally published in 1955 under the title: The
Mongol mission.
Reprint ed. of: New York: Harper & Row, 1966.
Includes bibliographical references and index.
ISBN 0-8020-6436-1

1. Mongols – History. 2. Missionaries – Asia.
3. Asia – Description and travel. I. Dawson,
Christopher, 1889–1970. II. Medieval Academy of
America. III. Title: The Mongol mission. IV. Series.

DS6.D3 1980   915.1'7'04   C81-001508-0

CONTENTS

INTRODUCTION

THE narratives by John of Plano Carpini and William of Rubruck of their journeys to Mongolia in the middle of the thirteenth century differ from the majority of works in this series. The authors were not canonized saints or *beati* and their travels were not missionary journeys in the strict sense, but were more of the nature of political embassies. Nevertheless they were servants of Christendom as few men have been. They endured all the hardships of which St. Paul speaks, in an entirely selfless devotion to the service of Christendom. They were, moreover, disciples of St. Francis of the first generation who possessed the genuine Franciscan spirit of simplicity and poverty and self-abnegation. But above all they give an absolutely first-hand authentic account of the first contact between Western Christendom and the Far East, and this at the moment when the whole oriental world from Korea to Hungary was being turned upside down and remade by one of the greatest catastrophes in the history of the world.

I. THE RELATION OF EUROPE TO ASIA: THE TWO EUROPES AND THE TWO ASIAS

To understand these events we must go back a long way in history. The ancient civilizations were oases in a wilderness of barbarism. It was only gradually that these oases were connected with one another by a common culture and became an *oecumene*, an *orbis terrarum*, a civilized world. The world from which we came is the *orbis terrarum* of the Mediterranean lands, which attained political unification in the Roman Empire in the first century B.C. At the other end of the old world a similar unity was constituted by China—the Middle Kingdom—which attained political unity much earlier than the West, though later than the Hellenistic world (i.e. in 216 B.C.). Similarly in Southern Asia a unity of the same kind was formed in India and extended its influence to the South-East to Cambodia and Java; but this cultural unity never achieved political unification. Finally between India and the Roman Empire there was the civilization of Persia which was in origin the oasis culture of the Iranian plateau but which tended to expand at the expense of the Indian civilization in the East and the Roman Hellenistic civilization to the West. To the north of this chain of oasis civilizations from the Roman frontiers to the Great Wall of China there stretched for thousands of miles the outer wilderness " like the ocean sea " as William of Rubruck says, which was the domain of the barbarians. Each of the oasis civilizations had its own barbarian neighbours who preyed upon it or were dominated by it, until eventually they became almost domesticated. But at intervals some change would take place in the depth of the wilderness and a new flood of barbarism would come sweeping in from the steppes, driving the half-civilized barbarians before it and piling up against the defences of the settled civilizations until they broke. Perhaps the most famous of these cataclysms was the barbarian invasion of the fourth century, when the Huns coming from the outer steppes drove the Goths before them out of the Russian steppes across the Danube and thus brought about the downfall of the Roman Empire. And a similar movement was in process at the same time in the Far East when the Eastern Huns overran Northern China, and somewhat later in India when the so-called White Huns conquered Northern India. Such moments have occurred again and again throughout the course of history and no civilization has ever been strong enough to be immune from their effects. After the Huns came the Avars, and after the Avars the Bulgars, and after the Bulgars the Magyars, and after the Magyars the Turks. And while the civilizations are by their nature highly differentiated and naturally incapable of combining for their material defence, the peoples of the steppe are relatively undifferentiated and their culture changes so little through the centuries that the description which Ammianus Marcellinus[1] gives of the Huns is almost inter-

[1] Ammianus Marcellinus, Book XXXI, ii.

changeable with that which Matthew Paris gives of the Mongols nine hundred years later.

The regular character of these cycles of invasion has suggested that there is some common factor behind them, and many years ago the theory was put forward by Professor Ellsworth Hunting-don and others that they were due to the climatic conditions which have caused the desiccation of Central Asia, so that if we had the necessary data it would be possible to establish an exact concord-ance between the hygrometric and ethnological change. But although there is no doubt that the desert has been advancing in Central Asia and that this exerts a continual pressure on the peoples of the steppe, it is impossible to make the climatic factor the exclusive cause of historical change. The evidence seems rather to suggest that the decisive factors are human ones; on the one side the weakening of the resistance of the oasis cultures from political causes, and, on the other, the periodical appearance among the barbarians of some military leader who could unite the barbarians in a movement of expansion and conquest. And when-ever such a leader appeared he found an inexhaustible reserve of military material in the nomad horsemen of the steppes, who were the finest light cavalry in the world. When such a movement had started, it grew irresistibly like an avalanche, since, as each new tribe was conquered, its forces were added to the original nucleus. Now in almost every case we find that the original starting point of the movement was in North-Western Mongolia, the land beyond the steppes. This forms a kind of oasis of barbarian culture, shut off by the great ranges of the Altai and Khingan Mountains from the rest of Inner Asia. It was here that all the great nomad empires of Asia had their centre, from the Huns in the third century B.C. to the East Turks and the Uighurs in the early Middle Ages and finally to the Mongols in the thirteenth century. And it is remark-able that all these four empires had their capitals within a few miles of one another in the valley of the Upper Orkhon—where the tombs and inscriptions of the early Turkish and Uighur Khans have been discovered.

Thus the empires of the steppes were never quite as barbarous as their victims in the civilized world believed. They had their own ancient traditions of culture which were never entirely lost in spite of all the changes of race and language. Already at the dawn of the Christian era, the tombs of the Hun princes which were discovered in 1924 at Noin Ula near Urga show an extraordinarily wide range of cultural contacts, not only with China but with Iran and Syria and Eastern Europe. At a later period the great East Turkish inscriptions of Kocho-Tsaidam near Karakorum, dating from the eighth century, are works of high literary quality which testify to the existence of a strong and original type of culture. Finally, during the same century, the Uighurs, who replaced the East Turks as the ruling power in Mongolia, adopted Manicheanism as their state religion and became a sedentary people, so that in their own words: " This land of barbarous customs, smoking with blood, was transformed into a vegetarian state, and this land of slaughter became a land devoted to good works".[1]

A pacific culture of this kind could not maintain itself in Outer Mongolia and the Uighurs were forced to retreat to the oases of Turfan and Hami where they remained throughout the Middle Ages. But they handed on their cultural tradition to their successors in Outer Mongolia, like the Kerait and the Naiman, and these in turn exercised a civilizing influence on the still more primitive Mongols who were later comers in Mongolia and had probably originated in the forest country north and east of Lake Baikal.

Thus, when Chingis Khan united all the peoples of Mongolia, both Mongol and Turk, and led them east and west to conquer the world, he inherited a tradition of culture as well as a tradition of empire, and employed the more civilized Kerait and Uighur Turks in the organization and administration of his empire.[2] At the same time he had inherited the highly specialized military tradition of the old warrior peoples of the steppes, who had learnt to manoeuvre great masses of cavalry with a speed and discipline which was unknown to the heavy armoured chivalry of the West. Where he differed from his predecessors was in the extraordinary speed and fury of his attack.

---

[1] From the Uighur inscription at Kara-Balsaghun quoted by Grousset, *L'Empire des Steppes*, p. 174.

[2] Thus e.g. the Mongols adopted the Uighur script for writing their language.

Temuchin, as Chingis was originally called, was born, probably in 1167, the son of a Mongol chief of royal descent but of little power, who was killed by the Tartars when his son was still a child. After an adventurous and hazardous youth, he became the vassal of Togrul, the Khan of the Kerait, the Christian tribe who at that time were the dominant power in Outer Mongolia. In alliance with the Kerait, he conquered many of the neighbouring Mongol tribes and eventually destroyed his hereditary enemies, the Tartars, who occupied Eastern Mongolia. Finally in 1203 he broke with his suzerain, Togrul, and brought the Kerait under his rule. In the following year he defeated the Naiman, who were the dominant people in Western Mongolia, and finally, in a great assembly or Kuriltay held on the River Onon in 1206, he was proclaimed Emperor under the name of Chingis Khan and set out on his career of world conquest.

In 1211 he began the great war with Northern China, which was then ruled by the Manchu people, known as the Chin, a war which was to last with brief interruptions for twenty years. The turning point was however reached as early as 1215 with the capture of Peking and the extension of Mongol rule over most of north China and Manchuria. After the fall of Peking, Chingis Khan turned his arms against the West and subdued the Kara Khitayan kingdom in Turkestan. This brought him into direct contact with the greatest Moslem power in Central Asia, the empire of Khorezm or Khiva. The campaign which followed from 1214 to 1222 was one of the most astounding feats of arms recorded in history. After totally destroying the Khorezmian empire, he pursued the defeated enemy across the Hindu Kush into North-West India, while at the same time he sent another army under his lieutenants Jebe and Subutay on a great raid round the south end of the Caspian, through Georgia, across the Caucasus, into south Russia, so that the great double campaign of 1222–3 extended from the Indus almost to the Dnieper. Even this did not exhaust his energies. For in 1226 he turned once more to the East, and was engaged in the destruction of the Tibetan kingdom of Tangut, which had its centre in Kansu, when he died in 1227.

In spite of the primitive means at his disposal, it is possible that he succeeded in destroying a larger portion of the human race than any modern expert in total warfare. Within a dozen years from the opening of his first campaign against China, the Mongol armies had reached the Pacific, the Indus and the Black Sea and had destroyed many of the greatest cities in India. For Europe especially the shock was overwhelming. For in the thirteenth century the West had mastered its own barbarians and was now pushing forward the frontiers of Christendom against Islam, which was the only enemy that it still feared. Consequently the sudden appearance of the Mongols was a bolt from the blue. Suddenly, without the least warning, an army of unknown barbarians appeared, in the spring of 1222, on the south-eastern borders of Russia. In the words of a Russian chronicler: "For our sins, unknown tribes came, none knows who they are or whence they came—nor what their language is, nor of what race they are nor what their faith is—God alone knows who they are and whence they came out."[1] The Russian princes went to the aid of their barbarian neighbours, the Cumans or Kypchak Turks, and there was a great battle on the River Kalka in the southern steppe, close to the Sea of Azov. The Russians and their allies were defeated and the Prince of Kiev and the other princes who surrendered were laid under boards and suffocated while the Mongols feasted on top. "This evil happened on May 31st, St. Jeremy's day. And the Tartars turned back from the river Dnieper, and we know not whence they came, nor where they hid themselves again. God knows whence He fetched them against us for our sins."[2]

Nothing more was heard of them for fifteen years. From the Russian point of view, it was an isolated raid of unknown savages. They did not know that behind those events there was the organizing mind of the great Chingis Khan, who had already unified Central Asia and conquered Northern China and was at that moment destroying the great Moslem civilization of Eastern Iran. It was not until after the death of Chingis Khan that Europe heard of the Mongols again. Then at last in 1236–7 the main

---

[1] *The Chronicle of Novgorod*, Eng. trans. Camden Society, 1914, p. 64.
[2] *Ibid.*, p. 66.

Mongol armies moved against the West under the command of Batu and Subutay. In December 1237 the Tartars sent envoys to Riazan—"a woman, a sorceress and two men with her", demanding from them "one-tenth of everything, of men and princes and horses—of everything one-tenth".[1] And when the Russian princes refused these terms, they proceeded methodically to invest and destroy the Russian cities one by one—Riazan and Moscow, Suzdal and Vladimir, Yaroslav and Tver—massacring the inhabitants without distinction of age and sex. In the course of little more than two months the whole of Central and Northern Russia to within sixty miles of Novgorod was a shambles.

Again there was a pause for more than two years while the Mongols secured their hold on the lands between the Volga and the Dnieper by the systematic slaughter of the inhabitants. When the Friars travelled through the country a few years later, they passed in the track of this great killing and found "many skulls and bones of dead men lying on the ground". From the Dnieper to the Oxus they travelled through an empty land where the cities were destroyed and they saw the "bones of dead men lying on the ground like dung".[2]

At last in the winter of 1240–1 the Mongols were ready for their last advance against the West. Kiev, the mother of Russian cities, was taken and destroyed on December 6th, and thence the army passed onwards to conquer the West. Their right wing passed through Galicia into Poland and met and defeated the combined forces of the Poles and the Germans at Legnica (Liegnitz) in Silesia on April 9th, 1241. At the same time the main army under Batu and Subutay entered Moravia and Hungary and destroyed the Magyar army at Mohi near Buda on April 11th. Hungary was occupied for more than a year and devastated as thoroughly as Southern Russia. A Mongol army even followed the flight of the King of Hungary into Dalmatia and destroyed Cattaro in the spring of 1242, while another detachment rode north into Austria as far as Klosterneuburg. Fortunately for Europe the death of the great Khan Ugedey in December 1241, and the dissensions between the

[1] *The Chronicle of Novgorod*, Eng. trans. Camden Society, 1914, p. 81.
[2] See p. 58 *infra*.

Mongol leaders in the West, Batu and Guyuk and Buri, caused the withdrawal of the Mongol armies, at least as far as Russia, in 1242. But the Western princes were by now alive to their imminent peril and from 1242 onwards they began to make belated attempts to organize measures of defence.

The first news of the peril reached Western Europe from widely different sources. Perhaps the most unexpected were the envoys from the Ismailians of Syria—better known as the Assassins— who in 1238 brought proposals to the kings of France and England for a grand alliance of Christians and Moslems against the common enemies of civilization. But they met with little sympathy. The attitude of the Westerners before they knew what was coming was brutally expressed by the Bishop of Winchester to Henry III, "Let these dogs destroy one another and be utterly exterminated and then we shall see the universal Catholic Church founded on their ruins and there will be one fold and one shepherd".[1]

Nevertheless, in spite of this arrogance in high places, there was a widespread feeling of disquiet, for in the same year—1238— Matthew Paris records that there was a glut of herrings at Yarmouth owing to the absence of the German fish merchants, who stayed at home for fear of the Tartars. And during the following years the news of disaster in the East and the desperate appeals from Christian rulers such as the Queen of Georgia and the Prince of Galicia aroused both the Pope and the Emperor to the gravity of the situation.[2] Unfortunately at this moment Western Christendom was split in two by the war between Frederick II and the Papacy. Indeed, in the letter which the Emperor wrote to Henry II and Louis IX, proposing common action against the Tartars, he complains that the crusade which should have been preached against the infidel had been turned by the Pope against the Empire and that the Tartars had been encouraged to attack Christendom by their knowledge of its divided and defenceless state.[3] As we have seen, the death of Ugedey Khan in December 1241 and the rivalry of the Mongol princes distracted their attention from the

[1] Matthew Paris, *Chron. Maj.*, iv, 112, 119.
[2] MGH, *Epist. saec. xiii e regestis P.R.* i, 765, 796, 821–3, 826.
[3] *op. cit.*, ii, 2, 102, 105.

West to the centre of the Empire. But Batu remained encamped on the Volga. Christian Russia had become a province of the Mongol Empire and there was nothing to prevent a further onslaught on the West as soon as the question of succession had been decided.

II. THE MISSION OF JOHN OF PLANO CARPINI (1245–7)

This was recognized by the new Pope, Innocent IV, and the first of the missions described in this volume was despatched by him in 1245 to avert the threatened danger.

For this purpose he chose two Franciscans, Lawrence of Portugal and John of Plano Carpini. "Men proved by years of regular observance and well versed in Holy Scripture, for we believed that they would be of greater help to you, seeing that they follow the humility of our Saviour. If we had thought that ecclesiastical prelates or other powerful men would be more profitable and more acceptable to you we would have sent them." Thus Innocent IV concludes the first of the two bulls to the Emperor of the Tartars, which will be found on pp. 73–6 of this volume, and it is difficult to say whether his words are an expression of naïve simplicity or statesmanlike imagination. Perhaps the Mongol princes were no less disconcerted by these barefooted emissaries of the lord of the Christian world than were the Russian princes by the sorceress who brought the Tartar ultimatum to Riazan in 1237. At least we cannot fail to be impressed by the courage of this disciple of St. Francis who, at the age of sixty-five, without any knowledge of oriental languages or any resource except his faith, embarked on this tremendous journey to the heart of the barbarian world. It is true that John of Plano Carpini was familiar with Northern Europe; and his companion, Benedict the Pole, who joined him at Breslau, had contacts with the Christian princes of Eastern Europe, Wenceslas of Bohemia, Boleslas of Silesia, Daniel of Galicia and Vasilko of Volhynia. But the information that they gave him cannot have been reassuring. As he writes in his prologue: "We feared that we might be killed by the Tartars or other people, or imprisoned for life, or afflicted with hunger, thirst, cold, heat, injuries and exceeding great trials almost beyond our powers of endurance—all of which with the exception of death and imprisonment for life fell to our lot in various ways in a much greater degree than we had conceived beforehand."

After spending the greater part of the winter in Poland and Galicia, they set out into the steppe "not knowing whether they were going to death or life" at the beginning of Lent, 1240, and immediately fell in with the Tartar outposts, who "came rushing upon us in a horrible manner, wanting to know what kind of men we were". But at least they met with no obstruction; the outpost despatched them to his commander "Corenza", who sent them to Sartak, who sent them on without delay to his father the great Batu, the ruler of the Western Ulus who held his camp on the lower Volga. Even here they remained only a few days, for Batu decided that they should be sent to the Great Khan Guyuk himself, in time to be present at the inauguration ceremony at the Golden Horde. They were forced to ride at top speed with five or six relays of horses every day. "We were so weak we could hardly ride. During the whole of that Lent our food had been nothing but millet with water and salt, and it was the same on other fast days, and we had nothing to drink except snow melted in a kettle."[1] And so they continued month after month for thousands of miles through a desert land without rest or intermission. It would have been an ordeal for the toughest of horsemen, but for an elderly clergyman who was extremely fat and in poor health, it is one of the most remarkable feats of physical endurance on record.

Travelling through Central Asia north of the Caspian and the Sea of Aral, they reached the camp of Orda, the elder brother of Batu, in the region of Lake Ala Kul in Dzungaria, at midsummer, and after a single day's rest they went on faster than ever, "rising early and travelling until night without eating anything and often we came so late to our lodgings that we had not time to eat that night, but were given in the morning the food we should have eaten the previous night".[2] Thanks to this relentless haste they

[1] See pp. 57-8.   [2] See pp. 60-1.

arrived at the camp of Guyuk near Karakorum on July 22nd in time to be present at the great assembly at which Guyuk was proclaimed and enthroned as Great Khan. And thus we have a firsthand record by a Western observer of this historic occasion which had brought together not only the leaders of the Mongols but the representatives of all the subject peoples of the Empire from Russia and Georgia to Manchuria and China.

Although their reception seemed churlish enough to the Friars, it is clear that their coming was welcome, and that the Mongols were anxious to establish relations with the great priest who ruled the Christians of the Far West. Their motives, however, are not so clear and it is possible that John of Plano Carpini was right in believing that a great campaign was being planned against the West and that their main object was to prepare the way for a formal offer of submission. However this may be, the Friars remained firm in their refusal to take back the Mongol envoys with them and finally on November 17th they were dismissed with the Khan's letter to the Pope, which we still possess and of which a translation is given below. They travelled back over the open steppes all through the winter with incredible hardships, sleeping in the snow "save when in the open plain when there were no trees we could scrape a place with our feet".

They reached Batu's camp on the Volga on the feast of the Ascension (May 9th, 1247), and after staying there a month, they at last received safe conducts for their return to Kiev. "We reached Kiev fifteen days before the feast of St. John the Baptist, and the men of Kiev when they heard of our arrival came out to meet us rejoicing and congratulating us as if we had risen from the dead, and so they did throughout Russia, Poland and Bohemia." And when Daniel of Galicia and his brother Vasilko had heard their account of the embassy, after taking council with their bishops, they sent their own letters to the Pope by the Friars, accepting his supremacy and that of the Roman Church. This was the first reunion between the Russians and the Western Church, and since Daniel at this time was the most powerful of the remaining Russian princes, it was perhaps the only positive and concrete result of this heroic venture.

Meanwhile Mongol policy was at a standstill owing to the strained relations between the Great Khan and his cousin Batu. There had been a bitter quarrel between the two princes during the invasion of Hungary five years earlier and it was impossible to undertake any large-scale expedition to the West so long as this issue was undecided. Thus what actually happened was not a war between the Mongols and the West but a breach between the two leading branches of the family of Chingis Khan—the house of Ugedey represented by Guyuk, and the house of Juchi represented by Batu. Civil war was only averted by the death of the Great Khan under very suspicious circumstances at the moment when Batu was advancing to meet him in Central Asia, and during the following three years (1248–51) Batu succeeded in bringing about the fall of the house of Ugedey and the election of his own candidate, Mongka the son of Tuluy, to be the supreme Khan.

III. The Missions of the Dominicans, Ascelin and Andrew
     of Longjumeau

It is possible that this change of government and the semi-independent position which Batu had achieved in the West saved Europe from further peril. For with the coming of the new dynasty, the drive of Mongol aggression turned southwards so that the existence of Islam rather than that of Christendom was endangered.

But the Christian West could not know this. Nothing could be more alarming than the report of John of Plano Carpini or more menacing than the letter of the Great Khan to the great Pope. And the result of the second mission which Innocent IV sent two years later was at first even more discouraging. This time the envoys were Dominicans,[1] Fr. Ascelin, Simon of Tournai and three others, and they were ordered to visit the camp of the nearest Mongol army on the frontier of Asia Minor and to demand the

[1] There is some obscurity about the relation of this mission of 1247 to the earlier Franciscan one. Lawrence of Portugal, the Franciscan who was charged with the original mission, does not seem to have visited the Mongols. But we are told that in 1247 he was sent by the Pope as legate to Asia Minor, and it was in this year that the mission of Ascelin and his companions to the Mongol leader in Asia Minor took place.

cessation of hostilities against Christendom. Ascelin reached the camp of Baiju, west of the Caspian Sea, on May 24th, 1247, but as he refused the usual act of homage and behaved in a somewhat uncompromising manner he met with a very harsh reception, so that at one moment the exasperated Mongol threatened to have them all executed. The situation seems to have changed with the coming of a higher officer, Aljigiday, the envoy of the Great Khan, who realized the importance of establishing relations with the Christians of the West. Accordingly Ascelin was sent back with an answer similar to that which had already been brought by John of Plano Carpini, together with two Mongol envoys—one of them, Sargis or Sergius, a Christian—who were received by Pope Innocent IV in Italy in the following year—1248. At the same time Aljigiday took steps to establish friendly relations with St. Louis, who had set out on his crusade against Egypt. Aljigiday's envoys, David and Mark, met King Louis in Cyprus and delivered a letter which declared that the Great Khan intended to protect all Christians, Latin and Greek, Armenian, Nestorian and Jacobite, and offered his help against the Saracens for the recovery of Jerusalem.

The fact that Guyuk Khan was no longer alive and that the house of Ugedey was tottering to its fall deprived this embassy of real authority, but the King of France could not realize this and he was naturally overjoyed to hear such "good and gracious words" from the East, which seemed to justify all that the legends of Prester John had promised. In reply he sent back with the Mongol envoys the most important mission that Christendom had sent hitherto. It was led by a Dominican, Andrew of Longjumeau, who knew Persian and had already visited the camp of Baiju, apparently as a member of Br. Ascelin's mission. With him went two other Dominicans, two clerks and two sergeants-at-arms, together with rich presents—above all a wonderful tent-chapel of scarlet cloth in which all the mysteries of the Christian faith were depicted for the instruction of the Tartars. This is the embassy which is described at some length by Joinville and other contemporary historians, so that it seems to have made more impression on public opinion than either of the Franciscan missions recorded in this volume. The envoys set out from Antioch early in 1248, "and from Antioch it took them a full year, riding ten leagues a day, to reach the great Khan of the Tartars. And they found all the land subject to the Tartars and many cities that they had destroyed and great heaps of dead men's bones". Nevertheless the journey of Andrew and his companions was not so long as that of the two Franciscan missions, since the Regent, Ogul Gamish, the widow of Guyuk Khan, was not in Mongolia but held her court on the River Imil south-east of Lake Balkash, at the point which John of Plano Carpini speaks of as "the first orda of the Emperor".

The Regent received the embassy in the normal Mongol and Chinese fashion as an act of homage and their presents as tribute, but she seems to have treated them honourably enough and sent them back with gifts and the remarkable answer recorded by Joinville as follows:

"Peace is good; for when a country is at peace those who go on four feet eat the grass in peace, and those who go on two feet till the ground, from which good things come, in peace.

"This we send you for a warning, for you cannot have peace if you are not at peace with us. Prester John rose against us, and such and such kings (giving the names of many) and all we have put to the sword. We bid you, then, every year to send us of your gold and of your silver so much as may win you our friendship. If you do not do this we shall destroy you and your people, as we have done to those we have named."[1]

St. Louis was naturally disappointed with the results of this mission, and Joinville says that he greatly repented having sent it. Nevertheless the accounts that he had received of the existence of a large Christian population in "Tartary" were not altogether discouraging, and these were confirmed by the reports of the Armenian missions led by the Constable of Armenia, Sempad, who was the brother of King Hethum I and the brother-in-law of the King of Cyprus.

The little kingdom of Cilician Armenia formed a valuable link between the crusading states of Syria and the interior of Asia,

[1] Joinville, *Life of St. Louis*, trans. R. Hague (Sheed and Ward), pp. 149.

owing to its strategic position on the highway from Antioch and Syria to Asia Minor and the Caspian. The coming of the Mongols had been a godsend to the Armenians, since it had delivered them from the continual threat of the Seljuk sultans of Iconium, and after the defeat of the latter by Baiju in 1243, King Hethum of Armenia had become a loyal and favoured vassal of the Great Khan. The embassy of Sempad the Constable took place in 1247 and 1248, so that it coincided with those of Ascelin and Andrew of Longjumeau, and the letter which he wrote from Samarkand in February 1248 to his brother-in-law in Cyprus stressed the importance of the Christian element among the Mongols. From these sources St. Louis learnt that Sartak, the son of Batu, was himself a Christian, and this fact or report encouraged the French King to send a further mission of a more definitely religious character than that of Andrew of Longjumeau to establish relations with the Christians in Central Asia.

IV. THE MISSION OF BROTHER WILLIAM OF RUBRUCK

This is the mission of the Franciscan William of Rubruck, which forms the greater part of the present volume and provides the fullest and most authentic information on the Mongol Empire in its pre-Chinese phase that we possess. The mission consisted of two Franciscans, William of Rubruck and Bartholomew of Cremona, a clerk named Gosset who was in charge of the King's presents to the Khan, and an interpreter or dragoman—"turgemannus"—called Homo Dei (i.e. Abdullah) who proved inefficient and unreliable.

In contrast to the earlier missions, this one was purely religious in character, for though they carried letters from St. Louis to Sartak, they were careful to insist that they were not ambassadors but men of religion whose sole work was "to preach the work of God and to instruct men to live by His will".

In many respects William of Rubruck was better equipped for his mission than John of Plano Carpini had been. Apart from the knowledge already acquired from the earlier missions, he had the great advantage of beginning his journey from the East, from

the court of St. Louis at Acre, where he was in touch with
Armenians, Syrians and Greeks, so that he was able to have his
letters of credence translated into Persian (or "Arabic" as he calls
it) and Syrian. Instead of entering the Mongol world through
the Iron Curtain of Eastern Europe and Russia, he travelled by
the old highway to Central Asia through Constantinople and the
Crimea, and at Constantinople he was able to get further information and letters of safe conduct from the Emperor Baldwin II
to the commander of the Mongol outposts. The party left
Constantinople on May 7th for Sudak (Soldaia), the great merchant
port in the Crimea which was the terminus of the land route to
Russia and Asia. They left Sudak on June 1st and reached the
Tartar outposts on the third day. "And when I came among
them," writes Friar William, "it seemed to me, indeed, as if I
were entering another world." From this point Brother William's
journey and his experiences correspond very closely with those
of Brother John of Plano Carpini eight years before. Both of
them went to the great camp of Batu on the Volga, the centre
of Mongol power in the West. Both were sent on by Batu to
the court of the Great Khan in Mongolia and both experienced
the same intense hardships in their travel through the steppes
and the same difficulties and misunderstandings in their dealings
with the arrogant Mongol chiefs and their greedy and unscru-
pulous underlings. Nevertheless the contents and manner of the
two narratives are very different. Brother John was chiefly concerned to make a full report to the Pope on the Mongols and
their empire considered as an immediate danger to Christendom,
and with special reference to their methods of making war and
how their attacks could best be met. Brother William's book
(with the exception of the nine short introductory chapters which
deal with Mongol manners and customs) is a straightforward
account of his journey and his personal experiences in full detail.
He was an exceptionally observant man with the temperament
and eye of an artist. "In fact," he says himself, "I would have
made you" (St. Louis) "pictures of everything if I only knew how
to paint."

The result is that he has written one of the most living and moving narratives in the whole literature of travel, even more direct and convincing than that of Marco Polo in his own time or Huc and Gabet in the nineteenth century. In spite of his writing in a "learned" language, we still see sharp and clear through his eyes the scene when the Friars at last came before the terrible Batu, on his high seat "long and wide like a couch", with his lady beside him. "We stood there in our habits, barefooted and heads uncovered, and we were a great gazing-stock for their eyes. . . . So we stood there before him for the space of a *Miserere mei Deus* and they all kept the deepest silence." We see the endless drinking parties at Karakorum and the men of every race and religion who met together there. We have a most vivid account of the great disputation held between the representatives of the three religions, Christians, Moslems and Buddhists. And finally we have the account of his last meeting with the Great Khan himself at Pentecost, which is surely one of the most remarkable interviews in history.

V. THE MONGOLS AND CHRISTENDOM

Here, we feel, we are standing at one of the great crossroads of history. For the new world-empire which stretched from the Pacific to the Black Sea and the Baltic and which ruled over Confucianists and Buddhists and Moslems and Christians was still uncommitted to any particular religion and culture. The primitive Shamanism of the Mongols was incapable of providing any principle of spiritual unity, just as their original tribal organization provided no basis for an imperial administration.[1] Nevertheless the Great Khans, in spite of their lack of culture, were fully aware of the importance of the religious factor and followed a broad policy of general toleration. Chingis Khan himself laid down as part of his law that all religions were to be respected

[1] Nevertheless we must not underestimate the persistence and strength of this primitive religious tradition. It seems clear from Marco Polo's discussion with Kubilay Khan that the latter adhered to Buddhism in a Shamanist spirit, and even in our own time (in 1913), Miss Czaplica has described how a Siberian of thoroughly European ancestry and Nordic type preferred the spiritual ministrations of the local Tungus Shaman to that of the Russian priest, on the ground that the latter could not master the local spirits in the way the Shaman did (Czaplica, *My Siberian Year*, pp. 190–193).

without favouritism and that the priests and holy men were to be
treated with deference, a principle to which all his descendants
adhered faithfully both in the East and the West for successive
generations.[1]

This attitude is probably due to the fact that Mongolia and
Turkestan were the meeting place of the world religions, and the
Mongols themselves as newcomers found Buddhism and Christianity and Manicheism and Mohammedanism already established
among the peoples from whom they acquired the rudiments of
civilization. The oldest and most civilized people of Mongolia,
the Uighur Turks, had adopted Manicheism when they were
the ruling people of Mongolia in the eighth and ninth centuries,
and now that they had withdrawn south of the Gobi to the oases
of Turfan and Hami they had become Buddhist and Christian.
Their successors in Western Mongolia, the Kerait and the Naiman,
who were most closely allied to the Mongols by culture and
political relations, were mainly Christian, as were also the Ongut
Turks on the northern frontier of China. The other ruling
peoples, the Kara Khitay or Khitan and the Jurjen or Chin, who
had been subjected to the influence of Chinese culture, were
Buddhist or Taoist, while the Western Turks, from Trans-
Oxiana to Asia Minor, were Moslems who came into the orbit of
Persian culture. Thus the position of Christianity in Mongolia
was relatively a strong one and offered even greater opportunities
for missionary activity than Western Christendom realized. Owing
to their intermarriages with the Kerait royal house many of the
wives and mothers of the Great Khans were Christians, including
some of the most influential of them all, like " Seroctan"[2] or
Soyorgatani, Baigi, the mother of Mongka, Kubilay and Hulagu
and the chief wife of Hulagu, Dokuz Khatun, who is described
by the Armenian chroniclers as a second St. Helena.

In the same way many of the leading Mongol officials under
the early Khans were Christians, like Chinkay, the Kerait

---

[1] "A singular conformity may be found," writes Gibbon, "between the
religious laws of Zingis Khan and of Mr. Locke"!

[2] Whom John of Plano Carpini describes as more renowned than any among
the Tartars except the mother of the Emperor and more powerful than any
except Batu.

chancellor of Guyuk Khan, who received John of Plano Carpini;
Bolgay, the chancellor of Mongka, who received William of
Rubruck; and Kitbuka, the Naiman lieutenant of Hulagu. It is
true that this Nestorian Christianity of Central Asia had been cut
off for centuries from the centres of Christian culture and William
of Rubruck's account of the Nestorian monks and clergy, mainly
Syrians, whom he met at the Mongol court, is a very unfavourable
one. Nevertheless this outlying province of Christendom
experienced a brief period of revival and expansion during the
Mongol period, which was due not only to the general Mongol
policy of toleration but still more to the fact that they were
determined to destroy the temporal power of Islam which they saw
as the main obstacle to Chingis Khan's idea of world empire.
Already while William of Rubruck was at Karakorum plans were
being laid by Mongka and his brother Hulagu for the destruction of the two leaders of the Moslem world—the Khalif of
Bagdad, the head of orthodox Islam, and the Grand Master of the
Assassins, who was the chief of the Ismailian or Shi'ite sect.

Later in the same year (1254), when King Hethum of Armenia
visited the Khan, he was informed of the projected expedition,
and received assurances from Mongka that the Mongols would
protect the Christians and their churches and would restore
Palestine and the Holy Places to the Christians. In fact Hulagu,
though he was himself a Buddhist, was genuinely favourable to
the Christians owing to the influence of his wife, the Kerait
princess Dokuz Khatun, who was devoted to her ancestral faith.
This princess, like so many of the ladies of the family of the
Mongol Khans, enjoyed great political influence. Indeed Rashid
al-Din, the official historian of the Mongols, states that Mongka
expressly charged his brother to consult her in every circumstance
and to follow her advice.

Consequently when in the autumn of 1257 the Mongol armies
advanced into Mesopotamia, after destroying the strongholds of
the Assassins which had hitherto been impregnable, the Christians
benefited by the great disaster that fell upon the Moslem world.

They hailed the fall of Baghdad and the destruction of the
Abbasid Khalifate, which took place in February 1258, as a just

retribution for the oppression that they had suffered for so many centuries. The Armenian chronicler Kirakos of Kantzag writes of the catastrophe in the spirit in which the Hebrew prophet described the fall of Nineveh. For five hundred and fifteen years the city had ruled all the nations and sucked the blood and treasure of the whole world. Now at length the measure of her iniquity was fulfilled and she was punished for all the blood she had shed and the evil she had done.[1]

Never had the prospects of Islam seemed darker than at this moment. All the Eastern Moslem sultanates west of the Indus had already been destroyed, and the Turks of Asia Minor had been forced to acknowledge the Mongol supremacy. Only Egypt remained, and after the fall of Baghdad Hulagu was determined to make an end of her. In the following year (1259) he advanced into Syria, capturing Martyropolis and Edessa and Harran, the home-lands of Syrian Christianity. In the following year Hulagu's Christian general, the Naiman Kitbuka, assisted by the King of Armenia and Bohemond of Antioch, captured Aleppo and Damascus, the two capitals of Moslem Syria. At this moment the whole future of the Middle East was at stake. The only remaining bulwark of Islam, the Mameluk sultanate of Egypt, was rich and possessed an efficient army, but it was an alien and artificial power controlled by foreign mercenaries and possessed no national roots, so that it could hardly have survived a combined push from the Mongols and the Franks in Syria. A Christian reconquest in the Near East, like that which was taking place at the same period in Andalusia, was by no means impossible. Rubruck remarks that not one-tenth of the inhabitants of Turkey were Moslems, almost all were Armenians and Greeks; and in the same way in Mesopotamia and Northern Syria the Syrian Christian element was still numerous.

In fact it was at this period that the Nestorian Church enjoyed its greatest prosperity and became for a time a real factor in world affairs. It enjoyed the favour not only of Hulagu and his successors Abaga and Argun, the Khans of Persia, but also of their suzerain Kubilay and his successors in China and the Far East. Under the

[1] Grousset, *Histoire des Croisades*, iii, p. 575.

patriarchate of Mar Denha (1265–81) its hierarchy was reorganized and extended from the Persian Gulf and the Indian Ocean to the Caspian and the Pacific. An archbishopric was established in 1275 at Kubilay's new capital of Khanbalik or Peking and churches were founded by Christian officials and merchants in many of the principal cities of China.

Nor were these friendly relations confined to the Nestorian Christians of the East. In the second half of the thirteenth century the Mongol Khans of Persia regarded the Christians of the West as their natural allies against Egypt and Islam and made a serious effort to establish diplomatic relations with them and to organize a common front in Syria. Thus the policy of St. Louis and the initiative of William of Rubruck at last bore fruit, and though Antioch, the strategic key to the Middle East, had fallen to Beybars in 1268, there was still a possibility of saving the crusading states in Syria with the help of the Mongols. Unfortunately St. Louis, who was now a dying man, allowed his last crusade to be diverted from Palestine to Tunis, perhaps owing to the sinister influence of his brother Charles of Anjou, who was intent on his selfish ambition to create a Mediterranean empire,[1] and Edward I of England was left with insufficient resources to carry on the tradition of the Palestinian crusade. He alone of the Western princes seems to have realized the importance of the Mongol alliance, and so long as he lived there was no cessation in the negotiations between the Mongols and the West. As soon as he arrived in Palestine in the early summer of 1271 he sent his envoys, Reginald Russel and John Parker, to Abaga and arrangements were made for a joint campaign against the Egyptians. Unfortunately at this moment Abaga was forced to turn his attention to Central Asia owing to the civil war that had arisen with Jagatay Khan of Turkestan, so that he was only able

---

[1] This is denied by Bréhier and Grousset (Hist. des Croisades, iii, 651–2) on the ground that the crusade interfered with Charles of Anjou's plans for an attack on the Byzantine Empire. And granted that Charles would have preferred an expedition against Constantinople, the conquest of Tunis was quite in accordance with the traditional policy of the Sicilian monarchy which had always aimed at the control of Tunisia. And Grousset fully recognizes the disastrous character of the decision, which he compares with the diversion of the Fourth Crusade from Egypt to the conquest of Constantinople.

to send a token force of Mongol horsemen to Syria. Nevertheless, as Grousset says, in spite of the lack of man-power which caused its failure, this crusade of Edward I was one of the most intelligently planned of all the later crusades, both from the strategic and the diplomatic point of view.[1]

In spite of the failure of Edward I's crusade, the Mongols continued to pursue negotiations for a Western alliance. In 1274 Abaga sent his envoys to the Council of Lyons, where they were present at the Act of Union between the Eastern and Western Churches which took place on July 6th. In 1277 he sent six envoys to England with apologies to Edward I for his failure to give adequate support to him when he was in Palestine. Finally in 1286 his son Argun Khan sent the most important of all the Mongol embassies to the West under the leadership of Rabban Sauma, a monk, who was the intimate friend of the Nestorian patriarch and in close relations with the Mongol court. We have a detailed account of this embassy in the contemporary biography of the patriarch Mar Yaballaha III, of which a Syriac version has been preserved,[2] and it provides a Mongol counterpart to William of Rubruck's narrative of his embassy from St. Louis to Mongka Khan.

Rabban Sauma, in spite of his Syriac name, was a Mongolian Turk, probably an Ongut, who had been born at Peking and who had come on pilgrimage with his fellow-countryman Rabban Markos to visit the Holy Places, about the year 1278. When they were still in Syria, the head of the Nestorian Church, Mar Denha, died, and Markos was elected to take his place under the name of Mar Yaballaha III in 1281. After the accession of Argun in 1284 the new patriarch, who was no mere Syrian, but a representative of the ruling race and came from the capital of the Mongol empire, acquired considerable influence at the court of the Il Khan. Consequently when Argun decided to send a new embassy to the West, the friend of the patriarch,

---

[1] Grousset, *op. cit.*, p. 662.
[2] *History of the Life and Travels of Rabban Sawma, Envoy of the Mongol Khans to the Kings of Europe, and Markos, Patriarch of the Nestorian Church in Asia.* Trans. from the Syriac by Sir E. A. Wallis Budge, 1928. See also A. C. Moule, *Christians in China before 1550* (1930).

Rabban Sauma, was chosen as its leader since he represented not merely Argun himself but the larger international unity of the whole Mongolian world. The mission reached Rome in 1287 soon after the death of Honorius IV and stayed in Western Europe for about a year, visiting Philip IV, Edward I and the newly elected Pope Nicholas IV. Thus the account of his experiences is a document of incomparable importance for the religious history of the Mongol empire and its relations with Western Christendom. In the first place it shows that the ancient theological antagonisms which had divided Eastern and Western Christendom had now become half-forgotten. Rabban Sauma celebrated the East Syrian liturgy in the presence of the Pope and the cardinals, and received Communion from the Pope. And at Bordeaux he did the same and Edward I received Communion from him.[1] Secondly it shows, even more than the embassies that preceded and followed it, how close were the relations between the Eastern Christians and the Mongols and how genuine were the Khan's efforts to establish a common front in Syria against the Saracens. Thus, when the cardinals expressed surprise that a Christian priest, attached to the patriarchate, should have come as an envoy from "the King of the Tartars", Rabban Sauma replied: "Know ye that many of our fathers in times past entered the lands of the Turks, the Mongols and the Chinese and have instructed them in the faith. To-day many Mongols are Christian. There are queens and children of kings who have been baptised and confess Christ. The Khans have churches in their camps. They honour Christians highly and there are many and faithful among them. And as the King is united in friendship with the Catholics and purposes to take possession of Syria and Palestine, he asks your aid for the conquest of Jerusalem." Fortunately the new Pope, Nicholas IV, who was elected in February 1285 soon after Rabban Sauma had

[1] "It was on this occasion that Edward I made the following remarkable reply to Rabban Sauma's request that he should be shown the shrines and holy places so that 'when we go back to the Children of the East we may give them descriptions of them'. And the King replied, 'Thus shall you say to King Arghôn and unto all the Orientals: We have seen a thing than which nothing is more wonderful, that is to say that in the countries of the Franks there are not two confessions of Faith, but only one confession of Faith, namely that which confesses Jesus Christ; and all the Christians confess it.'" E. A. W. Budge, *The Monks of Kublai Khan*, pp. 186–7.

returned to Rome, was a man who was well aware of the importance of the East, since he was the head of the Franciscan Order, Jerome of Ascoli, who had conducted the negotiations at Constantinople which had prepared the way for the Council of Lyons. He treated Rabban Sauma with the greatest cordiality and sent him back with letters to Argun and to the Christian widow of Abaga and with a letter to Yaballaha "confirming his patriarchal authority over all the Orientals".

Argun seems to have been well satisfied with the results of this mission. He made Rabban Sauma his chaplain and made a chapel for him communicating with the royal tent, and he had his son Oljaitu baptized Nicholas in honour of the Pope. Moreover it seems from the Pope's letter of April 2nd, 1288, that he had himself promised to receive baptism at Jerusalem when it had been won by the allied forces of the Mongols and the West.[1]

Finally, in the following year he sent further letters to the West, making concrete proposals for a joint campaign in Palestine in 1291. This letter, written in Mongol in the Uighur script, still exists and offers convincing proof of the serious character of the Mongol proposals.

"By the power of the Eternal God under the auspices of the supreme Khan [Kubilay] this is our word: King of France! By the envoy Mar Bar Sauma you have announced 'when the troops of the Il Khan open the campaign against Egypt, then we will set forth to join him'. Having accepted this message on your part, I say that, trusting in God, we propose to set forth in the last month of winter in the year of the Panther [January 1291] and to camp before Damascus on about the fifteenth day of the first month of spring. If you keep your word and send troops at the appointed time and God favours us, when we have taken Jerusalem from this people, we will give it to you. But if you fail to meet us, our troops will have marched in vain. Would that be becoming? And if afterwards we do not know what to do, what use will it be?"[2]

[1] Chabot, "Relations du roi Argoun avec l'occident", in *Revue de l'Orient Latin* (1894), p. 584. Grousset, *Hist. des Croisades*, iii, 722.
[2] Chabot, op. cit., p. 604; and A. C. Moule, *Christians in China*, p. 117.

At the same time the Khan offered to provide provisions for the crusading army and remounts for upwards of 20,000 horsemen. But on the Western side these offers met with little response. The powers of the West were absorbed in the miserable quarrel over Sicily which was the bitter fruit of the unfortunate alliance between the Papacy and Charles of Anjou. The only Western prince who was genuinely concerned with the crusade and who realized the possibilities of the Mongol alliance was Edward I of England, who again took the cross in 1289 and laboured for years to bring about a settlement by arbitration of the Sicilian conflict and to unite Western Christendom for the crusade. But his efforts were frustrated by the intransigence of the Papacy. There was no crusade, and Acre, the last Christian stronghold in Palestine, fell before the Egyptians on May 18th, 1291—almost at the moment when Argun had planned to recover Jerusalem. By this time Argun himself was dead and the opportunity was lost. Argun's son, Oljaitu, who had been baptized Nicholas in the name of the Pope himself, became a Moslem and thenceforth the Mongols in Persia, as well as in Russia and Turkestan, were gradually absorbed by the environment of Moslem culture.

VI. THE MISSION OF JOHN OF MONTE CORVINO TO THE FAR EAST

Nevertheless, on the religious side the work of William of Rubruck and Rabban Sauma was not altogether fruitless. The year after the latter's return Pope Nicholas IV sent further letters not only to Argun but also to Kubilay, the Great Khan, and to Kaidu, the last great representative of the house of Ugedey in Central Asia.[1] The bearer of these letters, the Franciscan John of Monte Corvino, had already spent years working in the East, and this last expedition, from which he never returned, was destined to be the longest and the most successful of all the missionary journeys of the Friars. Setting out from Rome in 1289 he first visited Argun at his capital at Tauris or Tabriz. He set out again in 1291 to visit the Great Khan, Kubilay, in China; and as he

[1] Kaidu was the most long-lived of all the house of Chingis Khan, since he had taken part in Batu's invasion of Hungary in 1241 and survived until 1301.

was unable to cross Central Asia owing to the great war between Kubilay and Kaidu, which had also interfered with the return of Marco Polo from China to Europe, he decided to go by way of India and spent more than a year at Mylapur in Madras, whence he sent back to Rome the first reliable account of the "Christians of St. Thomas" to reach the West. Owing to this immense detour he did not reach China until after the death of Kubilay.

This was a tragedy, for of all the Mongol Khans, Kubilay alone possessed the imagination and the breadth of mind which would have enabled him to use this opportunity. Early in his reign in 1266 he had despatched the uncles of Marco Polo to Rome with a request for a hundred men of learning, devoted to the Christian faith, and acquainted with the liberal arts, who would be capable of "proving to the learned of his dominions by just and fair argument that the faith professed by Christians is superior to and founded on more evident truth than any other".[1]

It staggers the imagination to consider what might have been the results if such a mission had actually been sent and if the Great Khan had used Western scholars instead of the Tibetan lamas whom he actually employed to lay the foundations of higher culture in Mongolia. But the Western response was too little and too late. John of Monte Corvino met with a favourable reception from Kubilay's successor, Timur (1294–1307), but he had to carry on his mission alone for twelve years with no helper save a friendly Italian merchant, Pietro de Lucalongo. Even so, he met with remarkable success. The year after his arrival, he converted one of the most important men in the Mongol Empire, the Nestorian prince, Kerguz or George, the son-in-law of the emperor and the ruler of the Ongut Turks of north-west China, the people to which the patriarch Mar Yaballaha belonged. George himself was killed soon afterwards in the great war with Kaidu, so that this promising beginning was uncompleted. But John of Monte Corvino continued his work alone at the capital, and succeeded in establishing an active centre of Tartar Catholicism at the heart of the empire in spite of every kind of difficulty and opposition.

[1] Of course we have only Marco Polo's word for this, but there can be no doubt that the Polos were actually sent to the Pope from Kubilay and that this is how they understood their mission.

Finally in 1307 Rome at last became aware of the existence of John of Monte Corvino and appointed him Archbishop of Khanbalik, as well as sending him the helpers whom he had so long desired.

Thenceforward the Chinese Mongol mission flourished for twenty years under John of Monte Corvino and continued for another forty years under his successors. We have a valuable account of the situation at the end of his episcopate in the journal of the Blessed Odoric of Pordenone in Friuli (1265–1331), who went to China by way of India about 1321 and returned by the overland route through Central Asia about 1328 to 1330. At that time he found the Franciscans established with a cathedral and two houses at Zaytun, the great medieval port of Southern China near Amoy, as well as at Yang Chow, where there were also three Nestorian churches. But it is clear from his narrative that the success of the Franciscan mission was mainly with the ruling class of Turco-Mongols[1] and the foreign population, which consisted of many different races, including large contingents of troops from Russia and the West. One of the most important of these groups, the Alans from the region of the Black Sea, were converted by John of Monte Corvino and sent an embassy to Rome in 1338, asking for a bishop and complaining that they had been left without spiritual help and without a superior since the death of John of Monte Corvino, though they were well instructed in the Catholic faith. This led to the last important medieval mission to the Far East of which we have a record, that of John of Marignolli, who left Avignon in 1338 and reached Peking by the land route in 1342, bringing as a gift from the Pope to the Emperor a great Western war horse which is recorded in the Chinese annals as a great horse from the kingdom of Fulan (=Farang=Frank land), $11\frac{1}{2}$ feet long and 6 feet 8 inches high.[2]

---

[1] When the Western missionaries speak of Tartars it is impossible to say whether they mean Mongols or Turks. Naturally enough they failed to distinguish the two races. In the same way, when John of Monte Corvino speaks of his translation of the breviary, etc., into the " Tartar" language he may mean Uighur or Jagatay or Mongol.

[2] The Chinese seem to have been more impressed by the horse than by the mission, for M. Pelliot has discovered a curious poem on it entitled " An Ode to the Supernatural Horse ".

John of Marignolli left China in 1347 and returned by way of India, reaching Avignon in 1353, after having been plundered of all his gifts in Ceylon by "a certain tyrant, Coya Jaan, a eunuch and an accursed Saracen".[1] By this time the Mongol empire in China was in a state of advanced decline, and the Christians, both Catholic and Nestorian, were involved in its fall. In 1362 the last Catholic Bishop of Zaytun, James of Florence, was martyred when the Chinese nationalists recovered the city, and a few years later, in 1369, the Christians were expelled from Peking, not to return until the coming of the Jesuits at the end of the sixteenth century.

At the same time the revival of Islam and the growth of Moslem intolerance were making the work of the Friars increasingly difficult in the rest of Asia. As early as 1321 Thomas of Tolentino and his companion were martyred at Tana near Bombay on their way to join John of Monte Corvino in China. In 1340 the Franciscan, Richard of Burgundy, who had been sent by the Pope to be bishop of Almalig near Kuldja in the sultanate of Jagatay was massacred with a number of Friars, one of whom was an "Indian", and an Italian merchant.

Finally, in the second half of the century, the whole of Central Asian Christianity and the eastern provinces of the Nestorian Church were destroyed by the conquests of Tamerlane or Timur, a conqueror who combined the ruthlessness of Chingis Khan with the religious intolerance and exclusiveness of an Aurangzeb. Timur was no illiterate barbarian, like the primitive Mongols, but a civilized oriental sovereign, the splendour of whose court aroused the admiration of the Spanish envoy, Clavijo. Nevertheless he was one of the great destroyers in history, and his career was like a tornado which passed across Asia from the Ganges to the Aegean, leaving ruin behind it. The Mongols, for all their atrocities, had a sense of their world responsibilities and performed a definite service to civilization. They drove a broad road from one end of Asia to the other, and after their armies had passed they opened the way to the merchant and the missionary, and made it possible for the East and the West to

---

[1] Yule, *Cathay and the Way Thither* (1866), ii, p. 394.

communicate both economically and spiritually. But everything that they had done was undone by Tamerlane, and from the fifteenth century the East and the West were more cut off from one another than they had been at any period in the Middle Ages.

No doubt some of the responsibility must fall on Western Christendom for its failure to take advantage of the opportunity when it was offered. But the following narratives show that the failure was not a complete one, and that an heroic effort was made by a few men with small resources in the face of enormous material difficulties to use the new road which had been so unexpectedly opened for the service of Christ and the Church. The spirit in which these earliest emissaries of Western Christendom approached their mission was stated with admirable simplicity and directness by William of Rubruck in his interview with the Great Khan. "My lord, we are not men of war. We wish that those should have dominion over the world who rule it most justly, in accordance with the will of God. Our office is to teach men to live after the will of God. For that we have come here and willingly would we remain here if it pleased you." If there had been more men of similar courage and faith to carry on this work in the same spirit, the whole history of the world, and especially of the relations between Europe and the Far East, might have been changed. But at least a beginning was made, so that the story of the expansion of medieval Christendom is not to be found only in the bloody history of the Crusades or in that of the forcible conversion of the pagan peoples of Eastern Germany and the Baltic provinces.

CHRISTOPHER DAWSON

BIBLIOGRAPHY

ANASTASIUS VAN DEN WYNGAERT, *Sinica Franciscana*, Vol. I: *Itinera et Relationes Fratrum Minorum saec. XIII et XIV* (Quaracchi-Firenze, 1929)

ANASTASIUS VAN DER WYNGAERT, *Jean de Monte Corvin, O.F.M., premier Evêque de Khanbalig* (1247–1328). Lille, 1924

E. A. W. BUDGE, *The Monks of Kûblâi Khân: Life and Travels of Rabban Sawma and Markôs*. Trans. from the Syriac by Budge, 1928

E. KOMROFF, *Some Contemporaries of Marco Polo* (Travellers' Library). (Translations of the principal narratives.)

The Chronicle of Novgorod. English translation by R. Mitchell and N. Forbes, with Introduction by C. R. Beazley. Camden Society, 1914

A. GAUBIL, S. J., *Histoire de Gentchiscan et de toute la dynastie des Mongous ses successeurs, conquérants de la Chine*. Paris, 1739. (This is the first European work to use the Chinese sources)

GRIGOR OF AKANC, *History of the Nation of the Archers*. Ed. and trans. R. P. BLAKE and R. N. FRYE. Harvard Journal of Asiatic Studies, 1949.

L. WADDING, *Annales Minorum*. Lyons, 8 vols., 1654; Rome, 19 vols., 1731–45

The Secret History of the Mongols. Mongol text ed. E. HAENISCH. 2 vols., Leipzig, 1935–9. German trans. by E. HAENISCH, Leipzig, 1948. French trans. of first part by P. Pelliot, Paris, 1948. This is the primary Mongol source, dated about 1240

The Journey of William of Rubruck to the Eastern Parts of the World, etc., ed. by WILLIAM W. ROCKHILL (Hakluyt Society, London, 1900)

C. R. BEAZLEY, *The Texts and Versions of John de Plano Carpini and William de Rubruquis* (Hakluyt Society, 1903)

The Book of Ser Marco Polo the Venetian Concerning the Kingdoms and Marvels of the East. Translated and edited with notes, by COL. SIR HENRY YULE, 3rd edition revised by H. CORDIER (2 vols., London, New York, 1927)

MARCO POLO, *The Description of the World*, ed. by A. C. MOULE and P. PELLIOT (2 vols., London, 1938) containing: Vol. I, the English translation: Vol. II, a translation of Z, the Latin codex in the Cathedral Library at Toledo

SIR HENRY YULE, *Cathay and the Way Thither*, etc. New edition by H. CORDIER (4 vols., Hakluyt Society, London, 1913-16)

H. GROUSSET, *L'Empire Mongol* (*Histoire du Monde*, ed. M. E. CAVAIGNAC, Tome VIII, 3, 1941)

H. GROUSSET, *L'Empire des Steppes* (1939)

H. GROUSSET, *Histoire de l'Extrême Orient* (2 vols., 1929)

H. GROUSSET, *Histoire des Croisades*, Tome III (1948)

A. C. MOURADJA D'OHSSON, *Histoire des Mongoles depuis Tchinguiz Khan jusqu'à Timour Bey* (4 vols., 1834-5 and 1852)

M. H. HOWORTH, *History of the Mongols* (3 vols., 1876-88)

L. OLSCHKI, *Marco Polo's Precursors* (1943)

L. OLSCHKI, *Guillaume Boucher: French Artist at the Court of the Khans* (1946)

G. VERNADSKY, *The Mongols and Russia* (1953)

P. PELLIOT, " Les Mongoles et la Papauté ", in *Revue de l'Orient Chrétien* (1922-3), 3-4; (1931-2), 66 and 79

P. PELLIOT, " Chrétiens d'Asie Centrale et d'Extrême Orient", in *T'oung Pao*, (1914), 628

C. R. BEAZLEY, *The Dawn of Modern Geography*, Vol. II, 320-52, 449-52. Also Vol. III *passim*.

B. VLADIMIRTSOV, *Le Régime Social des Mongoles* (Paris, 1948: trans. from Russian)

A. C. MOULE, *Christians in China Before 1550* (London, 1930)

S. RUNCIMAN, *History of the Crusades*, vol. III. 1954

M. A. CZAPLICA, *The Turks of Central Asia* (Oxford 1918) (very full bibliography)

EDITOR'S NOTE

THE text used is that of Father A. van den Wyngaert's *Sinica Franciscana*, Vol. I: *Itinera et Relationes Fratrum Minorum saec. XIII et XIV*, published by the Franciscan Press, Quaracchi. We wish to express our indebtedness to both editor and publisher.

The *History of the Mongols* by John of Plano Carpini and the *Journey* of William of Rubruck were translated by a Nun of Stanbrook Abbey. The Narrative of Benedict the Pole and the Letters of John of Monte Corvino, Brother Peregrine and Andrew of Perugia were translated by the Editor. The version of Guyuk Khan's letter to Pope Innocent IV is based on a translation of the Persian text by Mr. D. A. Maitland Muller.

I am indebted to Professor T. Sulimirski for his assistance in preparing the notes to William of Rubruck, especially those dealing with geographical questions.

C. D.

TABLE I—THE

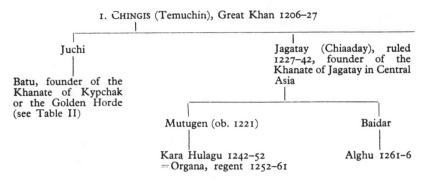

1. CHINGIS (Temuchin), Great Khan 1206–27

Juchi

Batu, founder of the Khanate of Kypchak or the Golden Horde (see Table II)

Jagatay (Chiaaday), ruled 1227–42, founder of the Khanate of Jagatay in Central Asia

Mutugen (ob. 1221)

Baidar

Kara Hulagu 1242–52 = Organa, regent 1252–61

Alghu 1261–6

TABLE II—THE KHANS OF KYPCHAK OR THE GOLDEN HORDE (RUSSIA AND KAZAKHSTAN) (CAPITAL: SARAI ON THE VOLGA)

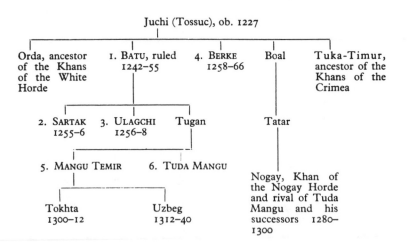

Juchi (Tossuc), ob. 1227

Orda, ancestor of the Khans of the White Horde

1. BATU, ruled 1242–55

4. BERKE 1258–66

Boal

Tuka-Timur, ancestor of the Khans of the Crimea

2. SARTAK 1255–6

3. ULAGCHI 1256–8

Tugan

Tatar

5. MANGU TEMIR

6. TUDA MANGU

Tokhta 1300–12

Uzbeg 1312–40

Nogay, Khan of the Nogay Horde and rival of Tuda Mangu and his successors 1280–1300

MONGOL EMPIRE

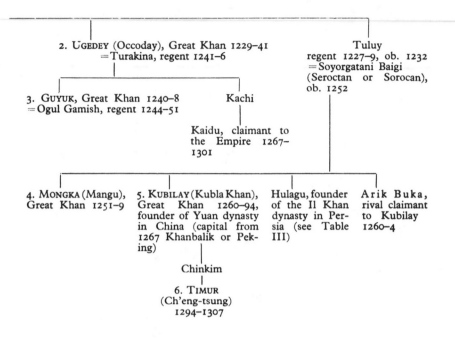

2. UGEDEY (Occoday), Great Khan 1229–41
= Turakina, regent 1241–6

Tuluy
regent 1227–9, ob. 1232
= Soyorgatani Baigi
(Seroctan or Sorocan),
ob. 1252

3. GUYUK, Great Khan 1240–8
= Ogul Gamish, regent 1244–51

Kachi

Kaidu, claimant to the Empire 1267–1301

4. MONGKA (Mangu), Great Khan 1251–9

5. KUBILAY (Kubla Khan), Great Khan 1260–94, founder of Yuan dynasty in China (capital from 1267 Khanbalik or Peking)

Hulagu, founder of the Il Khan dynasty in Persia (see Table III)

Arik Buka, rival claimant to Kubilay 1260–4

Chinkim

6. TIMUR
(Ch'eng-tsung)
1294–1307

TABLE III—THE IL KHANS OF PERSIA
(CAPITAL: TABRIZ)

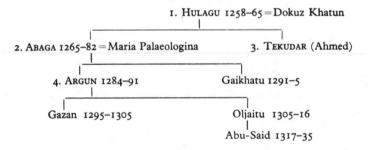

1. HULAGU 1258–65 = Dokuz Khatun

2. ABAGA 1265–82 = Maria Palaeologina

3. TEKUDAR (Ahmed)

4. ARGUN 1284–91

Gaikhatu 1291–5

Gazan 1295–1305

Oljaitu 1305–16

Abu-Said 1317–35

Note.—These Tables do not pretend to be complete, but they include most of the names mentioned in the text and show how they are related to Chingis Khan and to one another.

C. D.

HISTORY OF THE MONGOLS
By John of Plano Carpini

John of Plano Carpini, who derives his name from Piano di Carpini near Perugia, was a man of ripe age who had taken a leading part in the establishment of the Franciscan Order in Western Europe. He was chosen Guardian of the new province of Saxony in 1222. In 1228 he became Provincial of Germany. In 1230 he was sent to Spain as Provincial, but in 1233 he returned to Saxony as Provincial. His companion, Brother Giordino di Giano, the chronicler, describes him as "Ordinis sui dilatator maximus", sending Friars all over Northern and Eastern Europe, to Bohemia, Poland, Hungary, Denmark and Norway, watching over the brethren, as a hen over her chicks, and standing "constanter et personaliter" before bishops and princes in defence of his Order. Since he was a corpulent man he used to ride an ass, "and the men of those days were moved by greater devotion towards his ass—on account of the humility of the rider and the newness of the Order—than they are nowadays by the assiduity of the Friars towards the persons of the Ministers". After his return from the Mongol mission we get a vivid picture of him in the pages of Fra Salimbene who met him near Lyons, after he had made his report to Pope Innocent IV. Salimbene says that he often heard him describe his experiences, and when he was tired of talking he would have his book read aloud and would explain any points that his hearers did not understand. Salimbene says that he was well received by the Great Khan and treated honourably and courteously.

On his return the Pope sent Brother John on a mission to St. Louis and in 1248 he was made Archbishop of Antivari in Dalmatia. But his last years were unhappy. He became involved in a serious conflict with the Archbishop of Ragusa on questions of jurisdiction, and he died on August 1st, 1252, while his case was still being tried by the Roman Curia.

John of Plano Carpini's book was by far the most widely known of all the early accounts of Mongols. This is due to the fact that it was incorporated by Vincent of Beauvais in his *Speculum Historiale*, which was one of the most popular encyclopaedic works of the Middle Ages. Vincent was a Dominican who was closely connected with the family of St. Louis and was lector at the royal foundation of Royaumont in the middle of the thirteenth century. As John himself notes at the close of his work, there are two versions of the *History of the Mongols*, a longer and a shorter one, and both survive in a number of MSS. The best MS. and the longer version, on which Fr. van den Wyngaert's printed text is based, is the Corpus Christi, Cambridge, MS. 181, which also contains one of the few surviving texts of William of Rubruck's *Itinerary*. This MS. originally belonged to St. Mary's Abbey at York.

HISTORY OF THE MONGOLS

By John of Plano Carpini

Prologue

Friar John of Plano Carpini, of the Order of Friars Minor, envoy of the Apostolic See to the Tartars and other nations of the east, to all the faithful of Christ to whom this present writing may come, the grace of God be to you in this present life and glory in the world to come and a triumphant victory over the enemies of God and of Our Lord Jesus Christ.

When by command of the Apostolic See we went to the Tartars and the other oriental nations, knowing the desire of the Lord Pope and the venerable Cardinals, we chose first to make our way to the Tartars, for we were afraid that in the near future the Church of God would be threatened by danger from that quarter. And although we feared we might be killed by the Tartars or other people, or imprisoned for life, or afflicted with hunger, thirst, cold, heat, injuries and exceeding great trials almost beyond our powers of endurance—all of which, with the exception of death and imprisonment for life, fell to our lot in various ways in a much greater degree than we had conceived beforehand—nevertheless we did not spare ourselves in order to carry out the will of God as laid down in the Lord Pope's mandate, and be of some service to Christians, that, at all events, having learned the truth about the desire and intention of the Tartars, we could make this known to the Christians; then if by chance they made a sudden attack they would not find the Christian people unprepared (as happened on another occasion on account of the sins of men) and inflict a great defeat on them.

Therefore whatever, with your welfare in mind, we shall write to you to put you on your guard, you ought to believe all the more

3

confidently inasmuch as we have either seen everything with our own eyes, for during a year and four months and more we travelled about both through the midst of them and in company with them and we were among them, or we have heard it from Christians who are with them as captives and are, so we believe, to be relied upon. For we had instructions from the Supreme Pontiff to examine everything and to look at everything carefully, and this we zealously carried out, both I and Friar Benedict the Pole of the same Order, who was our companion in our tribulations and our interpreter.

But if for the attention of our readers we write anything which is not known in your parts, you ought not on that account to call us liars, for we are reporting for you things we ourselves have seen or have heard from others whom we believe to be worthy of credence. Indeed it is a very cruel thing that a man should be brought into ill-repute by others on account of the good that he has done.

CHAPTER I

THE LAND OF THE TARTARS, ITS POSITION, PHYSICAL FEATURES AND CLIMATE

SINCE therefore we wish to write an account of the Tartars in such a way that the reader can easily find his way about it, we will arrange it in chapters as follows. In the first we will speak of the country, in the second of the people, in the third of their religion, in the fourth of their customs, in the fifth of their empire, in the sixth of their wars, in the seventh of the countries which they have subjugated to their dominion, in the eighth of how war should be waged against them, and in the last of the journey we made, of the court of the Emperor and of the eye-witnesses we came across in the land of the Tartars.

We propose treating of the country in this manner: in the first place we will say something of its position, secondly we will speak of its physical features, and thirdly of the nature of the climate there.

Now the aforesaid country lies in that part of the east where, so we believe, the east joins the north. To the east of it lies the country of the Kitayans and also that of the Solangi; to the south the land of the Saracens; to the south-west there is the territory of the Uigurs; to the west the province of the Naimans;[1] on the north it is bounded by the ocean.

In some parts the country is extremely mountainous, in others it is flat, but practically the whole of it is composed of very sandy gravel. In some districts there are small woods, but otherwise it is completely bare of trees. They cook their food and they all, the Emperor as well as the nobles and other men, sit at a fire made of the dung of oxen and horses. Not one hundredth part of the land is fertile, nor can it bear fruit unless it be irrigated by running water, and brooks and streams are few there, and rivers very rare. And so there are no towns or cities there with the exception of one which is said to be quite big and is called Caracarom[2]. We however did not see it, but we were as near as half-a-day's journey to it when we were at the Syra Orda[3], which is the largest of the camps of their Emperor. Although the land is otherwise barren, it is fit for grazing cattle; even if not very good, at least sufficiently so.

The weather there is astonishingly irregular, for in the middle of summer, when other places are normally enjoying very great heat, there is fierce thunder and lightning which cause the death of many men, and at the same time there are very heavy falls of snow. There are also hurricanes of bitterly cold winds, so violent that at times men can ride on horseback only with great effort. When we were before the orda—that is what the camps of the Emperor and chief men are called—we lay prostrate on account

---

[1] The Kitayans are the Chinese and the Solangi are probably Koreans.
"The country of the Saracens" here no doubt refers to Persia and Southern Turkestan. The Uighur Turks, whom John calls the Huii, at this time occupied the oases of Turfan north of the river Tarim. The Naiman were one of the leading peoples of Mongolia occupying the western parts of Mongolia and the upper Irtish valley. Thus the description is very accurate, except that it extends Mongolia to include the adjacent part of Siberia, now occupied by the Yakut and the Tungus.

[2] Caracarom: cf. *infra* p. 183.

[3] Syra Orda: lit. " the Yellow Camp ", so called because yellow was the imperial colour.

of the force of the wind and we could scarcely see owing to the
great clouds of dust. There it never rains in the winter, but often
in the summer, though it is so little that sometimes the dust and
the roots of the grass are hardly moistened. Very heavy hail also
often falls there. At the time when the Emperor was elected and
was to be enthroned and we were in the orda, there was such a
heavy hailstorm that as a result of its sudden melting, so we
clearly understood, more than a hundred and sixty men in that
camp were drowned, and many dwellings and much property
were washed away. Then also in summer there is suddenly great
heat, and suddenly extreme cold. In winter in some parts there
are heavy falls of snow, in others however but slight.

To conclude briefly about this country: it is large, but otherwise—as we saw with our own eyes, for during five and a half
months we travelled about it—it is more wretched than I can
possibly say.

CHAPTER II

OF THEIR PERSONS, THEIR CLOTHES, THEIR DWELLING-PLACES,
POSSESSIONS AND MARRIAGE

HAVING spoken of the country, it is now for us to speak of the
people. First we will describe their personal appearance, secondly
we will add something about their marriages, thirdly their clothes,
fourthly their dwellings, and fifthly their possessions.

In appearance the Tartars are quite different from all other
men, for they are broader than other people between the eyes and
across the cheek-bones. Their cheeks also are rather prominent
above their jaws; they have a flat and small nose, their eyes are
little and their eyelids raised up to the eyebrows. For the most
part, but with a few exceptions, they are slender about the waist;
almost all are of medium height. Hardly any of them grow
beards, although some have a little hair on the upper lip and chin
and this they do not trim. On the top of the head they have a
tonsure like clerics, and as a general rule all shave from one ear
to the other to the breadth of three fingers, and this shaving joins

on to the aforesaid tonsure. Above the forehead also they all likewise shave to two fingers' breadth, but the hair between this shaving and the tonsure they allow to grow until it reaches their eyebrows, and, cutting more from each side of the forehead than in the middle, they make the hair in the middle long; the rest of their hair they allow to grow like women, and they make it into two braids which they bind, one behind each ear. They also have small feet.

Each man has as many wives as he can keep, one a hundred, another fifty, another ten—one more, another less. It is the general custom for them to marry any of their relations, with the exception of their mother, daughter and sister by the same mother. They can however take in marriage their sisters who have only the same father, and even their father's wives after his death; also a younger brother may marry his brother's wife after his death; or another younger relation is expected to take her. All other women they take as wives without any distinction and they buy them at a very high price from their parents. After the death of their husbands the women do not easily enter into a second union, unless a man wishes to take his stepmother to wife.

The clothes of both the men and the women are made in the same style. They do not use capes, cloaks or hoods, but wear tunics of buckram, velvet or brocade[1] made in the following fashion: they are open from top to bottom and are folded over the breast; they are fastened on the left with one tie, on the right with three, on the left side also they are open as far as the waist. Garments of all kinds of fur are made in the same style; the upper one however has the hairy part outside and is open at the back; it also has a tail at the back reaching to the knees.

The married women have a very full tunic, open to the ground in front. On their head they have a round thing made of twigs or bark, which is an ell in height and ends on top in a square; it gradually increases in circumference from the bottom to the top, and on the top there is a long and slender cane of gold or silver or wood, or even a feather, and it is sewn on to a cap which reaches to the shoulders. The cap as well as this object is covered

---

[1] "*Bucarano purpura vel baldakino.*"

with buckram, velvet or brocade, and without this headgear they never go into the presence of men and by it they are distinguished from other women. It is hard to tell unmarried women and young girls from men, for they are dressed in every respect like them. The caps they have are different from those of other nations, but I am unable to describe what they are like in such a way as you would understand.

Their dwelling-places are round like tents and are made of twigs and slender sticks. At the top in the middle there is a round opening which lets in the light, and is also to enable the smoke to escape, for they always make their fire in the middle. Both the sides and the roof are covered with felt, and the doors also are made of felt. Some of these dwellings are large, others small, according to the importance or significance of the people; some can be speedily taken down and put up again and are carried on baggage animals; others cannot be taken down but are moved on carts. To carry them on a cart, for the smaller ones one ox is sufficient, for the larger ones three, four or even more according to the size. Wherever they go, be it to war or anywhere else, they always take their dwellings with them.

They are extremely rich in animals, camels, oxen, sheep, goats; they have such a number of horses and mares that I do not believe there are so many in all the rest of the world; they do not have pigs or other farm animals.

The Emperor, the nobles and other important men own large quantities of gold and silver, silk, precious stones and jewels.

CHAPTER III

OF THEIR WORSHIP OF GOD, THOSE THINGS WHICH THEY CONSIDER TO BE SINS, DIVINATIONS AND PURIFICATIONS, FUNERAL RITES, ETC.

HAVING spoken of the men, we must now add something about their religion, and we will deal with it in this way: first we will speak of their worship of God, next of those things which they believe to be sins, thirdly of divinations and purifications for sins, and fourthly of their funeral rites.

They believe in one God, and they believe that He is the maker of all things visible, and invisible; and that it is He who is the giver of the good things of this world as well as the hardships; they do not, however, worship Him with prayers or praises or any kind of ceremony. Their belief in God does not prevent them from having idols of felt made in the image of man, and these they place on each side of the door of the dwelling; below them they put a felt model of an udder, and they believe that these are the guardians of the cattle and grant them the benefit of milk and foals; yet others they make out of silken materials and to these they pay great honour. Some put them in a beautiful covered cart before the door of their dwelling and if anyone steals anything from that cart he is put to death without any mercy. When they wish to make these idols, all the chief ladies in the different dwellings meet together and reverently make them; and when they have finished they kill a sheep and eat it and burn its bones in the fire. Also when any child is ill they make an idol as I have described and fasten it above his bed. Chiefs, captains of a thousand men and captains of a hundred, always have a shrine [hercium] in the middle of their dwelling.

They always offer to their idols the first milk of every cow and mare. When they are going to eat and drink they first make an offering to them of some of the food and drink. When they kill any animal they offer its heart in a cup to the idol in the cart; they leave it there until the morning, when they remove it from its presence, cook it and eat it. They have also made an idol to the first Emperor, which they have placed in a cart in a place of honour before a dwelling, as we saw before the present Emperor's court, and they offer many gifts to it; they also present horses to it and no one dare mount these till their death; they also give other animals to it, and if they slaughter these for food they do not break any of their bones but burn them in a fire. They bow to it towards the south as to God, and they make other nobles who are visiting them do the same.

Whence it recently came about that when Michael[1], one of the chief dukes of Russia, came on a visit to Bati, they made him first pass between two fires. After that they told him to bow towards the south to Chingis Chan; he replied that he would gladly bow to Bati and his attendants but he would not make an inclination to the image of a dead man, for it was not lawful for Christians to do this. When they had told him many times that he was to bow and he would not, the chief Bati sent him word through the son of Jaroslaus[2] that if he did not bow he would be put to death. He answered that he would rather die than do what was not lawful. Bati sent one of his attendants who went on kicking him in the stomach against his heart until he began to weaken. Thereupon one of his soldiers who was standing by encouraged him, saying "Be constant, for this suffering will last but a short time and eternal joy will follow hard upon it." Then they cut off his head with a knife, and the soldier also was beheaded.

In addition they venerate and adore the sun, the moon, fire, water and the earth, making them the first offerings of food and drink, especially in the morning before they eat or even drink. Since they observe no law with regard to the worship of God they have up to now, so we understood, compelled no one to deny his faith or law with the exception of Michael of whom we have just spoken. What they may ultimately do we do not know, but there are some who are of the opinion that, if they became sole rulers, which God forbid, they would make everyone bow down to that idol.

During our stay in the country it happened that Andrew, Duke of Cherneglone[3] which is in Russia, was accused before Bati of taking Tartar horses out of the country and selling them elsewhere; and although the charge was not proved he was put to

[1] Michael Duke of Chernigov and his companion, the boyar Feodor, have always been honoured as saints and martyrs by the Russian Church. Michael's loyalty was suspect to Batu, as he had been a refugee in the West and his son Rotislav had married a Hungarian princess, so it is probable that his refusal of homage to the *ongon* of Chingis Khan was treated as a sign of political disloyalty. His martyrdom seems to have occurred while John of Plano Carpini was at Karakorum in September 1246.

[2] Constantine, the son of the Grand Duke Yaroslav and the brother of Alexander Nevski.

[3] Andrew of Chernigov, the son of Mistislav.

death. Hearing this, his younger brother came with the widow of the slain man to the chief Bati to petition him not to take away their territory from them. Bati told the boy to take the widow of the slain man, the boy's own brother, as his wife; and bade the woman take him as her husband according to Tartar custom. She said that she would rather die than break the law. But none the less he gave her to him [as wife], although both of them refused as much as they could. And they put them both to bed together and forced them to consummate the marriage in spite of her tears and cries.

Although they have no law concerning the doing of what is right or the avoidance of sin, nevertheless there are certain traditional things, invented by them or their ancestors, which they say are sins; for example, to stick a knife into a fire, or even in any way to touch fire with a knife, or to extract meat from the cauldron with a knife, or to chop with an axe near a fire; for they believe that, if these things were done, the fire would be beheaded; likewise to lean on a whip with which a horse is lashed, for they do not use spurs: also to touch arrows with a whip; again to catch or kill young birds, to strike a horse with a bridle; also to break a bone with another bone, to pour out upon the ground milk or any kind of drink or food; to pass water inside a dwelling. If a man does this on purpose he is put to death, otherwise he has to pay a large sum of money to the soothsayer, who purifies him and has the dwelling and its contents carried between two fires; but before this purification has been carried out no one dare enter the dwelling or take away anything from it: again, if anyone takes a morsel and, unable to swallow it, spits it out of his mouth, a hole is made under the dwelling and he is dragged out by that hole and without any mercy put to death; also if a man treads on the threshold of a dwelling belonging to any chief he is put to death in the same way. They have many things like this which it would be tedious to tell of.

On the other hand, to kill men, to invade the countries of other people, to take the property of others in any unlawful way, to commit fornication, to revile other men, to act contrary to the prohibitions and commandments of God, is considered no sin by them.

They know nothing of everlasting life and eternal damnation, but they believe that after death they will live in another world and increase their flocks, and eat and drink and do the other things which are done by men living in this world.

They pay great attention to divinations, auguries, soothsayings, sorceries and incantations, and when they receive an answer from the demons they believe that a god is speaking to them. This god they call Itoga—the Comans however call him Kam[1]—and they have a wondrous fear and reverence for him and offer him many oblations and the first portion of their food and drink, and they do everything according to the answers he gives. When the moon is new, or at full moon, they embark on anything fresh they wish to do, and so they call the moon the great Emperor and bend the knee and pray to it. They also say that the sun is the mother of the moon because it receives its light from the sun. They believe, to put it shortly, that everything is purified by fire. Consequently when envoys or princes or any persons whatsoever come to them, they are obliged to pass between two fires, together with the gifts they are bringing, in order to be purified, lest perchance they have practised sorcery or brought poison or anything else injurious. Also if fire falls from heaven on cattle or men, a thing which often happens there, or any similar thing befalls them by which they are considered unclean or unlucky, they have to be purified in the same way by the diviners. They place almost all their hope in such things.

When anyone is sick past cure, they put a spear there and wind black felt round it and from then onwards no outsider dares to enter within the bounds of his dwellings. When the death agony begins almost everybody leaves him, for none of those who are present at his death can enter the orda of any chief or of the Emperor until the new moon.

When he is dead, if he is one of the less important men, he is buried in secret in the open country wherever it seems good to them. He is buried with one of his dwellings, sitting in the middle of it, and they place a table in front of him, and a dish filled with meat and a goblet of mare's milk. And they bury with him a mare and

---

[1] Kam is the modern Mongol word for a Shaman.

her foal and a horse with bridle and saddle, and another horse they eat and fill its skin with straw, and this they stick up on two or four poles, so that in the next world he may have a dwelling in which to make his abode and a mare to provide him with milk, and that he may be able to increase his horses and have horses on which to ride. The bones of the horse which they eat they burn for his soul; and also the women often assemble to burn bones for the men's souls, as we saw with our own eyes and learned from others there. We also saw that Occodai Chan, the father of the present Emperor, left behind a grove to grow for his soul, and he ordered that no one was to cut there, and anyone who cuts a twig there, as we ourselves saw, is beaten, stripped and maltreated. And when we were in great need of something with which to whip our horse, we did not dare to cut a switch from there. They also bury gold and silver in the same way with a dead man; the cart in which he rides is broken up and his dwelling destroyed, nor does anyone dare to pronounce his name until the third generation.

They have a different method of burying their chief men. They go in secret into the open country and there they remove the grass, roots and all, and they dig a large pit and in the side of this pit they hollow out a grave under the earth; and they put his favourite slave under him. He lies there under the body until he is almost at the point of death, then they drag him out to let him breathe, and this they do three times. If the slave escapes with his life, he is afterwards a free man and can do whatever he pleases and is an important man in his master's camp and among his relations. The dead man they place in the grave made in the side along with the things mentioned above. Then they fill the pit in front of his grave, and they put the grass over it as it was before so that no one may be able to discover the spot afterwards. The other things already described they also do, but his tent they leave above ground in the open.

In their country there are two cemeteries. One is where the Emperors, chiefs and all the nobles are interred, and wherever they die they are brought thither if this can fittingly be done. A great deal of gold and silver is buried with them. The other cemetery is the one where lie buried those who were killed in

Hungary, for many lost their lives there. No one dare go near these cemeteries except the keepers who have been put there to look after them. If anyone does approach them, he is seized, stripped, beaten and severely maltreated. We ourselves unwittingly entered the bounds of the cemetery of the men who were killed in Hungary, and they bore down upon us and would have shot at us with arrows, but, since we were envoys and did not know the customs of the land, they let us go free.

The relatives of the dead man and all those living in his dwellings have to be purified by fire. This purification is performed in the following manner: they make two fires and they put two spears near the fires, with a rope fastened on to the top of them, on to which they tie strips of buckram; under this rope and its ribbons and between the two fires pass men, animals and dwellings. And there are two women, one this side, the other that, who sprinkle water and recite incantations. If any carts break down there, or if anything falls to the ground on that spot, the enchanters get it. If anyone is killed by a thunderbolt, all the people living in his dwellings have to pass through the fires in the manner described; no one touches his tent, his bed, cart, felt, clothes or any other such things as he had; but they are spurned by all as unclean.

CHAPTER IV

Of Their Character, Good and Bad, Their Customs, Food, Etc.

Having spoken of their religion, now we must speak of their character, which we will deal with in this way: first we will tell of their good points, then of their bad, thirdly of their customs, and fourthly of their food.

These men, that is to say the Tartars, are more obedient to their masters than any other men in the world, be they religious or seculars; they show great respect to them nor do they lightly lie to them. They rarely or never contend with each other in word, and in action never. Fights, brawls, wounding, murder are never met with among them. Nor are robbers and thieves who steal on a large scale found there; consequently their dwellings and the carts in which they keep their valuables are not secured by bolts and bars. If any animals are lost, whoever comes across them either leaves them alone or takes them to men appointed for this purpose; the owners of the animals apply for them to these men and they get them back without any difficulty. They show considerable respect to each other and are very friendly together, and they willingly share their food with each other, although there is little enough of it. They are also long-suffering. When they are without food, eating nothing at all for one or two days, they do not easily show impatience, but they sing and make merry as if they had eaten well. On horseback they endure great cold and they also put up with excessive heat. Nor are they men fond of luxury; they are not envious of each other; there is practically no litigation among them. No one scorns another but helps him and promotes his good as far as circumstances permit.

Their women are chaste, nor does one hear any mention among them of any shameful behaviour on their part; some of them, however, in jest make use of vile and disgusting language. Discord among them seems to arise rarely or never, and although they may get very drunk, yet in their intoxication they never come to words or blows.

Now that the good characteristics of the Tartars have been described, it is time for something to be said about their bad. They are most arrogant to other people and look down on all, indeed they consider them as nought, be they of high rank or low born.

For at the Emperor's court we saw Jerozlaus[1], a man of noble birth, a mighty duke of Russia, also the son of the King and Queen of Georgia, and many important sultans; the chief also of the Solangi received no fitting honour from them, but the Tartars who were assigned to them, however base-born they were, went ahead of them and always had the first and highest place; indeed they were often obliged to sit behind their backs.

---

[1] Yaroslav I, Grand Duke of Vladimir 1238–47. He died at Karakorum during John of Plano Carpini's visit, as related *infra*, p. 65.

They are quickly roused to anger with other people and are of an impatient nature; they also tell lies to others and practically no truth is to be found in them. At first indeed they are smooth-tongued, but in the end they sting like a scorpion. They are full of slyness and deceit, and if they can, they get round everyone by their cunning. They are men who are dirty in the way they take food and drink and do other things. Any evil they intend to do to others they conceal in a wonderful way so that the latter can take no precautions nor devise anything to offset their cunning. Drunkenness is considered an honourable thing by them and when anyone drinks too much, he is sick there and then, nor does this prevent him from drinking again. They are exceedingly grasping and avaricious; they are extremely exacting in their demands, most tenacious in holding on to what they have and most niggardly in giving. They consider the slaughter of other people as nothing. In short, it is impossible to put down in writing all their evil characteristics on account of the very great number of them.

Their food consists of everything that can be eaten, for they eat dogs, wolves, foxes and horses and, when driven by necessity, they feed on human flesh. For instance, when they were fighting against a city of the Kitayans, where the Emperor was residing, they besieged it for so long that they themselves completely ran out of supplies and, since they had nothing at all to eat, they thereupon took one out of every ten men for food. They eat the filth which comes away from mares when they bring forth foals. Nay, I have even seen them eating lice. They would say, "Why should I not eat them since they eat the flesh of my son and drink his blood?" I have also seen them eat mice.

They do not use table-cloths or napkins. They have neither bread nor herbs nor vegetables nor anything else, nothing but meat, of which, however, they eat so little that other people would scarcely be able to exist on it. They make their hands very dirty with the grease of the meat, but when they eat they wipe them on their leggings or the grass or some other such thing. It is the custom for the more respectable among them to have small bits of cloth with which they wipe their hands at the end when they eat meat. One of them cuts the morsels and another takes them on the point of a knife and offers them to each, to some more, to some less, according to whether they wish to show them greater or less honour. They do not wash their dishes, and, if occasionally they rinse them with the meat broth, they put it back with the meat into the pot. Pots also or spoons or other articles intended for this use, if they are cleaned at all, are washed in the same manner. They consider it a great sin if any food or drink is allowed to be wasted in any way; consequently they do not allow bones to be given to dogs until the marrow has been extracted. They do not wash their clothes nor allow them to be washed, especially from the time when thunderstorms begin until the weather changes. They drink mare's milk in very great quantities if they have it; they also drink the milk of ewes, cows, goats and even camels. They do not have wine, ale or mead unless it is sent or given to them by other nations. In the winter, moreover, unless they are wealthy, they do not have mare's milk. They boil millet in water and make it so thin that they cannot eat it but have to drink it. Each one of them drinks one or two cups in the morning and they eat nothing more during the day; in the evening, however, they are all given a little meat, and they drink the meat broth. But in the summer, seeing they have plenty of mare's milk, they seldom eat meat, unless it happens to be given to them or they catch some animal or bird when hunting.

They also have a law or custom of putting to death any man and woman they find openly committing adultery; similarly if a virgin commit fornication with anyone, they kill both the man and the woman. If anyone is found in the act of plundering or stealing in the territory under their power, he is put to death without any mercy. Again, if anyone reveals their plans, especially when they intend going to war, he is given a hundred stripes on his back, as heavy as a peasant can give with a big stick. When any of the lower class offend in any way, they are not spared by their superiors, but are soundly beaten. There is no distinction between the son of a concubine and the son of a wife, but the father gives to each what he will; and if they are of a family of princes, then the son of a concubine is a prince just the same as the son of a legitimate wife. When a Tartar has many wives, each one has her own

dwelling and her household, and the husband eats and drinks
and sleeps one day with one, and the next with another. One,
however, is chief among the others and with her he stays more
often than with the others. In spite of their numbers, they never
easily quarrel among themselves.

The men do not make anything at all, with the exception of
arrows, and they also sometimes tend the flocks, but they hunt and
practise archery, for they are all, big and little, excellent archers,
and their children begin as soon as they are two or three years
old to ride and manage horses and to gallop on them, and they are
given bows to suit their stature and are taught to shoot; they are
extremely agile and also intrepid.

Young girls and women ride and gallop on horseback with
agility like the men. We even saw them carrying bows and arrows.
Both the men and the women are able to endure long stretches of
riding. They have very short stirrups; they look after their horses
very well, indeed they take the very greatest care of all their
possessions. Their women make everything, leather garments,
tunics, shoes, leggings and everything made of leather; they also
drive the carts and repair them, they load the camels, and in all
their tasks they are very swift and energetic. All the women wear
breeches and some of them shoot like the men.

CHAPTER V

THE BEGINNING OF THE EMPIRE OF THE TARTARS AND THEIR
CHIEF MEN, AND THE DOMINION EXERCISED BY THE EMPEROR AND
THE PRINCES[1]

HAVING spoken of their customs we must now add something
about their empire. First we will tell of its beginning, secondly
of its chief men, thirdly of the dominion exercised by the Emperor
and the princes.

[1] This is a most perplexing chapter, since it combines very accurate and
detailed information not found in any other Western writer with a number of
traveller's tales and purely legendary matter. The account of the Mongol
tribes and the derivation of their names is extremely accurate, except the
derivation of the name of the Tartars from the river Tartar, which is incorrect.

In the east there is a land, of which we have spoken above, which is called Mongolia. At one time there were in this land four tribes, one the Yekamongol, that means the Great Mongols; the second the Su-Mongol, that is to say the Mongols of the Water, but these called themselves Tartars from a certain river named the Tartur, which flows through their territory; another was called the Merkit; the fourth was the Mecrit. All these tribes were alike in appearance and had the same language, although they were separate from each other, having their own provinces and rulers.

In the land of the Yekamongols there was a man called Chingis. He became a mighty hunter before the Lord, and learned to steal and take men for prey. He also went into other territories and any men he could capture and get to join his band he did not let go again. He drew to himself men of his own nation and they followed him as their leader in all kinds of wrong-doing. When he had collected a great many followers he started fighting with the Sumongols or Tartars and he killed their leader and after much fighting he conquered all the Tartars and reduced them to subjection. After this he fought with all the others; he fought with the Merkits who were settled next to the territory of the Tartars, and these also he conquered in battle. Then he went on to attack the Mecrit and likewise defeated them.

When the Naimans heard that Chingis was behaving in this arrogant fashion they were angry, for they had had an extremely active Emperor to whom all the aforesaid tribes used to pay tribute. When he had paid the debt of all flesh, his sons succeeded in his place, but they were young men and foolish and did not know how to rule the people; instead they separated from and were at variance with each other. In the meantime Chingis had risen to great power; nevertheless the young men made assaults on the territories mentioned above, killing men, women and children and seizing plunder.

On hearing this, Chingis assembled all the men subject to him. The Naimans also and the Karakitayans[1], that is the Black Kitayans, assembled against him for battle in a certain narrow valley

[1] The Kara Khitay were a Mongol people who had been driven out of northern China and had established a powerful empire in Turkestan in the twelfth century. They were Buddhists in religion.

between two mountains, through which we passed on our way to their Emperor, and a battle was fought in which the Naimans and Karakitayans were defeated by the Mongols. The greater part of them were killed and others who could not make their escape were reduced to slavery.

Occodai Chan, the son of Chingis Chan, after he had been made Emperor, built a city in the land of the Karakitayans, which he called Omyl[1]. Near this city to the south is a vast desert, which, they say for a certainty, is inhabited by wild men, who do not speak at all and have no joints in their legs. If at any time they fall, they cannot get up again without the help of others, but they are intelligent enough to make felt out of camel's hair which they use to clothe themselves and as a protection against the wind. And if sometimes the Tartars pursue them and wound them with their arrows, they put grass in the wound and bravely flee before them.

The Mongols on their return to their own country prepared for war against the Kitayans,[2] and moving camp they entered their territory. When this came to the ears of the Emperor of the Kitayans he went to meet them with his army, and a hard battle was fought in which the Mongols were defeated and all the Mongol nobles in that army were killed with the exception of seven. This gives rise to the fact that, when anyone threatens them saying "If you invade that country you will be killed, for a vast number of people live there and they are men skilled in the art of fighting", they still give answer, "Once upon a time indeed we were killed and but seven of us were left, and now we have increased to a great multitude, so we are not afraid of such men."

Chingis however and the others who were left fled back to their own country and after a short rest Chingis again prepared for battle and set out to make war against the land of the Uighurs. These people, who are Christians of the Nestorian sect, he also

---

[1] Omyl, i.e. Imil on the river of the same name, in Tarbagatai.
[2] Northern China or *Cathay* was at this time ruled by an alien dynasty, the Chin, who originated in eastern Manchuria and had driven out their predecessors, the Khitan, a century earlier. Southern China or *Manji* still maintained its independence under the Later Sung dynasty, while western China was part of the Tangut kingdom, ruled by the Hsia. All three were later absorbed in the Mongol empire.

defeated in battle, and the Mongols took their alphabet, for formerly they had no written characters;[1] now however they call it the Mongol alphabet. Chingis then proceeded to make war on the land of Sari-Uigurs, the land of the Karanites, the land of the Voyrat and the land of Kanana, all of which countries he overcame in battle.

After that he returned to his own country and, after a short rest, he summoned all his men and they set out together to make war on the Kitayans. When they had fought for a long time against them, they conquered a large part of the territory of the Kitayans; they also hemmed in their Emperor in their largest town, which they besieged for such a long time that the army's supplies completely ran out. When they had nothing at all left to eat, Chingis Chan ordered that out of every ten men they should give one to be eaten. The men in the city, however, fought manfully against them with engines and arrows; and when they ran out of stones they threw silver instead, and especially melted-down silver, for this city contained much wealth. When they had fought for a long time and were unable to conquer it, the Mongols made a big subterranean passage from the army to the middle of the city and, suddenly making an opening in the ground—the inhabitants being all unawares—they leapt out into the middle of the city and fought with the men of the place. Those who were outside likewise attacked them and, breaking down the gates, they entered the city and, having killed the Emperor and many of the men, they took possession of it and carried off gold and silver and all its wealth; and when they had put some of their own men in command of the land of the Kitayans, they returned home. Then, once the Emperor of the Kitayans was defeated, Chingis Chan became Emperor. Part of the territory of the Kitayans, however, they have up to the present in no wise been able to conquer, for it is situated in the sea.

The Kitayans,[2] of whom we have just spoken, are pagans, and

---

[1] What John says of the derivation of the Mongol alphabet from Uighur is perfectly correct.

[2] This is the first Western account of the Chinese. At this period Buddhism was the dominant religion in China, especially in the Northern kingdom, but it had become so syncretistic and receptive to foreign influences that John of

they have their own special writing; it is said that they also have an Old and New Testament; and they have lives of Fathers and hermits and buildings made like churches, in which they pray at stated times; and they say they have some saints. They worship one God, they honour Our Lord Jesus Christ, and they believe in eternal life, but they are not baptised. They show honour and respect to our Scriptures, they love Christians and give much in alms. They seem to be most affable and kindly men. They have no beard and their physiognomy is much like that of the Mongols, though they are not so broad in the face. They have their own language. Better artificers are not to be found in the whole world in all the trades in which men are wont to be engaged. Their land is very rich in corn, wine, gold and silk and in all the things which usually support human life.

When Chingis had rested for a short time, he divided his armies. One of his sons, Tossuc[1] by name, who was also called Chan, that is, Emperor, he sent with an army against the Comans, and after much fighting Tossuc defeated them. When he had conquered them he returned home.

Chingis sent another son with an army to attack the Indians, and he conquered Lesser India. These black people are Saracens, and are called Ethiopians. This army advanced to make war on the Christians in Greater India. Hearing this, the king of that country, commonly called Prester John, assembled an army and went to meet them; and he made figures of men out of copper and set them in saddles on horses, putting fire inside them; and he placed men with bellows on the horses behind the copper figures, and with many such figures and horses fitted up like this they advanced to fight the Tartars. When they reached the battle-ground, they sent forward these horses, one next the other, while the men behind put I know not what on to the fire in the figures and blew hard with the bellows. As a result horses and men were

---

Plano Carpini's description is not unreasonable. Cf. Wieger, *Histoire des Croyances religieuses en Chine*, pp. 542–3 and 559.

The two Testaments are no doubt the Hinayana and Mahayana scriptures.

[1] This is Juchi, the eldest son of Chingis and the father of Batu. From this point the account of the Mongol campaigns becomes almost legendary, owing no doubt to John's reliance on the " Russian clerics ".

burned up by Greek fire, and the air was black with smoke. They then shot arrows at the Tartars which wounded and killed many of them, and thus they cast them out of their territory in confusion and we have never heard that they went back again later.

On their return journey through the desert they came to a land where—so we were definitely told at the Emperor's court by Russian clerics and others who had been living among them for a long time—they found monsters who had the likeness of women. When they asked them by means of many interpreters where the men-folk of that country were, they replied that every female born there had a human form, but every male had the shape of a dog. Whilst they were prolonging their stay in this land, the dogs collected together in another part of the river and, in the severe winter weather, they plunged into the water; immediately after this they rolled in the dust, and the dust thus mixed with the water froze on them. When they had done this many times, they were covered with a thick coating of ice, and with a great rush they joined battle with the Tartars. But when the latter shot at them with their arrows, the arrows rebounded as if they had shot at stones; nor were their other arms able to injure them in any way. The dogs, however, springing upon the Tartars, bit them, wounding and killing many of them, and in this way they cast them out of their country. This gave rise to a saying which is still current among the Tartars: "Your father or brother was killed by the dogs". The women they captured they took to their country and they were there until they died.

While this army, that is to say the army of the Mongols, was returning, they came to the land of Burithabet[1], which they conquered in battle. The inhabitants are pagans; they have an incredible or rather discreditable custom, for when anyone's father pays the debt of human nature they collect all the family together and eat him; we were told this for a fact. They do not grow beards, indeed they carry in their hands, as we saw, an iron instrument, with which they always pluck their beards if any hair happens to grow there, and they are exceedingly misshapen. From there the army returned home.

[1] Possibly Tibet.

At the same time that he was dividing the other armies, Chingis Chan also went with an expedition towards the west through the land of the Kergis, whom he did not conquer, and, so we were told there, he reached as far as the Caspian Mountains. The mountains in that part towards which they were directing their course are of loadstone; consequently they attracted their arrows and iron weapons. The inhabitants hemmed in by the Caspian Mountains hearing, it is believed, the noise of the army, began to break through a mountain, and when the Tartars came back that way on another occasion ten years later, they found the mountain broken in pieces. When the Tartars, however, tried to get at them, they could not, for a cloud lay ahead of them, beyond which they could in no way progress, for as soon as they reached it they lost all power of sight. Those on the opposite side, however, believing that the Tartars were afraid of attacking them, rushed towards them, but as soon as they reached the cloud they could go no further, for the reason already given. Before reaching the aforesaid mountains the Tartars travelled for more than a month through a vast wilderness.

Going on from there still westwards, they journeyed for more than a month through a large desert, and they came to a land where —so we were told with absolute certainty—they saw beaten tracks, but were unable to find any people; however, they made a thorough search throughout the land, with the result that they came across one man with his wife and these were brought before Chingis Chan. When he asked them where were the inhabitants of that country, they replied that they dwelt in the earth under the mountains. Chingis Chan, keeping the woman, sent the husband to tell those men to come at his command. He went to them and repeated all Chingis Chan's messages to them. They replied saying that on such and such a day they would come to him to do his bidding. In the meantime, however, they assembled by secret, underground routes and coming to fight against the Tartars, they suddenly rushed upon them and killed many of them. They, that is to say Chingis Chan and his followers, realised that they could gain nothing but rather would lose men, and in addition to this, they could not bear the sound of the sun—indeed at the time when the sun was rising they were obliged to place one ear on the ground and stop up the other completely so as not to hear that terrible noise, and yet even by taking these measures they were unable to prevent many of them from meeting their death on account of it—so they took to flight and left the country. However, they carried off those people with them, that is to say the man and his wife, and they remained in the land of the Tartars until their death. When questioned as to why they dwelt underground they said that at one season of the year when the sun rises the noise is so great that men cannot on any account stand it, as we have already told was the case with the Tartars. Indeed at that time they even used to strike musical instruments and beat drums and other things in order not to hear the noise.

While Chingis Chan was on the way back from that country, they ran short of food and suffered great hunger. Then they happened to come across the fresh entrails of an animal; they took them and, putting aside only the dung, they cooked them and brought them before Chingis Chan, who ate them with his men. As a result of this Chingis decreed that neither the blood nor the entrails nor any part of an animal that can be eaten, with the exception of the dung, is to be thrown away.

He then returned to his own country and there made many laws and statutes, which are observed inviolably by the Tartars.[1] We will give only two of these. One is that if anyone, puffed up by pride, wishes to be Emperor on his own authority without an election by the princes, he shall be put to death without any mercy. Hence before Cuyuc Chan's election, in accordance with this law one of the princes, a nephew of Chingis Chan, paid the death penalty, for he wanted to rule without an election. Another decree is that they are to bring the whole world into subjection to them, nor are they to make peace with any nation unless they first submit to them, until the time for their own slaughter shall come. They have fought now for forty-two years and they are due to

---

[1] From this point John's narrative once more becomes authentic and based on reliable information. The " laws and statutes "—the *Yasa*—are famous in Mongol history, and the Persian historian Juwaini says that a copy was kept in the treasury of all Chingis Khan's descendants. There is a full discussion of the subject in G. Vernadsky, *The Mongols and Russia*, pp. 99–110.

rule for another eighteen years. After that, so they say, they are to be conquered by another nation, though they do not know which; this has been foretold them. Those who escape with their lives, they say, are to keep the same law which is kept by those who defeat them in battle. Chingis also decreed that their armies should be organised into groups under captains of a thousand, a hundred, and ten, and "darkness"—that is, ten thousand[1]. He also decreed many other things which it would be tedious to tell of, and in any case I do not know what they are. After this he was killed by a thunderbolt, having completed his decrees and statutes.

Chingis had four sons. One was called Occodai, the second Tossuc Chan, another Chiaaday and the name of the fourth I do not know. All the Mongol chiefs are descended from these four. The first, namely Occodai Chan, had the following sons: the eldest is Cuyuc, who is the present Emperor, and Cocten and Chirenum, and I do not know if he had any more sons. The sons of Tossuc Chan are: Bati, who is the richest and most powerful after the Emperor, Ordu, who is the eldest of all the chiefs, Siban, Bora, Berca, Thaube. I do not know the names of Tossuc Chan's other sons. The sons of Chiaaday are Burim and Cadan. I do not know the names of the rest of his children. The sons of Chingis Chan's other son, whose name I do not know, are as follows: one is called Mongu; his mother is Sorocan, and among the Tartars this lady is the most renowned, with the exception of the Emperor's mother, and more powerful than anyone else except Bati; another son is called Bichac; he had a number of other sons, but I do not know their names.[2]

---

[1] "Tuman". John of Plano Carpini wrote "tenebras", "darkness", owing to a confusion between "tuman"—the word for 10,000—and "duman", darkness. William of Rubruck (infra, p. 171) gives the word its proper significance.

[2] This is the most complete and accurate account of the dynasty of Chingis Khan to be found in any Western writer. See the genealogical table, pp. xl–xli.

Almost the only errors are that Chirenen (or Shiramun) was not the son of Ugedey but of Mutugen son of Jagatay (Chiaaday) and that Cadan was not the son of the last-named but of Ugedey, and is probably the same as the one whom John of Plano Carpini names Cocten.

In the list of chiefs Hubilai is Kubilay, the brother and successor of Mongka. Sibedei is Subuday or Subutay, the greatest of the Mongol generals, and his title of Knight (*Miles*) represents the Mongol *Bagatur* (Turk. *Bahadur*), which signifies both a hero and a commander.

The names of the chiefs are as follows: Ordu—he was in Poland and Hungary; Bati, Birin, Syban, Dinget, all of whom were in Hungary; Cirpodan who is still beyond the sea fighting against certain Sultans of the land of the Saracens, and others who are beyond the sea. The following have stayed in their own country: Mengu, Sirenen, Hubilai, Sirenum, Sinocur, Chuacenur, Caragai, Sibedei, an old man who is known among them as "the knight", Bora, Berca, Mauci, Corenza; this last named, however, is the least of them all. There are many other chiefs, but I do not know their names.

The Emperor of the Tartars has a remarkable power over everyone. No one dare stay anywhere except in the place he has assigned to them. It is he who appoints where the chiefs are to be, but the chiefs fix the positions of the captains of a thousand, the captains of a thousand those of the captains of a hundred, and the captains of a hundred those of the captains of ten. Moreover, whatever command he gives them, whatever the time, whatever the place, be it to battle, to life or to death, they obey without a word of objection. Even if he asks for an unmarried daughter or sister, they give her to him without a murmur. Indeed, each year or every few years he collects young girls from all parts of the land of the Tartars, and if he wants to keep any for himself he keeps them; the others he gives to his men just as it seems good to him to arrange.

Whatever envoys he despatches, to whatever place and wherever it may be, they are bound to give them without delay pack-horses and provisions. Also from whatever quarter envoys come to him bearing tribute, they have likewise to be provided with horses, carts and supplies. Envoys who come for any other reason, however, are in a most unhappy position as regards both food and clothing, for poor and inadequate provision is made for them; and particularly when they come to the princes and have to prolong their stay there, for then such a small quantity is given to ten men that two could scarcely live on it. Even in the princes' ordas and on the journey they are given nothing to eat except once a day, and that little enough. Moreover, if they suffer any injury they cannot easily make any complaint and so are obliged to bear it patiently.

In addition, they are asked for many presents both by the princes and others of high and lower rank and if these are not forthcoming they despise them, indeed they consider them of no account; if they have been sent by men of importance, the Tartars are unwilling to receive a small gift from them, saying "You come from an important man and you give so little". And they refuse to accept it and, if the envoys wish for success in their undertaking, they are bound to give larger gifts. On that account we had no choice but to bestow in gifts a great part of the things given to us by the faithful for our expenses.

This also ought to be known, that all things are in the hands of the Emperor to such an extent that no one dare say this is mine or his, but everything is the Emperor's; that is to say goods, men and animals. On this point indeed a decree of the Emperor was recently issued. The chiefs have like dominion over their men in all matters, for all the Tartars are divided into groups under chiefs. Both the Emperor's men and all others are bound, without raising any objection, to provide envoys of the chiefs—whatever the destination to which they are being despatched—with packhorses and provisions and men to look after the horses and to serve the envoys. The chiefs as well as the others are obliged to give mares to the Emperor as rent, so that he can have the milk for a year, or for two or three years as it pleases him; and the men under the chiefs are bound to do the same for their lords, for not a man among them is free. In short, whatever the Emperor and the chiefs desire, and however much they desire, that they receive from their subjects' property; and their persons they dispose of in all respects according to their own good pleasure.

After the death of the Emperor, as has been said above, the chiefs assembled and elected in his stead Occodai, a son of the said Chingis Chan. Occodai held a council of his princes and then divided up his armies. Bati, who ranked second to him, he sent against the country of the Great Sultan and the land of the Bisermins.[1] These latter were Saracens but spoke the Coman

---

[1] John's account of the campaign of Ugedey is somewhat confused. The conquest of the " great Sultan " of Korezm and " the land of the Bisermins " was the work of Chingis Khan and his sons in 1219–23, and it was followed up by a minor campaign by Chormagan-Noyan (John's " Cirpodan ", p. 31) in

language. Entering their territory, Bati fought with them and overcame them in battle. A certain city called Barchin held out a long time against him, for they dug a great number of pits around the town and covered them over, and when the Tartars were nearing the city they fell into the pits, and so were unable to take it until they had filled them in.

The inhabitants of another city called Sakint, hearing of this, came out to meet the Tartars and of their own accord surrendered to them. In consequence their city was not destroyed, but many men were killed and others transported. The Tartars plundered the city and filled it with fresh inhabitants; they then proceeded to attack the city of Ornas. This city was densely populated, for there were many Christians there, namely Gazarians, Ruthenians, Alans and others, and there were also Saracens there. The government of the city was in the hands of the Saracens. This city was moreover filled with great wealth for it is situated on a river which flows through Iankint and the land of the Bisermins and runs into the sea, which makes it as it were a port, and other Saracens used to carry on extensive trading with that place. The Tartars, unable to conquer the city by any other means, threw a dam across the river, which ran through the town, and submerged it with its inhabitants and property. Having accomplished this, the Tartars then entered the land of the Turks, who are pagans.

Subduing this country, they attacked Russia, where they made great havoc, destroying cities and fortresses and slaughtering men; and they laid siege to Kiev, the capital of Russia; after they had besieged the city for a long time, they took it and put the inhabitants to death. When we were journeying through that land we came across countless skulls and bones of dead men lying about on the ground. Kiev had been a very large and thickly populated

---

1230 and the following years in North Persia, Armenia and Georgia. But the great event of Ugedey's reign was the conquest of Russia and the invasion of Central Europe by Batu and Subutay. This was the campaign which was the turning point in Russian history and which determined the fate of Eastern Europe for the next two centuries. The Mongol attack came, not from the Caucasus as John suggests, but from the northern steppes. It began in 1236–7 with the conquest of the Cumans and the Bulgars on the Middle Volga, which John puts after the invasion of Europe. In fact the conquest of north-east Russia took place in the following year (1238), while the destruction of Kiev, and the invasion of Hungary and Poland, followed in 1240 to 1242.

town, but now it has been reduced almost to nothing, for there are at the present time scarce two hundred houses there and the inhabitants are kept in complete slavery. Going on from there, fighting as they went, the Tartars destroyed the whole of Russia.

Proceeding from Russia and Comania, the afore-mentioned chiefs made war on the Hungarians and Poles. A great number of the Tartars were killed in Poland and Hungary, and if the Hungarians had not taken flight and had resisted manfully, the Tartars would have left their country, for they were filled with such fear that they all tried to run away. Bati, however, drawing his sword, withstood them to the face saying: "Do not flee, for if you do, not one will escape, and if we are to die, let us all die, for that is about to happen which Chingis Chan foretold when he said we should be put to death: if the time has now come let us endure it." And so fresh heart was put into them and they stayed and destroyed Hungary.

Then on their way back they came to the land of the Mord-vinians,[1] who are pagans, and they conquered them in battle. They next proceeded against the Billeri, that is to say Great Bulgaria,[2] and destroyed it completely. Going further north they attacked Baschart,[3] that is Great Hungary, and also defeated them.

Leaving that country they went still further north and came to the Parossites. These people have small stomachs and tiny mouths, so we were told, and they cook meat but do not eat it; when it is cooked they lean over the pot and inhale the steam and this is their only refreshment. If indeed they do eat anything, it is extremely little.

The Tartars continuing in their way came to the Samoyedes. Now these men, so it is said, live entirely off their hunting; even the tents and clothes they have are made of nothing but animal skins. Pressing on, the Tartars reached a land bordering on the

[1] The Finno-Ugrian people who still exist as an autonomous Republic of the U.S.S.R.
[2] Great Bulgaria was a Moslem State on the Middle Volga and was a very important centre of trade between Europe and Asia during the early Middle Ages.
[3] The modern Bashkirs who have given their name to the Soviet Autonomous Republic of Bashkiria in south-east Russia.

ocean, where they came across monsters, who, we were told for a fact, had a human shape in every respect except that the extremities of their feet were like the hooves of oxen and, although they had human heads, they had the faces of dogs. They would speak two words like human beings and the third they would bark like a dog, and they broke into barking in this way at intervals; however, they always came back to the matter in hand, so it was possible to understand what they were talking about. From there the Tartars returned to Comania and some of them have stayed there even until now.

At the same time Occodai Chan sent Cirpodan with an army to the south against the Kergis[1] and he defeated them in battle. These men are pagans and have no beards; they have a custom that when a man loses his father by death, out of grief he removes from his face a strip of skin from one ear to the other as a sign of mourning.

Having conquered the Kergis, Cirpodan proceeded south against the Armenians. When the Tartars were crossing a desert, they came upon certain monsters, so we were told as a certain truth, who had a human shape, but only one arm with a hand, in the middle of the breast, and one foot, and two of them shot with one bow; and they ran at such a rate that horses could not keep on their track, for they ran by hopping on their one foot and, when they grew tired with this method of progress, then they got along on the hand and foot turning cart-wheels. (Isidore called them Cyclopedes.) When this had exhausted them, they ran again in their former fashion. The Tartars managed to kill some of them, and we were told by the Russian clerics who live in the orda with the Emperor that in the legation at the Emperor's court several of the envoys of whom we made mention above came from them to make peace with him.

Moving on from there, the Tartars reached Armenia, which they conquered in battle; they also defeated part of Georgia, and the rest of the country came to do their bidding, and they gave them forty thousand *yperpera* each year as tribute and still do the same.

[1] The Circassians or Cherkess.

Continuing their march, the Tartars came to the land of the Sultan of Rum[1], a man of considerable might and power; and they fought against him and defeated him. They pushed on further, subduing and conquering, as far as the country of the Sultan of Aleppo, of which they are at the present moment taking possession, and it is their intention to attack other countries beyond this. Never up to the present day have they returned to their own country. The same army attacked the territory of the Caliph of Baghdad, which it also subdued. Every day they pay them as tribute four hundred besants, in addition to brocades and other gifts. Every year the Tartars send envoys telling the Caliph to come to them, and every year he sends magnificent presents with the tribute, begging them to release him from this obligation. The Emperor accepts the presents, nevertheless he sends for him to come.

CHAPTER VI

OF WAR, THEIR BATTLE ARRAY, ARMS, THEIR CUNNING IN ENGAGEMENTS, CRUELTY TO CAPTIVES, ASSAULT ON FORTIFICATIONS, THEIR BAD FAITH WITH THOSE WHO SURRENDER TO THEM, ETC.

HAVING spoken of their empire, we will now deal with war in the following manner: first we will tell of their battle array, second of their arms, thirdly of their cunning in engagements, fourthly of the cruelty they show to captives, fifthly of how they make assaults on forts and cities, and sixthly of the bad faith they show to those who surrender to them.

Chingis Chan ordained that the army should be organised in such a way that over ten men should be set one man and he is what we call a captain of ten; over ten of these should be placed one, named a captain of a hundred; at the head of ten captains of a hundred is placed a soldier known as a captain of a thousand, and over ten captains of a thousand is one man, and the word they

---

[1] The Seljuk Sultanate of Iconium, conquered by the Mongols in 1243-4.

use for this number means "darkness."[1] Two or three chiefs are in command of the whole army, yet in such a way that one holds the supreme command.

When they are in battle, if one or two or three or even more out of a group of ten run away, all are put to death; and if a whole group of ten flees, the rest of the group of a hundred are all put to death, if they do not flee too. In a word, unless they retreat in a body, all who take flight are put to death. Likewise if one or two or more go forward boldly to the fight, then the rest of the ten are put to death if they do not follow and, if one or more of the ten are captured, their companions are put to death if they do not rescue them.

They all have to possess the following arms at least: two or three bows, or at least one good one, three large quivers full of arrows, an axe and ropes for hauling engines of war. As for the wealthy, they have swords pointed at the end but sharp only on one side and somewhat curved, and they have a horse with armour; their legs also are covered and they have helmets and cuirasses. Some have cuirasses, and protection for their horses, fashioned out of leather in the following manner: they take strips of ox-hide, or of the skin of another animal, a hand's breadth wide and cover three or four together with pitch, and they fasten them with leather thongs or cord; in the upper strip they put the lace at one end, in the next they put it in the middle and so on to the end; consequently, when they bend, the lower strips come up over the upper ones and thus there is a double or triple thickness over the body.

They make the covering for their horses in five sections, one on one side of the horse and one on the other, and these stretch from the tail to the head and are fastened to the saddle and behind the saddle on its back and also on the neck; another section they put over its hindquarters where the ties of the two parts are fastened and in this last-named piece they make a hole for the tail

---

[1] " Darkness ": see note on p. 26 above. John has confused " duman " (darkness) with " tuman ", which means 10,000. Apart from this mistake, the whole of this chapter with its minute details of Mongol armaments and tactics is extremely accurate and well informed, as is also the following chapter with its account of the " Tartar Yoke " in Russia during its earliest and most " totalitarian " phase.

to come through; covering the breast there is another section. All these pieces reach down as far as the knees or joints of the leg. On its forehead they put an iron plate which is tied to the afore-mentioned sections on each side of the neck.

The cuirass is made in four parts. One piece stretches from the thigh to the neck, but is shaped to fit the human figure, being narrow across the chest and curved round the body from the arms downwards; behind, over the loins, they have another piece which reaches from the neck and meets the first piece encircling the body; these two sections, namely the front one and the back, are fastened with clasps to two iron plates, one on each shoulder; also on each arm they have a piece stretching from the shoulder to the hand and open at the bottom, and on each leg another piece. All these sections are fastened together by clasps.

The upper part of the helmet is of iron or steel, but the part affording protection to the neck and throat is of leather. All these leather sections are made in the manner described above.

Some of the Tartars have all the things we have mentioned made of iron in the following fashion: they make a number of thin plates of the metal, a finger's breadth wide and a hand's breadth in length, piercing eight little holes in each plate; as a foundation they put three strong narrow straps; they then place the plates one on top of the other so that they overlap, and they tie them to the straps by narrow thongs which they thread through the afore-mentioned holes; at the top they attach a thong, so that the metal plates hold together firmly and well. They make a strap out of these plates and then join them together to make sections of armour as has been described above. They make these into armour for horses as well as men and they make them shine so brightly that one can see one's reflection in them.

Some of them have lances which have a hook in the iron neck, and with this, if they can, they will drag a man from his saddle. The length of their arrows is two feet, one palm and two digits. Since feet are not all the same,[1] we will give the measurement of a geometrical foot; the length of a digit is two grains of barley, and sixteen digits make a geometrical foot. The heads of the

[1] This is the old Greek foot, consisting of four palms and sixteen digits.

arrows are very sharp and cut on both sides like a two-edged sword —the Tartars always carry files at the side of their quiver for sharpening their arrows. The iron heads have a pointed tail, a digit's breadth in length and this they stick into the shaft.

They have a shield made of wicker or twigs, but I do not think they carry it except in camp and when guarding the Emperor and the princes, and this only at night. They also have other arrows for shooting birds and animals and unarmed men; these are three digits wide; in addition they have various other kinds of arrows for shooting birds and animals.

When they are going to make war, they send ahead an advance guard and these carry nothing with them but their tents, horses and arms. They seize no plunder, burn no houses and slaughter no animals; they only wound and kill men or, if they can do nothing else, put them to flight. They much prefer, however, to kill than to put to flight. The army follows after them, taking everything they come across, and they take prisoner or kill any inhabitants who are to be found. Not content with this, the chiefs of the army next send plunderers in all directions to find men and animals, and they are most ingenious at searching them out.

When they come to a river, they cross it in the following manner, even if it is wide. The nobles have a circular piece of light leather, round the edge of which they make numerous loops, through which they thread a rope; they draw this up so that it makes a pouch, which they fill with their clothes and other things, pressing them down very tightly together; on top of these, in the middle, they put their saddles and other hard things. The men also sit in the middle and they tie the boat they have made in this way to the tail of a horse. They make one man swim in front with the horse to guide it, or sometimes they have a couple of oars with which they row to the other side of the water and so cross the river. The horses, however, they drive into the water, and a man swims by the side of one horse, which he guides, and the others all follow it; in this way they cross both narrow and wide rivers. The poorer men have a leather bag securely sewn—everybody is expected to possess one of these—and into this bag or satchel they put their clothes and all their belongings; having tied the sack tightly at the top, they hang it on to a horse's tail and cross in the manner described above.

It should be known that when they come in sight of the enemy they attack at once, each one shooting three or four arrows at their adversaries; if they see that they are not going to be able to defeat them, they retire, going back to their own line. They do this as a blind to make the enemy follow them as far as the places where they have prepared ambushes. If the enemy pursues them to these ambushes, they surround and wound and kill them. Similarly if they see that they are opposed by a large army, they sometimes turn aside and, putting a day's or two days' journey between them, they attack and pillage another part of the country and they kill men and destroy and lay waste the land. If they perceive that they cannot even do this, then they retreat for some ten or twelve days and stay in a safe place until the army of the enemy has disbanded, whereupon they come secretly and ravage the whole land. They are indeed the most cunning in war, for they have now been fighting against other nations for forty years and more.

When however they are going to join battle, they draw up all the battle lines just as they are to fight. The chiefs or princes of the army do not take part in the fighting but take up their stand some distance away facing the enemy, and they have beside them their children on horseback and their womenfolk and horses; and sometimes they make figures of men and set them on horses. They do this to give the impression that a great crowd of fighting-men is assembled there. They send a detachment of captives and men of other nationalities who are fighting with them to meet the enemy head-on, and some Tartars may perhaps accompany them. Other columns of stronger men they dispatch far off to the right and the left so that they are not seen by the enemy and in this way they surround them and close in and so the fighting begins from all sides. Sometimes when they are few in number they are thought by the enemy, who are surrounded, to be many, especially when the latter catch sight of the children, women, horses and dummy figures described above, which are with the chief or prince of the army and which they think are combatants; and alarmed by this they are thrown into disorder. If it happens that the enemy fight well, the Tartars make a way of escape for them; then as soon as they begin to take flight and are separated from each other they fall upon them and more are slaughtered in flight than could be killed in battle. However, it should be known that, if they can avoid it, the Tartars do not like to fight hand to hand but they wound and kill men and horses with their arrows; they only come to close quarters when men and horses have been weakened by arrows.

They reduce fortresses in the following manner. If the position of the fortress allows it, they surround it, sometimes even fencing it round so that no one can enter or leave. They make a strong attack with engines and arrows and they do not leave off fighting by day or night, so that those inside the fortress get no sleep; the Tartars however have some rest, for they divide up their forces and they take it in turns to fight so that they do not get too tired. If they cannot capture it in this way they throw Greek fire; sometimes they even take the fat of the people they kill and, melting it, throw it on to the houses, and wherever the fire falls on this fat it is almost inextinguishable. It can however be put out, so they say, if wine or ale is poured on it. If it falls on flesh, it can be put out by being rubbed with the palm of the hand.

If they are still unsuccessful and the city or fort has a river, they dam it or alter its course and submerge the fortress if possible. Should they not be able to do this, they undermine the city and armed men enter it from underground; once inside, some of them start fires to burn the fortress while the rest fight the inhabitants. If however they are not able to conquer it even in this way, they establish a fort or fortification of their own facing the city, so as not to suffer any injury from the missiles of the enemy; and they stay for a long time over against the city, unless by chance it has outside help from an army which fights against the Tartars and removes them by force. While they are pitched before the fortification they speak enticing words to the inhabitants making them many promises to induce them to surrender into their hands. If they do surrender to them, they say: "Come out, so that we may count you according to our custom," and when they come out to them they seek out the artificers among them and keep these, but the others, with the exception of those they wish to have as slaves, they kill with the axe. If they do spare any others they never spare the noble and illustrious men, so we are told, and if by chance the unexpected happens and some nobles are kept, they can never afterwards escape from captivity either by entreaty or by bribe.

All those they take prisoner in battle they put to death unless they happen to want to keep some as slaves. They divide those who are to be killed among the captains of a hundred to be executed by them with a battle-axe; they in their turn divide them among the captives, giving each slave to kill ten or more or less as the officers think fit.

CHAPTER VII

How They Make Peace, the Names of the Countries They have Conquered, the Tyranny They Exercise over the Inhabitants, and the Countries Which Have Manfully Resisted Them

Having described how the Tartars fight, I have now to tell of the countries they have brought under their sway and I will write of this in the following manner: first I will tell how they make peace, secondly I will give the names of the countries they have subjected, thirdly I will tell of the tyranny they exercise over them and fourthly of the countries which have manfully resisted them.

It should be known that the Tartars never make peace except with those who submit to them, for, as has been said above, they have Chingis Chan's command to bring all nations into subjection if possible. They make the following demands of them, first that, when the Tartars so wish, they shall proceed with them in their army against any nation, and secondly that they shall hand over a tenth part of everything, men as well as possessions. They count ten boys and take one of them, and they do the same with girls, and, taking them away to their own country, they keep them as slaves; the rest they number and dispose of according to their custom.

When they have complete dominion over them, if they make them any promises, they do not keep them; rather do they find reasons for making all possible extraordinary demands on them whenever they can. For example, when we were in Russia, a Saracen was sent there, on behalf, so they said, of Cuyuc Chan and Bati and we were told later that from every man who had three boys this official took one; he also took away all the unmarried men and he did the same with the women who had not got legitimate husbands; and the poor, even those who procured their daily bread by begging, he deported in like manner; the rest he numbered according to their custom and issued the command that everyone, great and small, even children but a day old, rich or poor, should pay the following tribute: that is, they should give the skin of a white bear, a black beaver, a black sable, a black fox and the black pelt of a certain animal, which has its burrow in the ground and the name of which I do not know how to translate into Latin, but the Poles and Ruthenians call it *dorcori*. Whoever does not produce these things is to be led off to the Tartars and reduced to slavery among them.

They also send for the rulers of countries, bidding them come to them without delay. When they come they do not receive the honour which is their due but are treated like other low-born people and are obliged to give substantial presents both to the chiefs and their wives and to the captains of a thousand and the captains of a hundred; indeed it is the general rule for all, even the very slaves, to pester them with requests for gifts, and this applies not only to rulers but also to the envoys sent to the Tartars by powerful princes.

Against some they trump up reasons for putting them to death, as has been told of Michael and others; some however they allow to return in order to entice others; some they murder by means of potions and poison, for it is the Tartars' intention that they alone shall rule the world. Of those whom they allow to return they demand sons or brothers and they never afterwards give these their liberty; this is how they have treated the son of Jerozlaus and a chief of the Alans and many others. If the father or brother dies without an heir they never set free the son or brother, nay rather they themselves take over the rule completely, as we saw done in the case of a chief of the Solangi.

The Tartars place *bastaki*[1] or prefects of their own in the countries of those whom they allow to return and the rulers as well as the others are obliged to obey their commands. If the men of any city or country do not do what these *bastaki* wish, the latter accuse them of being unfaithful to the Tartars, and consequently that city or country is destroyed and the inhabitants put to death by a strong force of Tartars who, summoned by the governor to whom the land is subject, arrive, unknown to the inhabitants, and suddenly rush upon them; this happened recently when we were in the land of the Tartars to a certain town of Ruthenians which the Tartars themselves had established in the land of the Comans. And not only the Tartar prince who had usurped the government of the land, or the prefect, but any noble Tartar passing through that city or country acts as if he were its ruler, especially if he is one of the more important Tartars.

Moreover they demand and receive without any gainsaying gold and silver and other things they want, when they please and as much as they please. Also if the rulers who have surrendered to them have any disputes among themselves, then they have to go to the Emperor of the Tartars to plead their case, as happened lately in the affair of the two sons of the King of Georgia. One of them was legitimate and the other born out of wedlock; the latter was called David, while the name of the legitimate son was Melic. Now the father had left part of the land to the son of the concubine; the other, who was younger, seeing that the said David had set out on the journey to the Emperor of the Tartars, also started to come to him accompanied by his mother. Melic's mother, that is to say the Queen of Georgia, died on the way; it was through her that her husband held the royal power, for that

---

[1] These are the *baskaks* or tax-inspectors who were responsible for the Mongol tax census and for the levying of taxes and recruits. There is an interesting account in the *Novgorod Chronicle* of the disturbances that occurred there in 1259 when "the accursed ones began to ride through the streets, numbering the Christian houses" (*op. cit.*, pp. 96–7).

throne could be held through wives. When the two sons reached the Emperor, they gave him magnificent presents, especially the legitimate son who was claiming back the land which his father had left to his son David, on the grounds that the latter ought not to hold it, being the son of a mistress. To this David gave reply: "Granted I am the son of a concubine, nevertheless I ask that I be shown justice in accordance with the custom of the Tartars, who make no difference between the sons of a wife and those of a concubine". Consequently judgment was given against the legitimate son and he was to be subordinate to David, who was older than he and who was to govern the land which his father had given him in peace and harmony. Thus Melic lost both the gifts he had given and the case he had against his brother.

The Tartars take tribute from and deal leniently with nations a long distance away from them which border on countries not subject to the Tartars and somewhat feared by them; they do this so that these neighbouring countries will not bring an army against them or be afraid to surrender to them; they have dealt in this way with the Obesi or Georgians, from whom they receive as tribute forty thousand *yperperas* or bezants. Otherwise at the moment they allow them to live in peace but, according to my information, the Georgians intend rebelling against them.

The names of the countries [and races] they have conquered are as follows: Kitay, the Naimans, the Solangi, the Karakitayans or black Kitay, Comania, Cumae, Voyrat, Karanites, Uigurs, Su-Mongols, Merkits, Mecrits, Sari-Uigurs, Bascart that is Great Hungary, Kergis, Cosmir, the Saracens, the Bisermins, the Turcomans, Byleri that is Great Bulgaria, Catora, Tomiti, Buri-thabet, Parossites, Cassi, the Alans or Assi, Obesi or Georgians, Nestorians, Armenians, Kangit, Comans, Brutachi who are Jews, the Mordvinians, the Turks, the Gazars, the Samoyedes, the Persians, the Tarci, Lesser India or Ethiopia, the Circassians, Ruthenians, Baghdad, and the Sarti. There are many other countries, but I do not know their names. We saw men and women from almost all the countries just mentioned.

Now follow the names of those countries which have manfully resisted the Tartars and are at the present time not subject to them: Great India, part of the Alans, part of the Kitayans and the Saxi[1]. When we were there we were told that the Tartars besieged a certain city of these Saxi and tried to subdue it. The inhabitants however made engines to match those of the Tartars, all of which they broke, and the Tartars were not able to get near the city to fight owing to these engines and missiles. At last they made an underground passage and bursting forth into the city they tried to set fire to it, while others fought, but the inhabitants posted a group to put out the fire, and the rest fought valiantly with those who had penetrated into the city and, killing many of them and wounding others, they forced them to retire to their own army. The Tartars, realising that they could do nothing against them and that many of their men were dying, withdrew from the city.

In the land of the Saracens and other nations the Tartars, who live among them as their lords and masters, take all the best craftsmen and employ them in their own service, while the rest of the artificers pay tribute out of their work. They store all their crops in the barns of their masters, who however allow them seed and as much as will furnish them with a reasonable living. In the case of others they give to each a very small quantity of bread every day and nothing else, except the small amount of meat with which they provide them three times a week, and this they do only for those artificers who live in the towns. Moreover, when it pleases the masters they take all the young men with their wives and children and compel them to follow them with all their household; from henceforth they are counted as Tartars, or rather as captives, for although they are numbered among the Tartars, they are never shown the respect that these enjoy but are treated as slaves and are sent into every kind of danger like other prisoners; they are first in battle and if a swamp or dangerous river has to be crossed, they have to try the passage first. They are also obliged to do all the work that has to be done and if they offend in any matter or do not obey a command they are flogged like donkeys.

---

[1] According to Benedict the Pole (infra, p. 80), the Saxi were the Goths who still survived in the Crimea at this period, but the list of peoples given in *The Secret History of the Mongols* (section 262) suggests that they were the Chechen of the Caucasus (Sas or Sasoun).

In short, it is little that they eat and little that they drink, and they are wretchedly clad, unless it happen that they can earn something as do the goldsmiths and other skilled craftsmen. Some however have such wicked masters that they allow them nothing and, on account of the great number of tasks which have to be carried out for their masters, they have no time to work for themselves unless they steal it from the hours when they ought to be resting or sleeping—they can do this if they have wives and their own dwelling. But the others who are kept in their master's house as slaves are in a most unhappy condition. I saw them very often wearing leather trousers with the rest of the body naked in the extreme heat of the sun, and in winter they suffer from the intense cold. I saw some of the men who had lost toes and fingers owing to the great cold and I heard that some had died or had lost the use of all their members from the same cause.

CHAPTER VIII

How to Wage War Against the Tartars; the Intentions of the Tartars; Arms and Army Organisations, How to Meet their Cunning in Battle, the Fortification of Camps and Cities, and What Should be Done with Tartar Prisoners

HAVING spoken of the countries subject to the Tartars, I must now add a description of how to wage war against them, and it seems to me it should be dealt with in the following manner: first as to their plans, secondly, as to arms and army organisation, thirdly how to meet their cunning in engagements, fourthly of the fortification of camps and cities, fifthly of what ought to be done with prisoners.

It is the intention of the Tartars to bring the whole world into subjection if they can and, as has been mentioned above, on this point they have received a command from Chingis Chan. It is for this reason that their Emperor writes in his letters: "The strength of God, the Emperor of all men" and this is the inscription on his seal: "God in heaven and Cuyuc Chan on earth, the strength of God, the seal of the Emperor of all men". This also accounts for their refusing to make peace with any nation unless, as has been told, they surrender into their hands. Since there is no country on earth which they fear with the exception of Christendom, they are preparing to make war on us. Wherefore be it known unto everyone that, while we were in the land of the Tartars, we attended a solemn court, which had been announced several years back and at which, in our presence, they chose Cuyuc as Emperor, or Chan as it is in their language. The said Cuyuc Chan, together with all the princes, raised the standard to proceed against the Church of God and the Roman Empire, and against all Christian kingdoms and nations of the West, unless they carry out the instructions he is sending to the Lord Pope, the rulers and the Christian peoples of the West.

In my opinion, these instructions ought on no account to be observed, first because of the extreme, nay intolerable, hitherto unheard-of servitude to which they reduce all nations they conquer and which we have seen with our own eyes; then because they are not trustworthy and no nation can rely on their word—they break any promises they make as soon as they see that the tide is turned in their favour, and they are full of deceit in all their deeds and assurances; it is their object to wipe off the face of the earth all princes, nobles, knights and men of gentle birth, as has already been told, and they do this to those in their power in a sly and crafty manner: then because it is unfitting that Christians should be subject to them in view of the abominations they practise and seeing that the worship of God is brought to nought, souls are perishing and bodies are afflicted beyond belief in many ways; it is true at first they speak fair words, but afterwards they sting and hurt like a scorpion; and lastly because they are fewer in number and weaker in body than the Christian peoples.

At the aforementioned court the fighting-men and chiefs of the army were given their appointments. Out of ten men they are sending three with their servants from every country under their sway. One army is to penetrate by way of Hungary, and a second by way of Poland, so we were told. They will come prepared to fight without a break for eighteen years, and they have been assigned their time for setting out. Last March we came upon an army which had been called up from among all the Tartars through whose territory we travelled after leaving Russia. In three or four years' time they will reach Comania. From there they will make an attack on the countries mentioned above; I do not know however whether they will come immediately after the third winter is over, or wait some time longer so that they have a better chance of coming unexpectedly.

All these things are sure and certain, unless God, in His mercy, places some hindrance in their way as He did when they went into Hungary and Poland. It was their plan to continue fighting for thirty years, but their Emperor was killed by poison and consequently they have rested from battle until the present time. But now, since an Emperor has been newly appointed, they are beginning to prepare for the fight once again. It should be known that the Emperor said with his own lips that he wanted to send an army into Livonia and Prussia. Since it is their object to overthrow the whole world and reduce it to slavery—a slavery, as has already been said, unbearable for men of our race—they must therefore be met in battle.

If one province is not prepared to help another, then the country the Tartars are attacking will be vanquished and they will fight against another country with the prisoners they take and these will be placed in the front line. If they fight badly the Tartars kill them, but if they fight well, then they keep them by means of promises and flattery, and to prevent them from running away they go so far as to promise to make them mighty lords. But after this, when they can feel sure that they will not leave them, they turn them into most wretched slaves and they do the same with the women they wish to keep as servants and concubines. And so, with the inhabitants of the district they have conquered, they destroy another country and, in my opinion, there is no province able to resist them by itself unless God fight on its side for, as has already been said, men are collected together from every country to fight under their dominion. Therefore if Christians wish to save themselves, their country and Christendom, then ought kings, princes, barons and rulers of countries to assemble together and by common consent send men to fight against the Tartars before they begin to spread over the land, for once they begin to be scattered throughout a country it is impossible for anyone to give any effective help to another, for troops of Tartars search out the inhabitants everywhere and slaughter them. If the latter shut themselves up in fortresses, the Tartars station three or four thousand or more men round the fort or city to besiege it, at the same time continuing to spread all over the country killing men.

Whoever wishes to fight against the Tartars ought to have the following arms: good strong bows, crossbows, of which they are much afraid, a good supply of arrows, a serviceable axe of strong iron or a battle-axe with a long handle; the heads of the arrows for both bows and cross-bows ought to be tempered after the Tartar fashion, in salt water when they are hot, to make them hard enough to pierce the Tartar armour. They should also have swords and lances with a hook to drag the Tartars from their saddle, for they fall off very easily; knives, and cuirasses of a double thickness, for the Tartar arrows do not easily pierce such; a helmet and armour and other things to protect the body and the horses from their weapons and arrows. If there are any men not as well armed as we have described, they ought to do as the Tartars and go behind the others and shoot at the enemy with their bows and crossbows. There ought to be no stinting of money when purchasing weapons for the defence of souls and bodies and liberty and other possessions.

The army should be organised in the same way as the Tartar army, under captains of a thousand, captains of a hundred, captains of ten and the chiefs of the army. The last named ought on no account to take part in the battle, just as the Tartar chiefs take no part, but they should watch the army and direct it. They should make a law that all advance together either to battle or elsewhere in the order appointed. Severe punishment ought to be meted out to anyone who deserts another either going into battle or fighting, or takes flight when they are not retreating as a body, for if this happens a section of the Tartar force follows those fleeing and kills them with arrows while the rest fight with those who have remained on the field, and so both those who stay and those who run away are thrown into confusion and killed. Similarly anyone who turns aside to take plunder before the army of the enemy has been completely vanquished ought to be punished with a very heavy sentence; among the Tartars such a one is put to death without any mercy. The chiefs of the army should choose their battle ground, if possible a flat plain, every part of which they can watch, and if they can they should have a large forest behind them or on their flank, so situated however that the Tartars cannot come between them and the wood. The army ought not to assemble into one body, but many lines should be formed, separated from each other, only not too far apart. One line ought to be sent to meet the first line of Tartars to approach; if the Tartars feign flight they ought not to pursue them very far, certainly not further than they can see, in case the Tartars lead them into ambushes they have prepared, which is what they usually do. And let another line be in readiness to help the first if occasion require it.

Moreover they ought to have scouts in every direction, behind, to the right and to the left, to see when the other lines of Tartars are coming, and one line ought always to be sent to meet each Tartar line, for the Tartars always strive to surround their enemies; the greatest precautions ought to be taken to prevent their doing this, for in this way an army is easily vanquished. Each line should take care not to pursue them for long, on account of the ambushes they are wont to prepare, for they fight with deceit rather than courage.

The leaders of the army ought always to be ready to send help to those who are fighting if they need it. Another reason for avoiding too long a pursuit after the Tartars is so as not to tire the horses, for we have not the great quantity which they have. The horses the Tartars ride on one day they do not mount again for the next three or four days, consequently they do not mind if they tire them out seeing they have such a great number of animals. Even if the Tartars retreat our men ought not to separate from each other or be split up, for the Tartars pretend to withdraw in order to divide the army, so that afterwards they can come without any let or hindrance and destroy the whole land. The Christians should also beware of their usual tendency of over-expenditure, lest they be obliged to go home on account of lack of money and the Tartars destroy the whole earth and the name of God be blasphemed on account of their extravagance. They should take care to see that if it come to pass that some fighting men return home, others take their place.

Our leaders ought also to arrange that our army is guarded day and night, so that the Tartars do not make a sudden and unexpected attack upon them for, like the devils, they devise many ways of doing harm. Indeed our men ought to be on the alert as much during the night as in the daytime, they should never undress to lie down, nor sit at table enjoying themselves, so that they cannot be taken unawares, for the Tartars are always on the watch to see how they can inflict some damage. The inhabitants of a country who are apprehensive and fear that the Tartars are coming to attack them should have secret pits in which they should put their corn as well as other things, and this for two reasons: namely so that the Tartars cannot get hold of them and also that, if God shows them His favour, they themselves will be able to find them afterwards. If they have to flee from their country, they ought to burn the hay and straw or hide it away in a safe place so that the horses of the Tartars will find less to eat.

If they wish to fortify cities or fortresses, let them first examine them from the point of view of position, for fortified places ought to be so situated that they cannot be reduced by engines and arrows; they should have a good supply of water and wood and, if possible, it should be impossible to deprive them of an entrance and exit, and they should have sufficient inhabitants for them to take it in turns in fighting. They ought to keep a careful watch to prevent the Tartars from taking the fortress by stealth, by means of cunning. They should have sufficient supplies to last for many years, and let them keep them carefully and eat them in moderation, for they do not know how long they will have to be shut up inside their fortress. When the Tartars once begin, they lay siege to a fortress for many years, for example at the present time in the land of the Alans they have been besieging a hill for the past twelve years, the inhabitants of which have manfully resisted and killed many Tartars and nobles.

Other fortresses and cities which have not the situation described above ought to be strongly protected by means of deep, walled ditches and well-built walls and they should have a good supply of bows and arrows and slings and stones. They must take great care not to allow the Tartars to place their engines in position, but they should drive them off with their own engines. If it happen that the Tartars by some device or cunning erect their engines, then the inhabitants ought to destroy them with theirs if they can; they should also use cross-bows, slings and engines against them to prevent them from drawing near to the city. In other respects they ought to be prepared as has already been described. As for fortresses and cities situated on rivers, they should be careful to see that they cannot be flooded out. Moreover, in regard to this point it should be known that the Tartars much prefer men to shut themselves into their cities and fortresses rather than fight with them in the open, for then they say they have got their little pigs shut in their sty, and so they place men to look after them as I have told above.

If any Tartars are thrown from their horse during the battle, they ought to be taken prisoner immediately, for when they are on the ground they shoot vigorously with their arrows, wounding and killing men and horses. If they are kept they can be the means of obtaining uninterrupted peace or a large sum of money would be given for them, for they have great love for each other. As to how Tartars may be recognised, it has been told above in the place where a description is given of their appearance. When they are taken prisoner, a strict guard must be kept over them if they are to be prevented from escaping. There are men of many other nations with them and these can be distinguished from them by means of the description set down above. It is important to know that there are many men in the Tartar army who, if they saw their opportunity and could rely on our men not to kill them, would fight against the Tartars in every part of the army, as they themselves told us, and they would do them worse harm than those who are their declared enemies.

These things which have been written above we have reported merely as men who have seen and heard, not in order to instruct prudent men who, by their experience of the fight, are acquainted with the cunning devices of war; for we believe that those who are practised and well-versed in these matters will think of and carry out better and more useful ideas. Nevertheless the things we have told above will stimulate them and provide them with material for thought, for it is written: "A wise man shall hear and be wiser; and he that understandeth shall possess governments" [Prov. i. 5].

CHAPTER IX

THE COUNTRIES THROUGH WHICH WE PASSED, THEIR POSITION, THE WITNESSES WE CAME ACROSS, AND THE COURT OF THE EMPEROR OF THE TARTARS AND HIS PRINCES

HAVING described how to make war against the Tartars, to finish we will speak of the journey we made, of the countries through which we passed, the arrangement of the court of the Emperor and his princes and the witnesses who came our way in the land of the Tartars.

When we had planned, as has already been told in another chapter, to set out for the Tartars, we first came to the King of the Bohemians[1]. As this lord was a friend of ours from of old we sought his advice concerning the best route to follow, and he replied that it seemed to him it would be best to go through Poland and Russia, for he had relations in Poland by whose aid we would be able to enter Russia. He gave us a letter and safe-conduct for the journey so that we could cross Poland and he also arranged for victuals to be supplied to us throughout his country and cities, until we should reach his nephew Boleslaus[2], Duke of

---

[1] King Wenceslas, 1240–53. He was a great supporter of the Franciscans, and his sister, the Blessed Agnes of Bohemia, whom St. Clare called her "other self", was the first to introduce the Poor Clares north of the Alps at Prague in 1230.

[2] Boleslaus. Boleslav V the Chaste, the Duke not of Silesia but of Cracow and Little Poland, where he had been temporarily supplanted by his uncle Conrad of Mazovia, "Conrad Duke of Lenczy", who invited the Teutonic Knights to Prussia.

Silesia, who was also a friend and acquaintance of ours. The latter likewise gave us a letter, safe-conduct and supplies in his towns and cities until we should come to Conrad, Duke of Lenczy. We were favoured by the grace of God, for at that time the Lord Vasilko[1], Duke of Russia, was there and from him we did in fact learn a good deal about the Tartars, for he had sent envoys to them and they had returned to him and his brother Daniel, bringing a safe-conduct for the Lord Daniel to go to Bati. He told us that if we wished to go to them we ought to have valuable gifts to present to them, for they asked for such things with the most pressing importunity, and if they were not given them (as is indeed true) an envoy could not properly fulfil his mission, nay rather he would be held of no account.

We did not wish the business of the Lord Pope and the Church to be hindered on that score, so out of the money which had been given to us as alms to help us on our way so that we should not be in want, we bought some beaver pelts and also the skins of various other animals. Duke Conrad, the Duchess of Cracow, certain knights and the Bishop of Cracow, learning of this, also presented us with a number of skins of this kind. Duke Conrad and his son and the Bishop of Cracow most earnestly begged the aforementioned Duke Vasilko to do all in his power to help us make the journey to the Tartars, and he replied that he would gladly do this. And so he took us with him to his own country, and after he had kept us for some days as his guests so that we could rest a little, at our request he summoned his Bishops to meet us and we read to them the Lord Pope's letter in which he admonished them that they should return to the unity of Holy Mother Church. We gave them the same counsel and also led them round as well as we could to this point of view, both the Duke and the Bishops and all who had assembled. But since at the same time that the Duke had come to Poland his brother Daniel had gone to Bati and was consequently not present, they were unable to give a definite reply; for a complete answer his return would have to be awaited.

[1] Vasilko, Prince of Volhynia, the brother of Daniel of Galich, the most powerful of the Russian princes who survived the Mongol invasion.

After this the Duke sent a servant with us as far as Kiev; however, in spite of this we went in continual danger of death on account of the Ruthenians[1], who made frequent and secret raids as often as they could upon Russian territory, especially in those parts through which we had to pass. And since the majority of the men-folk of Russia had either been killed or taken into captivity by the Tartars, they were unable to offer any effective resistance. However, thanks to the said servant we were safe from the Ruthenians. And so, the grace of God favouring us and rescuing us from the enemies of the cross of Christ, we reached Kiev, the capital of Russia.

On arrival there we talked over our journey with the captain of a thousand, and other nobles in that place. They told us that if we were to take to the Tartars the horses which we had they would all die, for the snow was deep and they would not know how to dig up the grass from under the snow like the Tartar horses, nor would we be able to find anything else for them to eat since the Tartars have neither straw nor hay nor fodder. After this discussion we decided to leave the horses there with two servants to look after them. We had to give the captain presents, so as to make him disposed to give us pack-horses and an escort. Before we got as far as Kiev, however, I was desperately ill in Danilone[2]; nevertheless I had myself carried in a vehicle through the snow in the bitter cold. In order not to hinder the affairs of Christendom, we settled our business in Kiev and set out from there for the barbarian nations with the captain's horses and the escort the day after the feast of the Purification of Our Lady [February 3rd, 1246].

We reached a town which was directly under the Tartars and is called Kaniev. The prefect of the town gave us horses and an escort as far as another town. Here the prefect was a certain Alan, called Micheas, who was filled with all malice and iniquity, for he had sent some of his retinue to us in Kiev who lyingly told us, as

---

[1] Vincent of Beauvais' version in Book XXXI of the *Speculum Historiale* reads "Lithuanians" here. This makes more sense than "Ruthenians", since it was at this time that the heathen Lithuanians began raiding southwards into Volhynia until they eventually conquered the whole of Western Russia.

[2] Danilone—position doubtful: possibly Lvov.

from Corenza, that since we were envoys we were to go to him. He did this, although it was not true, in order to be able to extort presents from us. When however we did reach him, he made himself most difficult to please and was unwilling to be of service to us in any way, unless we promised him presents. We, seeing that otherwise we would not be able to proceed any further, promised to make some offering. When we gave him what seemed good to us he would not accept it unless we gave more; and so we had to increase it in accordance with his desire, and other things he took from us by cunning, stealth and knavery.

We then left with him on the Monday of Quinquagesima and he took us as far as the first Tartar camp. On the first Friday after Ash Wednesday we were putting up for the night as the sun was setting when some armed Tartars rushed upon us in a horrible manner, wanting to know what kind of men we were. When we replied that we were envoys of the Lord Pope, they accepted some of our food and went away immediately.

When day came we set off and when we had proceeded for a short distance the chief men from the camp came to meet us, asking why we were journeying to them and what was our business. We answered them saying that we were envoys of the Lord Pope, the lord and father of Christians, who was sending us both to the King and Princes and all the Tartars because it was his desire that all Christians should be friends of the Tartars and be at peace with them; moreover he desired that they should be great before God in heaven. For this reason the Lord Pope urged them, both through us and by his letter, to become Christians and to receive the faith of Our Lord Jesus Christ, for otherwise they could not be saved; moreover he told them that he was amazed at the great slaughter of men carried out by the Tartars, especially of Christians and above all of Hungarians, Moravians and Poles, who are his subjects, seeing that they had done the Tartars no harm nor even attempted to do so; and since the Lord God was grievously offended by this, he urged them to avoid such things for the future and to do penance for their past deeds. We added that the Lord Pope asked them to write back to him what they wished to do in the future and what was their intention and to give him an answer in their letter to all the above points.

Having heard our reasons and understood what we have noted above, they replied that on the strength of what we had said they were willing to provide us with pack-horses and an escort as far as Corenza, and immediately they asked for gifts, which they received from us, for we needs must comply with their wishes. And so having given the presents and received the pack-horses, from which they themselves dismounted, we set out with an escort of them on the journey to Corenza. However, they sent ahead a messenger riding swiftly, who took with him to the chief the message we had given them. This chief is lord of all those who are placed as a guard against all the peoples of the West, to prevent them from making a sudden and unexpected attack on the Tartars. He has under him, so we heard, six thousand armed men.

When we reached Corenza he had tents pitched for us a long way from him and he sent to us his servants who were stewards to enquire of us with what we wished to bow to him, in other words what gifts did we wish to give him. We replied that the Lord Pope had not sent any presents, not being sure that we would be able to get to them. Moreover our journey had led us through districts most dangerous on account of the Ruthenian terror[1], for they frequently make raids on the roads from Poland to within a short distance of the Tartars we had passed on the way. Nevertheless from among those things which by the grace of God and our Lord the Pope we had with us for our daily needs we would honour him as well as we could. When we had given him a number of things he was not satisfied with them but must ask for more, promising that if we granted his request he would have us conducted with honour; we were obliged to do this if we wanted to live and carry through the Lord Pope's command to a successful conclusion.

After they had received the gifts they led us to his orda or tent and we were instructed to genuflect three times on the left knee before the door of the dwelling and to pay great heed not to step on the threshold of the door; we were most careful about this for

[1] " The Ruthenian terror ": see note to p. 52 above.

the sentence of death is on those who knowingly tread on the threshold of the dwelling of any chief. After we had entered we had to repeat on bended knees, in the presence of the chief and all the other nobles who had been specially summoned for this purpose, the things we had previously said. We handed him the Lord Pope's letter, but since our paid interpreter whom we had brought from Kiev was not competent to translate the letter, and there was no one else at hand capable of doing it, it could not be translated. After this we were given horses and three Tartars; two of these were captains of ten while the third belonged to Bati, to whom they were to take us with great speed. This Bati is the most powerful of all the princes of the Tartars, with the exception of the Emperor whom he is bound to obey.

We set out on the journey to him on the Monday after the first Sunday in Lent [February 26th]. We rode as fast as the horses could trot, for we had fresh horses three or four times almost every day and we rode from morn till night, even very often during the night, yet we were not able to reach him before the Wednesday of Holy Week [April 4th].

We travelled right across the land of the Comans, which is flat and contains four large rivers. The first is called the Dnieper; along the Russian side of this Corenza roams and on the other side, over the plains, Mauci, who is mightier than Corenza; the second is the Don, along which roams a prince, Carbon by name, who has as wife a sister of Bati; the third is the Volga, a very large river, along which Bati goes; the fourth is called the Yaik and along this go two captains of a thousand, the one on one side of the river, the other on the other. All these men go south in the winter towards the sea, and in the summer they go up north along the banks of the same rivers to the mountains. The sea is the Great Sea, from which juts out the arm of St. George[1] which goes to Constantinople. For many days we went along the Dnieper on the ice. These rivers are large, and very full of fish, especially the Volga. They flow into the sea of Greece, which is called the

[1] The " arm of St. George " is the Bosphorus. John's error as to the Volga and the Yaik or Ural flowing into the Black Sea is found in other early writers. William of Rubruck, on the other hand, distinguishes the Caspian and the Black Seas very clearly.

Great Sea, on the shores of which we were in considerable danger for many days on account of the ice in a number of places, for it freezes round the shores for a good three leagues out.

Before we reached Bati two of our Tartars went on ahead to inform him of everything we had said to Corenza. When we got to Bati, on the borders of the land of the Comans, we were stationed a league away from his tents. When the time came for us to be taken to his court, we were told that we would have to pass between two fires, a thing we were on no account willing to do. But they said to us: "Go without any fear, for we are making you pass between two fires for no other reason than this that, if you are planning to do any evil to our lord or if you happen to be carrying poison, the fire may remove all that is harmful." To this we replied: "That being the reason, we will go through so as not to be suspected of such things."

When we arrived at the orda, his steward, who is called Eldegai, asked us with what we wished to bow, that is to say what gifts we were ready to give. I gave the same answer as I had given to Corenza, namely that the Lord Pope had not sent any presents, but we wished to honour him as well as we could from among those things which, by the grace of God and the Lord Pope, we had with us for our needs. The gifts offered and accepted, the steward Eldegai enquired of us the purpose of our coming and we gave him the same reasons we had given earlier to Corenza.

Having heard this they led us into the dwelling after we had first made a bow and received the warning about not treading on the threshold, as has been described. Entering we said what we had to say on our knees; that done we delivered the letter and asked to be given interpreters capable of translating it. We were given them on Good Friday, and carefully translated the letter with them into Ruthenian, Saracenic[1] and Tartar characters. This translation was presented to Bati, who read it and noted it carefully. At last we were led back to our tent, but they gave us no food, except once when they gave us a little millet in a bowl the first night we arrived.

---

[1] " Saracenic " probably denotes " Persian ", and " Tartar " means " Uighur ", since these were the languages used in the Mongol chancery.

Bati lives with considerable magnificence, having door-keepers and all officials just like their Emperor. He even sits raised up as if on a throne with one of his wives; the others, however, both his brothers and sons and others less noble, sit lower down on a bench in the middle; as for the rest they sit beyond them on the ground, the men on the right and the women on the left. He has large and very beautiful tents of linen which used to belong to the King of Hungary. No outsider, except a member of his household, however mighty and powerful he may be, dare approach his tent if he has not been summoned, unless he happens to know that that is Bati's desire. We, having declared our purpose, sat down on the left, for this is what all envoys do on their way to the Emperor, but on the way back we were always placed on the right. In the middle near the door of the tent is set a table on which drinks are placed in gold and silver vessels. Neither Bati nor any other Tartar prince ever drinks, especially in public, without there being singing and guitar-playing for them. When he goes out riding a sunshade or little tent is carried over his head on a stick, and the same is done in the case of all the chief princes of the Tartars and also their wives. Bati is kindly towards his own men, nevertheless he is greatly feared by them; in battle he is the most cruel of men, very shrewd and also extremely cunning in war, for he has now been fighting for many years.

On Holy Saturday we were summoned to the orda, and Bati's steward, whom we have mentioned before, coming out to us told us on his master's behalf that we were to go to the Emperor Cuyuc in their own country, and that they were detaining certain of our party under the pretence that they wished to send them back to the Lord Pope. We gave them a letter to take to him giving an account of all that we had done, but when they reached Mauci on the return journey they were kept there until we arrived.

On Easter Sunday we said office and made some kind of a meal and then, together with the two Tartars who had been assigned to us by Corenza, we left with many tears, for we knew not whether we were going to death or to life. We were so weak we could hardly ride. During the whole of that Lent our food had been nothing but millet with water and salt, and it was the same on other fast days, and we had nothing to drink except snow melted in a kettle.

North of Comania, immediately after Russia, are the Mordvinians, the Bylers, that is Great Bulgaria, the Bastarcs, that is Great Hungary; beyond the Bastarcs are the Parosites and the Samoyedes; after the Samoyedes are those men who are said to have faces like dogs and live in the wilderness along the shores of the ocean. To the south of Comania are the Alans, the Circassians, the Gazars, Greece, Constantinople and the land of the Iberians, the Caths, the Bruthachi who are said to be Jews and shave their heads, the land of the Sicci, of the Georgians and Armenians and the country of the Turks.[1] To the west it has Hungary and Russia. This land of the Comans is very large and long.

It took us from the beginning of Lent until eight days after Easter to cross Comania, riding hard, for we had fresh horses five or seven times a day, not indeed when we were going through the desert, as has already been told, but then we were given better and stronger horses able to maintain a prolonged effort. The Tartars killed these Comans; some did in fact flee from before them and others were reduced to slavery. Most of those who fled however have come back to them.

We next entered the country of the Kangits,[2] in many parts of which there is great scarcity of water and but few people dwell there. This was why many of the men of Jerozlaus, Duke of Russia, who were going to the land of the Tartars to join him, died of thirst in the desert. In this country as well as in Comania we came across many skulls and bones of dead men lying on the ground like dung. We were travelling through this country from eight days after Easter until about the Ascension of Our Lord. The inhabitants were pagans and neither the Comans nor the Kangits cultivated the land, but lived off their animals, nor did they build houses but dwelt in tents. The Tartars also wiped out

[1] Most of these peoples have been already mentioned in the list on p. 41. The Cathi may be either the Karthlians or the Khaketians of Georgia, the Sicci are the Zichians of the Kuban Steppe.
[2] The Kangli Turks, whose name still survives as that of one of the subdivisions of the Kaizaks. See p. 125 n. 2.

the Kangits and now inhabit their country; such Kangits as were left have been reduced to slavery.

On leaving the land of the Kangits we entered the country of the Bisermins.[1] These people used to speak the Coman language and still speak it, but they hold the faith of the Saracens. In this country we came across innumerable ruined cities and demolished forts and many deserted towns. There is there a large river—I do not know its name—on which lies a city called Iankinc, and another called Barchin and a third called Orpar and many others the names of which I do not know. This country used to have a ruler called the Great Sultan and he was destroyed, together with all his children, by the Tartars, but I do not know his name. There are very high mountains in this land. To the south of it lies Jerusalem, Baghdad and the whole country of the Saracens; near its borders are stationed the chiefs Burin and Cadan[2] who are blood-brothers. On the north it has part of the country of the Black Kitayans and the ocean; here Siban, Bati's brother, is stationed. We travelled through this country from about the feast of the Ascension until eight days before the feast of St. John the Baptist [May 17th–June 16th].

We next entered the land of the Black Kitayans,[3] where the Tartars have only recently built a city called Divult[4] and the Emperor has put up a house there to which we were invited for a drink. The Emperor's representative there made the nobles of the city and even his two sons clap their hands before us.

On leaving there we came to a lake,[5] not very large, and I do not know what it is called for we did not ask. On the shore of this lake there is a little hill in which there is an opening, so they say, and in winter such great storms of wind come out of it that men can hardly pass by and only at great peril. In summer the sound of the wind can always be heard there but it only blows

[1] "The country of the Bisermins"—the kingdom of Khorezm or Khiva. It is difficult to identify the different cities, but Orpar is probably Otrar on the river Syr Darya.

[2] "Burin and Cadan." This is incorrect, as Buri was the grandson of Jagatay, and Cadan the son of Ugedey.

[3] The former kingdom of the Kara Khitay extended from the Syr Darya to the upper Irtish and the borders of Mongolia.

[4] Divult—the city of Omyl or Imil in Tarbagatai.

[5] This lake is probably the Ala Kul.

gently out of the hole, or so we were told by the inhabitants. We journeyed for several days along the shores of this lake, which has in it a number of islands. We went away from it leaving it on our left. This country has an abundance of rivers, though they are not large; on both banks of the rivers there are woods, but they do not stretch far in depth. Ordu lives in this country; he is older than Bati, in fact he is the oldest of all the Tartar chiefs. The orda or court of his father is there and it is ruled by one of his wives, for it is a custom among the Tartars that the courts of princes or nobles are not destroyed but women are always appointed to control them and they are given their share of the offerings just as their lord was in the habit of giving them.

We next came to the Emperor's chief orda, where one of his wives was living. As we had not yet seen the Emperor they were unwilling to invite us or to allow us to enter the orda, but they did have us very well looked after in the Tartar fashion in our own tent and they kept us there throughout the day so that we could rest.

Leaving there on the Vigil of St. Peter [June 28th] we entered the country of the Naimans,[1] who are pagans. On the feast of the Apostles Peter and Paul there was a heavy fall of snow there and we experienced intense cold. This land is extremely mountainous and cold and there is very little flat country. The two nations last mentioned do not cultivate the land, but like the Tartars dwell in tents. They have both been overthrown by the Tartars. We journeyed through this country for many days.

Next we entered the land of the Mongols, whom we call Tartars. We were, I think, journeying through this country for three weeks riding hard, and on the feast of St. Mary Magdalene [July 22nd] we reached Cuyuc, who is now Emperor. We made the whole of this journey at great speed, for our Tartars had been ordered to take us quickly so that we could arrive in time for the solemn court which had been convened several years back for the election. And so we started at dawn and journeyed until night without a meal,

---

[1] The Naiman of Western Mongolia, whom John describes as pagans, are spoken of as Christians by William of Rubruck (cf. *infra*, p. 122). There is no doubt that Nestorian Christian influences were very strong amongst them.

and many a time we arrived so late that we did not eat that night but were given in the morning the food we should have eaten the previous evening. We went as fast as the horses could trot, for the horses were in no way spared since we had fresh ones several times a day, and those which fell out returned, as has already been described, and so we rode swiftly without a break.

On our arrival Cuyuc had us given a tent and provisions, such as it is the custom for the Tartars to give, but they treated us better than other envoys. Nevertheless we were not invited to visit him for he had not yet been elected, nor did he yet concern himself with the government. The translation of the Lord Pope's letter, however, and the things I had said had been sent to him by Bati. After we had stayed there for five or six days he sent us to his mother[1] where the solemn court was assembling. By the time we got there a large pavilion had already been put up made of white velvet, and in my opinion it was so big that more than two thousand men could have got into it. Around it had been erected a wooden palisade, on which various designs were painted. On the second or third day we went with the Tartars who had been appointed to look after us and there all the chiefs were assembled and each one was riding with his followers among the hills and over the plains round about.

On the first day they were all clothed in white velvet, on the second in red—that day Cuyuc came to the tent—on the third day they were all in blue velvet and on the fourth in the finest brocade. In the palisade round the pavilion were two large gates, through one of which the Emperor alone had the right to enter and there were no guards placed at it although it was open, for no one dare enter or leave by it; through the other gate all those who were granted admittance entered and there were guards there with swords and bows and arrows. If anyone approached the tent beyond the fixed limits, he was beaten if caught; if he ran away he was shot at, but with arrows however which had no heads. The horses were, I suppose, two arrow-flights away. The chiefs went about everywhere armed and accompanied by a number of their

[1] Turakina (or Toragana) Khatun, the Empress Dowager, who had exercised the regency during the interregnum since the death of Ugedey Khan.

men, but none, unless their group of ten was complete, could go as far as the horses; indeed those who attempted to do so were severely beaten. There were many of them who had, as far as I could judge, about twenty marks' worth of gold on their bits, breastplates, saddles and cruppers. The chiefs held their conference inside the tent and, so I believe, conducted the election. All the other people however were a long way away outside the afore-mentioned palisade. There they remained until almost mid-day and then they began to drink mare's milk and they drank until the evening, so much that it was amazing to see. We were invited inside and they gave us mead as we would not take mare's milk. They did this to show us great honour, but they kept on plying us with drinks to such an extent that we could not possibly stand it, not being used to it, so we gave them to understand that it was disagreeable to us and they left off pressing us.

Outside were Duke Jerozlaus of Susdal in Russia and several chiefs of the Kitayans and Solangi, also two sons of the King of Georgia, the ambassador of the Caliph of Baghdad, who was a Sultan, and more than ten other Sultans of the Saracens, so I believe and so we were told by the stewards. There were more than four thousand envoys there, counting those who were carrying tribute, those who were bringing gifts, the Sultans and other chiefs who were coming to submit to them, those summoned by the Tartars and the governors of territories. All these were put together outside the palisade and they were given drinks at the same time, but when we were outside with them we and Duke Jerozlaus were always given the best places. I think, if I remember rightly, that we had been there a good four weeks when, as I believe, the election took place; the result however was not made public at that time; the chief ground for my supposition was that whenever Cuyuc left the tent they sang before him and as long as he remained outside they dipped to him beautiful rods on the top of which was scarlet wool, which they did not do for any of the other chiefs. They call this court the Sira Orda.

Leaving there we rode all together for three or four leagues to another place, where on a pleasant plain near a river among the mountains another tent had been set up, which is called by them the Golden Orda;[1] it was here that Cuyuc was to be enthroned on the feast of the Assumption of Our Lady,[2] but owing to the hail which fell, as I have already related, the ceremony was put off. This tent was supported by columns covered with gold plates and fastened to other wooden beams with nails of gold, and the roof above and the sides on the interior were of brocade, but outside they were of other materials. We were there until the feast of St. Bartholomew,[3] on which day a vast crowd assembled. They stood facing south, so arranged that some of them were a stone's throw away from the others, and they kept moving forward, going further and further away, saying prayers and genuflecting towards the south. We however, not knowing whether they were uttering incantations or bending the knee to God or another, were unwilling to genuflect. After they had done this for a considerable time, they returned to the tent and placed Cuyuc on the imperial throne, and the chiefs knelt before him and after them all the people, with the exception of us who were not subject to them. Then they started drinking and, as is their custom, they drank without stopping until the evening. After that cooked meat was brought in carts without any salt and they gave one joint between four or five men. Inside however they gave meat with salted broth as sauce and they did this on all the days that they held a feast.

At that place we were summoned into the presence of the Emperor, and Chingay[4] the protonotary wrote down our names and the names of those who had sent us, also the names of the chief of the Solangi and of others, and then calling out in a loud voice he recited them before the Emperor and all the chiefs. When this was finished each one of us genuflected four times on the left knee and they warned us not to touch the lower part of the threshold. After we had been most thoroughly searched for knives

[1] Altyn Orda. This name—the Golden Horde—was transferred to the Mongols of the west after the break-up of the Empire, and is used by Russian historians in the traditional title of the Khanate of Kypchak, which was originally known as the Great Horde.
[2] August 15th.
[3] August 24th.
[4] Chingay was a Nestorian Christian and had already been chancellor under Ugedey. He was executed a few years later with Guyuk's other ministers when Mongka became Khan.

and they had found nothing at all, we entered by a door on the east side, for no one dare enter from the west with the sole exception of the Emperor or, if it is a chief's tent, the chief; those of lower rank do not pay much attention to such things. This was the first time since Cuyuc had been made Emperor that we had entered his tent in his presence. He also received all the envoys in that place, but very few entered his tent.

So many gifts were bestowed by the envoys there that it was marvellous to behold—gifts of silk, samite, velvet, brocade, girdles of silk threaded with gold, choice furs and other presents. The Emperor was also given a sunshade or little awning such as is carried over his head, and it was all decorated with precious stones. A certain governor of a province brought a number of camels for him, decked with brocade and with saddles on them having some kind of contrivance inside which men could sit, and there were, I should think, forty or fifty of them; he also brought many horses and mules covered with trappings or armour made of leather or of iron. We in our turn were asked if we wished to present any gifts, but we had by now used up practically everything, so had nothing to give him. There up on a hill a good distance away from the tents were stationed more than five hundred carts, which were all filled with gold and silver and silken garments, and these things were shared out among the Emperor and the chiefs. Each chief divided his share among his men, but according to his own good pleasure.

Leaving there we went to another place where a wonderful tent had been set up all of red velvet, and this had been given by the Kitayans; there also we were taken inside. Whenever we went in we were given mead and wine to drink, and cooked meat was offered us if we wished to have it. A lofty platform of boards had been erected, on which the Emperor's throne was placed. The throne, which was of ivory, was wonderfully carved and there was also gold on it, and precious stones, if I remember rightly, and pearls. Steps led up to it and it was rounded behind. Benches were also placed round the throne, and here the ladies sat in their seats on the left; nobody, however, sat on the right, but the chiefs were on benches in the middle and the rest of the people sat beyond them. Every day a great crowd of ladies came.

The three tents of which I have spoken were very large. The Emperor's wives however had other tents of white felt, which were quite big and beautiful. At that place they separated, the Emperor's mother going in one direction and the Emperor in another to administer justice. The mistress of the Emperor had been arrested; she had murdered his father with poison at the time when their army was in Hungary and as a result the army in these parts retreated. Judgment was passed on her along with a number of others and they were put to death.

At the same time the death occurred of Jerozlaus, Grand Duke in a part of Russia called Susdal. He was invited by the Emperor's mother, who gave him to eat and drink with her own hand as if to show him honour. On his return to his lodging he was immediately taken ill and died seven days later and his whole body turned bluish-grey in a strange fashion. This made everybody think that he had been poisoned there, so that the Tartars could obtain free and full possession of his lands. An additional proof of this is the fact that straightway, without the knowledge of Jerozlaus's suite there, the Emperor sent a messenger post haste to Russia to his son Alexander[1] telling him to come as he wished to give him his father's lands. Alexander was willing to go but waited, in the meantime sending a letter saying that he would come and receive his father's lands. Everybody, however, believed that if he did come he would be put to death or at least imprisoned for life.

After the death of Jerozlaus, if I remember the time correctly, our Tartars took us to the Emperor. When he heard from them that we had come to him he ordered us to go back to his mother, the reason being that he wished on the following day to raise his banner against the whole of the Western world—we were told this definitely by men who knew, as I have mentioned above—and he wanted us to be kept in ignorance of this. On our return we stayed

---

[1] Alexander, afterwards known as St. Alexander Nevski. He actually came to Karakorum more than a year later with his brother Andrew, when he was invested with the principality of Kiev, and his brother with that of Vladimir. In 1251 Andrew was dethroned, but Alexander, who succeeded him at Vladimir, always remained on good terms with his Mongol suzerains.

for a few days, then we went back to him again and remained with him for a good month, enduring such hunger and thirst that we could scarcely keep alive, for the food provided for four was barely sufficient for one, moreover we were unable to find anything to buy, for the market was a very long way off. If the Lord had not sent us a certain Russian, by name Cosmas, a goldsmith and a great favourite of the Emperor, who supported us to some extent, we would, I believe, have died, unless the Lord had helped us in some other way.

Before the enthronement Cosmas showed us the Emperor's throne which he himself had made and his seal which he had fashioned, and he also told us what the inscription was on the seal. We picked up many other bits of private information about the Emperor from men who had come with other chiefs, a number of Russians and Hungarians knowing Latin and French, and Russian clerics and others,[1] who had been among the Tartars, some for thirty years, through wars and other happenings, and who knew all about them, for they knew the language and had lived with them continually some twenty years, others ten, some more, some less. With the help of these men we were able to gain a thorough knowledge of everything. They told us about everything willingly and sometimes without being asked, for they knew what we wanted.

After this the Emperor sent for us, and through Chingay his protonotary told us to write down what we had to say and our business, and give it to him. We did this and wrote out for him all that we said earlier to Bati, as has already been told. A few days passed by; then he had us summoned again and told us through Kadac, the procurator of the whole empire, in the presence of Bala and Chingay his protonotaries and many other scribes, to say all we had to say: we did this willingly and gladly. Our interpreter on this as on the previous occasion was Temer, a knight of Jerozlaus': and there were also present a cleric who was with him

---

[1] The existence of the Europeans at the Mongol court is also vouched for by William of Rubruck. Some of the Russians may have been brought back from the first Mongol raid to the West in 1221–3, but most of them, and especially the Hungarians, were probably newcomers who had been captured a few years before during Batu's great European campaign of 1238–42.

and another cleric who was with the Emperor. On this occasion we were asked if there were any people with the Lord Pope who understood the writing of the Russians or Saracens or even of the Tartars. We gave answer that we used neither the Ruthenian nor Saracen writing; there were however Saracens in the country but they were a long way from the Lord Pope; but we said that it seemed to us that the most expedient course would be for them to write in Tartar and translate it for us, and we would write it down carefully in our own script and we would take both the letter and the translation to the Lord Pope. Thereupon they left us to go to the Emperor.

On St. Martin's day we were again summoned, and Kadac, Chingay and Bala, the aforementioned secretaries, came to us and translated the letter for us word by word. When we had written it in Latin, they had it translated so that they might hear a phrase at a time, for they wanted to know if we had made a mistake in any word. When both letters were written, they made us read it once and a second time in case we had left out anything, and they said to us: " See that you clearly understand everything, for it would be inconvenient if you did not understand everything, seeing you have to travel to such far-distant lands". When we replied "We understand everything clearly" they wrote the letter once again in Saracenic, in case anyone should be found in those parts who could read it, if the Lord Pope so wished.

It is the custom for the Emperor of the Tartars never to speak to a foreigner, however important he may be, except through an intermediary, and he listens and gives his answer, also through the intermediary. Whenever his subjects have any business to bring before Kadac, or while they are listening to the Emperor's reply, they stay on their knees until the end of the conversation, however important they may be. It is not possible nor indeed is it the custom for anyone to say anything about any matter after the Emperor has declared his decision. This Emperor not only has a procurator and protonotaries and secretaries, but all officials for dealing with both public and private matters, except that he has no advocates, for everything is settled according to the decision of the Emperor without the turmoil of legal trials. The other princes of the Tartars do the same in those matters concerning them.

The present Emperor may be forty or forty-five years old[1] or more; he is of medium height, very intelligent and extremely shrewd, and most serious and grave in his manner. He is never seen to laugh for a slight cause nor to indulge in any frivolity, so we were told by the Christians who are constantly with him. The Christians of his household also told us that they firmly believed he was about to become a Christian, and they have clear evidence of this, for he maintains Christian clerics and provides them with supplies of Christian things; in addition he always has a chapel before his chief tent and they sing openly and in public and beat the board for services after the Greek fashion like other Christians, however big a crowd of Tartars or other men be there. The other chiefs do not behave like this.

According to our Tartars the Emperor proposed sending ambassadors with us, to accompany us. I think, however, that they wanted us to request him to do this, for one of our Tartars, the eldest, advised us to make this petition. But since it did not seem good to us that they should come, we told him it was not for us to do the asking, but if the Emperor by his own desire should send them, we would by the help of God conduct them safely. There were several reasons why it did not seem expedient to us that they should come. In the first place we were afraid lest, seeing the dissensions and wars which are rife among us, they might be all the more encouraged to attack us. The second reason was that we feared that their real purpose might be to spy out the land. The third reason was that we were apprehensive that they might be killed, for our people are for the most part arrogant and proud. When at the request of the Cardinal, who is legate in Germany, the servants with us went to him wearing Tartar costume, they were very nearly stoned by the Germans on the way and obliged to take off the costume. Now it is the custom of the Tartars never to make peace with men who kill their envoys, until they have taken vengeance on them.

---

[1] " Forty or forty-five years old ". In reality Guyuk must have been considerably younger than this, hardly more than thirty years old.

The fourth reason is that we were afraid they might be taken from us by force, as happened on one occasion to a Saracen prince, who is still in captivity if he has not died. The fifth reason is that no good purpose would be served by their coming, since they would have no other mandate or authority than that of taking to the Lord Pope and to the other princes the letters which we had; and we believed that this might have harmful consequences. For these reasons we were not in favour of their coming.

Two days later, that is to say on the feast of St. Brice [November 13th], they gave us a permit to depart and a letter sealed with the Emperor's seal, and sent us to the Emperor's mother. She gave each of us a fox-skin cloak, which had the fur outside and was lined inside, and a length of velvet; our Tartars stole a good yard from each of the pieces of velvet and from the piece given to our servant they stole more than half. This did not escape our notice, but we preferred not to make a fuss about it.

We then set out on the return journey.[1] We travelled throughout the winter, often sleeping in the desert on the snow except when we were able to clear a place with our feet. When there were no trees but only open country we found ourselves many a time completely covered with snow driven by the wind. So on the Lord's Ascension[2] we reached Bati and we told him to send an answer to the Lord Pope. He replied that he did not wish to send any message other than that which the Emperor had written, and he added that we were to tell the Lord Pope and the other lords with great care what the Emperor had written. Having been given a letter of safe conduct we took our leave of him and we got as far as Mauci by the Saturday within the octave of Pentecost;[3] there were our companions and servants who had been detained, and we had them brought back to us.

From there we went to Corenza, who again asked us for presents. We did not give him any, for we had none. He provided us with two Comans, who counted as Tartars, to take us as far as Kiev in Russia. Our Tartar however did not leave us until we had left the last Tartar post. The others, who had been given to us by Corenza, took us in six days from the last post as far as Kiev, and

[1] May 9th, 1247.   [2] May 25th.   [3] June 9th.

we arrived there fifteen days before the feast of St. John the
Baptist.[1] When the inhabitants of Kiev became aware of our
arrival, they all came to meet us rejoicing and they congratulated
us as if we were risen from the dead. We met with the same reception throughout the whole of Poland, Bohemia and Russia.

Daniel and his brother Vasilko made a great feast for us and
kept us, against our will, for quite eight days. In the meantime
they discussed between themselves and with the bishops and
other worthy men the matter about which we had spoken to them
when we were setting out for the Tartars. They answered us
jointly declaring that they wished to have the Lord Pope as their
special lord and father, and the Holy Roman Church as their
lady and mistress, and they also confirmed everything which they
had previously despatched by their abbot concerning this matter.
In addition they sent with us a letter and envoys.

To avoid any doubt arising in the minds of anyone as to our
having been to the Tartars, we will write down the names of those
with whom we came into contact there. Near the orda of Carbon,
who is married to Bati's sister, we met with King Daniel of Russia
and all his knights and men who had accompanied him; when with
Corenza we met Nongrot, a captain of a hundred from Kiev, and
his companions, and they also escorted us part of the journey;
they reached Bati after us. At Bati's orda we came across the son
of Duke Jerozlaus; he was accompanied by a knight from Russia
called Sangor, who was a Coman by nationality but is now a
Christian, like the other Russian who was our interpreter with
Bati and came from the Susdal district. At the court of the
Emperor of the Tartars we met Duke Jerozlaus, who died there,
and one of his knights, by name Temer. This latter acted as our
interpreter with Cuyuc Chan, the Emperor namely of the Tartars,
both in translating the Emperor's letter to the Lord Pope and in
speaking and replying. There also were Dubuzlaus, a cleric of
the said Duke, and his servants James, Michael and another James.
On coming to the land of the Bisermins on our way back, in the

---

[1] This six months' winter journey across Asia is the most extraordinary of
all the achievements of the missionaries. Unfortunately we have no information
as to their route or how they surmounted the difficulties and hardships of their
journey.

city of Lemfinc, we met Coligneus who, by command of Jerozlaus and Bati, was on his way to join the said Jerozlaus; and also Cocteleban and all his suite. All of these have returned to the Susdal district in Russia and the truth could if necessary be learned from them. At Mauci's orda Duke Jerozlaus and his suite, and also a certain duke from Russia called Sancopoltus and his retinue met with our companions who had stayed behind there. On leaving Comania we came across Duke Romanus, who was going to the Tartars, together with his companions and Duke Olaha, who was leaving, with his suite. An envoy also of the Duke of Chernigov left Comania along with us and travelled across Russia with us for a considerable time; all these Dukes are Ruthenians.

The entire city of Kiev is a witness, for the inhabitants gave us an escort and horses as far as the first Tartar camp, and on our return they received us together with our Tartar escort and their horses which were being returned to them; likewise all those men of Russia who were on our route and received Bati's sealed letter and order saying that they were to provide us with horses and food, otherwise he would put them to death.

In addition there are as witnesses the merchants from Vratislavia, who accompanied us as far as Kiev and know that we were in the clutches of the Tartars, and also many other merchants, both from Poland and from Austria, who arrived at Kiev after we had gone to the Tartars. Further witnesses are the merchants from Constantinople who came to Russia via the Tartars and were in Kiev when we returned from the land of the Tartars. The names of these merchants are as follows: Michael the Genoese and Bartholomew, Manuel the Venetian, James Reverius of Acre, Nicolas Pisani, are the chief; the less important are: Mark, Henry, John, Vasius, another Henry Bonadies, Peter Paschami. There were many others, but I do not know their names.

We beg all those who read the foregoing account not to cut out or add anything, for, with truth as guide, we have written everything that we have seen or heard from others who we believe are to be trusted and, as God is witness, we have not knowingly added anything. People however whom we came across on our journey in Poland, Bohemia, Germany and in Liége and Champagne wanted to have the above account and so they copied it before it was complete and even in a very abbreviated form, for we had not then had a quiet time when we could finish it completely. Therefore let no one be surprised that in the present account there are more facts and they are more correct than in the former, for having some leisure we corrected this copy so that it is complete and perfect, at least more perfect than the unfinished one.

Here ends the account of the Mongols who by us are called the Tartars.

Two Bulls of Pope Innocent IV Addressed to the Emperor of the Tartars[1]

I

GOD the Father, of His graciousness regarding with unutterable loving-kindness the unhappy lot of the human race, brought low by the guilt of the first man, and desiring of His exceeding great charity mercifully to restore him whom the devil's envy overthrew by a crafty suggestion, sent from the lofty throne of heaven down to the lowly region of the world His only-begotten Son, consubstantial with Himself, who was conceived by the operation of the Holy Ghost in the womb of a fore-chosen virgin and there clothed in the garb of human flesh, and afterwards proceeding thence by the closed door of His mother's virginity, He showed Himself in a form visible to all men. For human nature, being endowed with reason, was meet to be nourished on eternal truth as its choicest food, but, held in mortal chains as a punishment for sin, its powers were thus far reduced that it had to strive to understand the invisible things of reason's food by means of inferences drawn from visible things. The Creator of that creature became visible, clothed in our flesh, not without change in His nature[2], in order that, having become visible, He might call back to Himself, the Invisible, those pursuing after visible things, moulding men by His salutary instructions and pointing out to them by means of His teaching the way of perfection: following the pattern of His holy way of life and His words of evangelical instruction, He deigned to suffer death by the torture of the cruel

[1] In *Epistolae Saeculi xiii e regestis Pontificorum Romanorum selectae,* t. ii, Nos. 102 and 105, *Monumenta Germaniae Historica.*
[2] *Non sine commutatione nature.*

cross, that, by a penal end to His present life, He might make an end of the penalty of eternal death, which the succeeding generations had incurred by the transgression of their first parent, and that man might drink of the sweetness of the life of eternity from the bitter chalice of His death in time. For it behoved the Mediator between us and God to possess both transient mortality and everlasting beatitude, in order that by means of the transient He might be like those doomed to die and might transfer us from among the dead to that which lasts for ever.

He therefore offered Himself as a victim for the redemption of mankind and, overthrowing the enemy of its salvation, He snatched it from the shame of servitude to the glory of liberty, and unbarred for it the gate of the heavenly fatherland. Then, rising from the dead and ascending into heaven, He left His vicar on earth, and to him, after he had borne witness to the constancy of his love by the proof of a threefold profession, He committed the care of souls, that he should with watchfulness pay heed to and with heed watch over their salvation, for which He had humbled His high dignity; and He handed to him the keys of the kingdom of heaven by which he and, through him, his successors, were to possess the power of opening and of closing the gate of that kingdom to all. Wherefore we, though unworthy, having become, by the Lord's disposition, the successor of this vicar, do turn our keen attention, before all else incumbent on us in virtue of our office, to your salvation and that of other men, and on this matter especially do we fix our mind, sedulously keeping watch over it with diligent zeal and zealous diligence, so that we may be able, with the help of God's grace, to lead those in error into the way of truth and gain all men for Him. But since we are unable to be present in person in different places at one and the same time—for the nature of our human condition does not allow this—in order that we may not appear to neglect in any way those absent from us we send to them in our stead prudent and discreet men by whose ministry we carry out the obligation of our apostolic mission to them. It is for this reason that we have thought fit to send to you our beloved son Friar Laurence of Portugal and his companions of the Order of Friars Minor, the bearers of this letter, men remarkable for their religious spirit, comely in their virtue and gifted with a knowledge of Holy Scripture, so that following their salutary instructions you may acknowledge Jesus Christ the very Son of God and worship His glorious name by practising the Christian religion. We therefore admonish you all, beg and earnestly entreat you to receive these Friars kindly and to treat them in considerate fashion out of reverence for God and for us, indeed as if receiving us in their persons, and to employ unfeigned honesty towards them in respect of those matters of which they will speak to you on our behalf; we also ask that, having treated with them concerning the aforesaid matters to your profit, you will furnish them with a safe-conduct and other necessities on both their outward and return journey, so that they can safely make their way back to our presence when they wish. We have thought fit to send to you the above-mentioned Friars, whom we specially chose out from among others as being men proved by years of regular observance and well versed in Holy Scripture, for we believed they would be of greater help to you, seeing that they follow the humility of our Saviour: if we had thought that ecclesiastical prelates or other powerful men would be more profitable and more acceptable to you we would have sent them.

Lyons, 5th March 1245

II

Seeing that not only men but even irrational animals, nay, the very elements which go to make up the world machine, are united by a certain innate law after the manner of the celestial spirits, all of which God the Creator has divided into choirs in the enduring stability of peaceful order, it is not without cause that we are driven to express in strong terms our amazement that you, as we have heard, have invaded many countries belonging both to Christians and to others and are laying them waste in a horrible desolation, and with a fury still unabated you do not cease from stretching out your destroying hand to more distant lands, but, breaking the bond of natural ties, sparing neither sex nor age, you rage against all indiscriminately with the sword of chastisement. We, therefore, following the example of the King of Peace, and desiring that all men should live united in concord in the fear of God, do admonish, beg and earnestly beseech all of you that for the future you desist entirely from assaults of this kind and especially from the persecution of Christians, and that after so many and such grievous offences you conciliate by a fitting penance the wrath of Divine Majesty, which without doubt you have seriously aroused by such provocation; nor should you be emboldened to commit further savagery by the fact that when the sword of your might has raged against other men Almighty God has up to the present allowed various nations to fall before your face; for sometimes He refrains from chastising the proud in this world for the moment, for this reason, that if they neglect to humble themselves of their own accord He may not only no longer put off the punishment of their wickedness in this life but may also take greater vengeance in the world to come. On this account we have thought fit to send to you our beloved son [John of Plano Carpini] and his companions the bearers of this letter, men remarkable for their religious spirit, comely in their virtue and gifted with a knowledge of Holy Scripture; receive them kindly and treat them with honour out of reverence for God, indeed as if receiving us in their persons, and deal honestly with them in those matters of which they will speak to you on our behalf, and when you have had profitable discussions with them concerning the aforesaid affairs, especially those pertaining to peace, make fully known to us through these same Friars what moved you to destroy other nations and what your intentions are for the future, furnishing them with a safe-conduct and other necessities on both their outward and return journey, so that they can safely make their way back to our presence when they wish.

Lyons, 13th March 1245

THE NARRATIVE OF BROTHER BENEDICT THE POLE

This brief relation by John of Plano Carpini's Polish companion was dictated by him to a prelate or scholastic of Cologne on his return from Asia. It was first published by d'Avezac in 1838 from a MS. in the Bibliothèque Nationale at Paris.

THE NARRATIVE OF BROTHER BENEDICT THE POLE

IN THE Year of Our Lord 1245 Brother John of the Order of Friars Minor, named of Plano Carpini, was sent to the Tartars by the Lord Pope, with another brother of the same Order, and leaving Lyons in Gaul where the Pope was, he went to Poland and there at Vratislavia[1] took a third brother of the same Order, named Benedict, a Pole by race, to be his interpreter and the companion of his labour and cares.

With the help of Conrad, Duke of the Poles, they reached Kiev, a city of Russia, which is now under the Tartar yoke, and the rulers of the city gave them guides for six days' journey to the Tartar frontier guard on the borders of the Coman country.

When the captains of this frontier guard heard that they were envoys of the Pope, they asked and received presents, and the two Friars John and Benedict left their companion, who was sick, with the horses and servants that they had brought with them, and were taken on horses provided by the Tartars with their baggage to the second camp.

And so by many camps and changes of horses. They came on the third day to the general of an army, who was in command of 8,000 troops, and when his servants had asked and received gifts they took them to their commander Corenza. He enquired of them the cause of their journey and the nature of their business, and on learning this, he sent with them three Tartars from his following so that they should have horses and provisions from one army to another until they came to Bati, who is one of the great princes of the Tartars and the one who laid waste Hungary.

On their way they crossed the rivers Nepere [Dnieper] and Don, and they spent five weeks and more on this journey—i.e. from the first Sunday in Lent to Maundy Thursday, when they

[1] Modern Wroclaw or Breslau.

reached Bati, finding him on the great river Ethil[1] which the Russians call the Volga, and which is supposed to be the Thanais.[2]

And when the servants of Bati received the presents that they demanded, namely forty beaver skins and eighty badger skins, they carried them between the two sacred fires, and the Friars were obliged to do likewise, since it is the custom of the Tartars to purify envoys and presents by fire. Beyond the fires there stood a chariot bearing a golden statue of the Emperor, which also it is their custom to worship. But as the Friars utterly refused to do so they were only compelled to bow their heads.

When Bati had heard the Pope's letters and examined them word by word, after five days, that is, on the Tuesday after Easter, he sent the Friars with his own litters and the same Tartar guides as before to the son of the great Emperor, whose name is Cuy[u]cchan[3], in the native land of the Tartars.

And so they were dismissed by Prince Bati and, binding their limbs with bandages to bear the strain of continual riding, they left the land of the Comans after two weeks. This is the land which was once named Pontus and in it there is a great deal of wormwood, as Ovid remarks in his Epistles: "The bitter wormwood shivers in the endless plains."

Now as the Friars traversed Comania they had on their right the land of the Saxi, whom we believe to be Goths and who are Christians: next the Alans who are Christians and then the Guzari [Khazars] who are likewise Christian. In their country is situated Ornas,[4] a rich city which the Tartars captured by flooding it with water. After, the Circassians, and they are Christians. And finally the Georgians, also Christians.

Before this in Russia, they had the Mordvins,[5] who are pagans and have the greater part of the back of their heads shorn. Then the Bylers[6] who are pagan, then the Bascards [Bashkirs] who are the ancient Hungarians, then the dog-headed Cynocephali, then

[1] Itil or Ityl, the Turkish name for the Volga.
[2] The Tanais is, of course, the Don, as William of Rubruck realized.
[3] Guyuk at this time had not yet been chosen as Great Khan.
[4] Ornas, see *supra*, p. 29 n.
[5] The Mordvins are a Finno-Ugrian people who still exist on the Volga.
[6] The Bylers are the Volga Bulgarians represented by the modern Chuvash. As William of Rubruck notes they were not pagans, but strongly Mohammedan.

the Parocitae, who have such small and narrow mouths that they cannot chew anything solid but take liquids, and inhale the steam of meat and fruit.

On the frontier of Comania, they crossed a river named Yaralk [Yaik or Ural] where the land of the Kangites[1] begins. Through this country they rode for twenty days, finding few men, but many marshes and saltings and salt rivers, which we believe to be the Meotide swamps;[2] moreover, for eight days they traversed a vast desert sandy and parched with drought.

After the land of the Kangites they reached Turkey [Turkestan] where they found for the first time a large city—Yankint—and they travelled through Turkey for about ten days. Now Turkey follows the law of Mahomet. After Turkey they entered a land which is called Kara Kitai—that is to say Black Cathay—and the inhabitants are pagans and they found no city there, but they found a sea on their left hand which we believe to be the Caspian.[3] After this they entered the land of the Naimans who were once lords of the Tartars and here also they found no villages or cities. Finally they entered the land of the Tartars on the Feast of Mary Magdalene [July 22nd], when they found the Emperor at a great encampment which is called Syra Orda. Here they stayed four months and were present at the election of Cuiu[c]kan their Emperor.

And the same Brother Benedict the Pole related to us by word of mouth how they had both seen about 5,000 princes and great men who were all clad in cloth of gold on the first day when they assembled for the election of the king. But neither on that day, nor on the next when they appeared in white samite, did they come to an agreement. But on the third day, when they wore red samite, they reached agreement and made the election. Moreover, the same Brother affirms that there were about 3,000 ambassador envoys from different parts of the world present, bringing letters, answers, and every kind of tribute and gifts to the court. And

[1] The Kangites are the Kangli Turks, occupying what is now the Kaizak country.
[2] Probably the salt lakes of the Turgai and the Kyzyl Kum desert.
[3] Probably Lake Balkash. The " we " of this passage and the preceding one are presumably the scribes who took down his verbal report.

among them were the aforesaid Friars who wore brocade over their habit as needs must, for no envoy is allowed to see the face of the elect and crowned king, unless he is correctly dressed.

Accordingly they were admitted to the Syra Orda which is the Emperor's abode, and saw him wearing his crown and shining in splendid robes. He was sitting in the midst of the tent on a dais richly ornamented with gold and silver and with a canopy over it. There were four separate sets of steps leading up to this dais. Three of them were in front, one in the middle by which the Emperor alone went up and down, and two at the sides for the grandees and lesser men, while by the fourth flight, which was at the back, his mother and his wife and family used to ascend. Likewise, the Syra Orda had three entrances, like doors, and the one in the middle, which is the largest and far exceeds the others, always stands open without any guard, for the king alone goes in and out by it, and if anyone else were to enter by it he would be slain without mercy. But the two side doors were closed with bars, and have most severe guards keeping watch with arms, and through these, men enter with awe for fear of the appointed penalty.

On the third day the mission of the Lord Pope was heard after discussion and deliberation through the official and interpreters, and afterwards the Friars were sent to the Emperor's mother whom they found in another place, also sitting in a great and very fair tent. And she treated them with great courtesy and friendliness and sent them back to her son.

While they were staying there they often met Georgians who lived among the Tartars and were highly respected by them as brave and warlike men. These people are called Georgians because they invoke St. George in their wars and have him as patron and honour him beyond all other saints. They use the Greek version of Holy Scripture and have crosses on their camps and their carts. They follow the Greek rites in divine worship among the Tartars.

And so when the business on which they had come had been completed the Friars were sent back by the Emperor to carry letters to the Lord Pope signed under his own seal. They set out westwards with the envoys of the Soldan of Babylon, and when they had travelled together for fifteen days, the envoys turned southwards and left them. But the Friars travelled on to the West, and after crossing the Rhine at Cologne they returned to the Lord Pope at Lyons and presented to him the letters of the Emperor of the Tartars, the purport of which according to the Latin translation that was made is as follows:

The Strength of God, the Emperor of all men, to the Great Pope, Authentic and True Letters

Having taken counsel for making peace with us, You Pope and all Christians have sent an envoy to us, as we have heard from him and as your letters declare. Wherefore, if you wish to have peace with us, You Pope and all kings and potentates, in no way delay to come to me to make terms of peace and then you shall hear alike our answer and our will. The contents of your letters stated that we ought to be baptized and become Christians. To this we answer briefly that we do not understand in what way we ought to do this. To the rest of the contents of your letters, viz: that you wonder at so great a slaughter of men, especially of Christians and in particular Poles, Moravians and Hungarians, we reply likewise that this also we do not understand. However, lest we may seem to pass it over in silence altogether, we give you this for our answer.

Because they did not obey the word of God and the command of Chingis Chan and the Chan, but took council to slay our envoys, therefore God ordered us to destroy them and gave them up into our hands. For otherwise if God had not done this, what could man do to man? But you men of the West believe that you alone are Christians and despise others. But how can you know to whom God deigns to confer His grace? But we worshipping God have destroyed the whole earth from the East to the West in the power of God. And if this were not the power of God, what could men have done? Therefore if you accept peace and are willing to surrender your fortresses to us, You Pope and Christian princes, in no way delay coming to me to conclude peace and then we shall know that you wish to have peace with us. But if you should not believe our letters and the command of God nor hearken to our counsel then we shall know for certain that you wish to have war. After that we do not know what will happen, God alone knows.

Chingis Chan, first Emperor, second Ochoday Chan, third Cuiuch Chan.

GUYUK KHAN'S LETTER TO POPE INNOCENT IV (1246)[1]

WE, by the power of the eternal heaven,

Khan of the great Ulus[2]

Our command:—

This is a version sent to the great Pope, that he may know and understand in the [Muslim] tongue, what has been written. The petition of the assembly held in the lands of the Emperor [for our support], has been heard from your emissaries.

If he reaches [you] with his own report, Thou, who art the great Pope, together with all the Princes, come in person to serve us. At that time I shall make known all the commands of the *Yasa*.

You have also said that supplication and prayer have been offered by you, that I might find a good entry into baptism. This prayer of thine I have not understood. Other words which thou hast sent me: "I am surprised that thou hast seized all the lands of the Magyar and the Christians. Tell us what their fault is." These words of thine I have also not understood. The eternal God has slain and annihilated these lands and peoples, because they have neither adhered to Chingis Khan, nor to the Khagan,[3] both of whom have been sent to make known God's command, nor to the command of God. Like thy words, they also were impudent, they were proud and they slew our messenger-emissaries. How could anybody seize or kill by his own power contrary to the command of God?

Though thou likewise sayest that I should become a trembling Nestorian Christian, worship God and be an ascetic, how knowest

[1] Translated from the Persian.
[2] Ulus is a large or small social group, here consisting of all the peoples under the supreme ruler as a community.
[3] Khagan is the supreme ruler.

thou whom God absolves, in truth to whom He shows mercy? How dost thou know that such words as thou speakest are with God's sanction? From the rising of the sun to its setting, all the lands have been made subject to me. Who could do this contrary to the command of God?

Now you should say with a sincere heart: "I will submit and serve you." Thou thyself, at the head of all the Princes, come at once to serve and wait upon us! At that time I shall recognize your submission.

If you do not observe God's command, and if you ignore my command, I shall know you as my enemy. Likewise I shall make you understand. If you do otherwise, God knows what I know.

At the end of Jumada the second in the year 644.[1]

The Seal

We, by the power of the eternal Tengri, universal Khan of the great Mongol Ulus—our command. If this reaches peoples who have made their submission, let them respect and stand in awe of it.

[1] The date at the end of the document corresponds to November A.D. 1246.

THE JOURNEY OF WILLIAM OF RUBRUCK

Hardly anything is known about this great man except what he tells us in his book. The dates of his birth and his death are unknown, but he seems to have been a much younger man than John of Plano Carpini. It is almost certain that he was a native of Flanders, deriving his name from Rubruc near Cassel, now in French Flanders, not from Ruisbroek in Brabant as has sometimes been supposed.

After his return from Mongolia he was detained by the Order in Palestine, as lector in Theology at Acre, and he was obliged to ask St. Louis to obtain permission for his return to Europe. This request was eventually granted, and he came to Paris. Here he met Roger Bacon who was intensely interested in his experiences, and refers to him at length in the *Opus Majus*. This is the last we hear of him. Indeed it is the only contemporary record of him that we possess. But Roger Bacon's account seems to have aroused the interest of his countrymen, for except in England William and his travels were practically forgotten until modern times. The three MSS. at Corpus Christi College, Cambridge, and the one in the British Museum, are the sources of all the existing MSS. and versions and it was in England that Hakluyt and Purchas first published their versions. Thus it is almost by accident that the work of one of the greatest of medieval travellers has survived, and it is only in our own time that the accuracy and historical importance of his work have been fully recognized.

THE JOURNEY OF WILLIAM OF RUBRUCK

FRIAR WILLIAM OF RUBRUCK, least in the Order of Friars Minor, to the most excellent Lord and most Christian Louis, by the grace of God illustrious King of the French, health and continual triumph in Christ.

It is written of the Wise Man in Ecclesiasticus: "He shall pass into strange countries, he shall try good and evil in all things." This have I fulfilled, my Lord King, but would that it were as a wise man and not as a fool: for many perform the same actions as a wise man, not however in a wise manner but rather foolishly, and I fear I am to be numbered among these. Nevertheless, whatever be the manner in which I have acted, since you told me when I took my leave of you that I was to write to you of everything I should see among the Tartars, and even admonished me not to be afraid of writing you a long letter, I am doing what you bade me, albeit with fear and diffidence, for words such as I ought to use when writing to so eminent a majesty do not readily spring to my mind.

CHAPTER I

THE PROVINCE OF GAZARIA

BE it known therefore to your holy Majesty that in the year of Our Lord one thousand two hundred and fifty-three on the seventh of May we entered the Sea of Pontus which is commonly called the Greater Sea. It is one thousand four hundred miles in length, as I learned from merchants, and is divided into two parts, for about the middle of it there are two points of land, one in the north and the other in the south. The one in the south is called Sinopolis [Sinope] and is a fortress and the port of the Sultan of Turkey:

as for the one in the north it is that province which is nowadays called Gazaria by the Latins, but by the Greeks who dwell on the sea coast is named Cassaria, that is to say, Caesarea.[1] There are also certain promontories stretching out into the sea towards the south in the direction of Sinopolis. There are three hundred miles between Sinopolis and Cassaria. It is, by and large, seven hundred miles from these points to Constantinople and seven hundred to the east, that is, to Hyberia which is the province of Georgia.

We sailed in the direction of the province of Gazaria or Cassaria, which is like a triangle, on the west side of which lies the city called Kersona [Sebastopol] where St. Clement met his martyrdom. As we sailed by we saw the island on which is the temple said to have been built by the hands of angels. In the middle of the south side, as it were at the apex, there is a city called Soldaia [Sudak], which looks towards Sinopolis, and all the merchants coming from Turkey and wishing to go to northern lands make their way thither, and similarly those coming from Russia and northern territories who wish to cross to Turkey. The latter bring squirrel and ermine and other valuable furs, while the former carry materials of cotton or bombax, silk stuffs and sweet-smelling spices. To the east of this province is a city called Matrica [Taman]; here the river Tanais [Don] empties itself into the Sea of Pontus [Black Sea] through an opening twelve miles wide.

Before this river reaches the Sea of Pontus it forms a kind of sea [Sea of Azov] towards the north, which is seven hundred miles in breadth and length and nowhere reaches a depth of more than six paces; consequently large vessels do not enter it, but merchants from Constantinople going to the aforesaid city of Matrica send their barks as far as the river Tanais in order to buy dried fish, namely sturgeon and barbot and other fish in enormous quantities.

The said province of Cassaria is therefore girt on three sides by the sea, namely on the west where lies Kersona the city of Clement; on the south where is the city of Soldaia towards which we were steering and which forms the apex of the province, and on the

---

[1] The Crimea was named Cassaria after the kingdom of the Khazars, which was the great power in south-east Russia in the early Middle Ages.

east by the Sea of Tanais where the city of Matrica is and the outlet of the Sea of Tanais.

Beyond the mouth is Ziquia which is not subject to the Tartars, and to the east are the Suevi and Iberi [Georgians], who also do not obey them. Then towards the south is Trebizond which has its own ruler, by name Guido,[1] who is of the stock of the Emperor of Constantinople and is subject to the Tartars. Next comes Sinopolis which belongs to the Sultan of Turkey who is likewise subject. Then there is the territory of Vastasius[2] whose son is called Ascar after his maternal grandfather; he is not subject to them. From the mouth of the Tanais westwards as far as the Danube all is theirs, even beyond the Danube in the direction of Constantinople—Blakia which is the land of the Assans,[3] Lesser Bulgaria even as far as Sclavonia, all pay them tribute: also in addition to the agreed tribute they have, in recent years, taken from each house one axe and all the unwrought iron which they found.

And so we reached Soldaia on May 21st. Certain merchants from Constantinople had arrived before us and had announced that envoys were coming thither from the Holy Land who wished to visit Sartach. Now I had preached publicly on Palm Sunday in St. Sophia's that I was not an envoy either of you or anybody else, but that I was going among these unbelievers in accordance with our Rule. Then when we landed the said merchants warned me to mind my words, for they had given out that I was an envoy, and if I were to deny that I was such, then I would not be allowed to proceed.

Thereupon I spoke in the following manner to the prefects of the city or rather to their deputies, for the prefects had gone to Baatu in the winter bearing their tribute and had not yet returned. "We heard it told of your lord Sartach in the Holy Land that he was a Christian and the Christians rejoiced exceedingly over this fact, especially the most Christian lord, the King of the French, who is on a pilgrimage there and is fighting against the

---

[1] By Guido, William appears to mean Andronicus Ghidos, who no longer ruled. His successor at this period was Emmanuel Comnenus.

[2] John Vatatzes, the Byzantine emperor, 1222–55. His son "Ascar" is Theodore Lâscaris.

[3] The second Bulgarian kingdom of John Asen and his successors.

Saracens in order to wrest the Holy Places from their hands: for this reason I desire to go to Sartach and bring to him a letter of my lord the King, in which he admonishes him concerning the good estate of the whole of Christendom." They received us with joy and lodged us in the episcopal church. The Bishop of that church had been to Sartach and he told me many good things about him which I, for my part, was not to discover later.

They then gave us the choice as to whether we would like carts with oxen, or pack horses, to carry our belongings. The merchants from Constantinople advised us to accept the carts and even to buy covered carts for ourselves like the ones the Ruthenians use for carrying their furs, and into these to put such of our things as I did not wish to unpack every day; for if I took the horses, I should have to unload them at every stopping place and pack them on to other horses; moreover I would be able to ride at a more gentle pace with the oxen. I followed their advice, but it was bad advice for I was on the road for two months before I reached Sartach : a journey I could have completed in one month if I had gone with horses.

On the advice of the merchants I had brought with me from Constantinople fruit, muscatel wine and choice biscuits to present to the chief men of the city so that I might be granted permission to travel about, since they look with no favourable eye upon anyone coming to them empty-handed. On failing to find the prefects of the city there, I placed all these things in a cart, as I was told that Sartach would be delighted with them, if only I could get them as far as him.

So we set off on our journey about June 1st with our own four covered carts and with two others I had received from them in which was carried bedding for sleeping on at night. They gave us five horses to ride on, for we were five in number, myself, my companion Friar Bartholomew of Cremona, Gosset the bearer of this letter, Abdullah the interpreter, and a boy, Nicholas, whom I had bought at Constantinople out of the alms you gave me. They also gave us two men who drove the carts and looked after the oxen and horses.

There are lofty promontories along by the sea from Kersona

as far as the mouth of the Tanais, and between Kersona and Soldaia there are forty small towns, practically each one of them having its own dialect; among them were many Goths who speak German.

Beyond these mountains towards the north is a most fair forest in a plain watered by springs and streams; on the other side of the forest is a vast plain which stretches northwards five days' journey to the boundary of this province where, having the sea to the east and west, it narrows so that there is a great dyke from one sea to the other. Before the Tartars came the Comans used to dwell in this plain and they obliged the aforementioned cities and fortresses to render them tribute; when the Tartars came the Comans entered this province, all fleeing as far as the sea-shore in such vast numbers that they ate each other, the living those who died, so I was told by a merchant who saw the living devouring and tearing with their teeth the raw flesh of the dead as dogs do corpses.

At the far end of this province are many large lakes, on the shores of which are salt-water springs; as soon as the water from these runs into the lake it turns into salt, hard like ice. Baatu and Sartach draw large revenues from these salt springs, for men come thither from the whole of Russia for salt, and for every cart-load they give two lengths of cotton valued at half an *yperpera*.[1] Many ships also come by sea for the salt, all giving payment according to the amount each takes.

And so on the third day after leaving Soldaia we came across the Tartars; when I came among them it seemed indeed to me as if I were stepping into some other world, the life and customs of which I will describe for you as well as I can.

CHAPTER II

THE TARTARS AND THEIR DWELLINGS

THE Tartars have no abiding city nor do they know of the one that is to come. They have divided among themselves Scythia, which

[1] *Yperpera*: a Byzantine gold coin; also called bezants in the Middle Ages.

stretches from the Danube as far as the rising of the sun. Each captain, according to whether he has more or fewer men under him, knows the limits of his pasturage and where to feed his flocks in winter, summer, spring and autumn, for in winter they come down to the warmer districts in the south, in summer they go up to the cooler ones in the north. They drive their cattle to graze on the pasture lands without water in winter when there is snow there, for the snow provides them with water.

The dwelling in which they sleep has as its base a circle of interlaced sticks, and it is made of the same material; these sticks converge into a little circle at the top and from this a neck juts up like a chimney; they cover it with white felt and quite often they also coat the felt with lime or white clay and powdered bone to make it a more gleaming white, and sometimes they make it black. The felt round the neck at the top they decorate with lovely and varied paintings. Before the doorway they also hang felt worked in multicoloured designs; they sew coloured felt on to the other, making vines and trees, birds and animals. They make these houses so large that sometimes they are thirty feet across; for I myself once measured the width between the wheel tracks of a cart, and it was twenty feet, and when the house was on the cart it stuck out at least five feet beyond the wheels on each side. I have counted to one cart twenty-two oxen drawing one house, eleven in a row across the width of the cart, and the other eleven in front of them. The axle of the cart was as big as the mast of a ship, and a man stood at the door of the house on the cart, driving the oxen.

In addition they make squares to the size of a large coffer out of slender split twigs; then over it, from one end to the other, they build up a rounded roof out of similar twigs and they make a little entrance at the front end; after that they cover this box or little house with black felt soaked in tallow or ewes' milk so that it is rain-proof, and this they decorate in the same way with multi-coloured handwork. Into these chests they put all their bedding and valuables; they bind them onto high carts which are drawn by camels so that they can cross rivers. These chests are never removed from the carts. When they take down their dwelling houses, they always put the door facing the south; then afterwards they draw up the carts with the chests on each side, half a stone's throw from the house, so that it stands between two rows of carts, as it were between two walls.

The married women make for themselves really beautiful carts which I would not know how to describe for you except by a picture; in fact I would have done you paintings of everything if I only knew how to paint. A wealthy Mongol or Tartar may well have a hundred or two hundred such carts with chests. Baatu has twenty-six wives and each of these has a large house, not counting the other small ones which are placed behind the large one and which are, as it were, chambers in which their attendants live; belonging to each of these houses are a good two hundred carts. When they pitch their houses the chief wife places her dwelling at the extreme west end and after her the others according to their rank, so that the last wife will be at the far east end, and there will be the space of a stone's throw between the establishment of one wife and that of another. And so the orda of a rich Mongol will look like a large town and yet there will be very few men in it.

One woman will drive twenty or thirty carts, for the country is flat. They tie together the carts, which are drawn by oxen or camels, one after the other, and the woman will sit on the front one driving the ox while all the others follow in step. If they happen to come on a bad bit of track they loose them and lead them across it one by one. They go at a very slow pace, as a sheep or an ox might walk.

When they have pitched their houses with the door facing south, they arrange the master's couch at the northern end. The women's place is always on the east side, that is, on the left of the master of the house when he is sitting on his couch looking towards the south; the men's place is on the west side, that is, to his right.

On entering a house the men would by no means hang up their quiver in the women's section. Over the head of the master there is always an idol like a doll or little image of felt which they call the master's brother, and a similar one over the head of the mistress, and this they call the mistress's brother; they are fastened on to the wall. Higher up between these two is a thin little one which is, as it were, the guardian of the whole house. The mistress of the house places on her right side, at the foot of the couch, in a prominent position, a goat-skin stuffed with wool or other material, and next to it a tiny image turned towards her attendants and the women. By the entrance on the women's side is still another idol with a cow's udder for the women who milk the cows, for this is the women's job. On the other side of the door towards the men is another image with a mare's udder for the men who milk the mares.

When they have foregathered for a drink they first sprinkle with the drink the idol over the master's head, then all the other idols in turn; after this an attendant goes out of the house with a cup and some drinks; he sprinkles thrice towards the south, genuflecting each time; this is in honour of fire; next towards the east in honour of the air, and after that to the west in honour of water; they cast it to the north for the dead. When the master is holding his cup in his hand and is about to drink, before he does so he first pours some out on the earth as its share. If he drinks while seated on a horse, before he drinks he pours some over the neck or mane of the horse. And so when the attendant has sprinkled towards the four quarters of the earth he returns into the house; two servants with two cups and as many plates are ready to carry the drink to the master and the wife sitting beside him upon his couch. If he has several wives, she with whom he sleeps at night sits next to him during the day, and on that day all the others have to come to her dwelling to drink, and the court is held there, and the gifts which are presented to the master are placed in the treasury of that wife. Standing in the entrance is a bench with a skin of milk or some other drink and some cups.

In the winter they make an excellent drink from rice, millet, wheat and honey, which is clear like wine. Wine, too, is conveyed to them from distant regions. In the summer they do not bother about anything except cosmos. Cosmos [koumiss] is always to be found inside the house before the entrance door, and near it stands a musician with his instrument. Our lutes and viols I did not see there but many other instruments such as are not known among us. When the master begins to drink, then one of the attendants cries out in a loud voice "Ha!" and the musician strikes his instrument. And when it is a big feast they are holding, they all clap their hands and also dance to the sound of the instrument, the men before the master and the women before the mistress. After the master has drunk, then the attendant cries out as before and the instrument-player breaks off. Then they drink all round, the men and the women, and sometimes vie with each other in drinking in a really disgusting and gluttonous manner.

When they want to incite anyone to drink they seize him by the ears and pull them vigorously to make his gullet open, and they clap and dance in front of him. Likewise when they want to make a great feast and entertainment for anyone, one man takes a full cup and two others stand, one on his right and one on his left, and in this manner the three, singing and dancing, advance right up to him to whom they are to offer the cup, and they sing and dance before him; when he stretches out his hand to take the cup they suddenly leap back, and then they advance again as before; and in this way they make fun of him, drawing back the cup three or four times until he is in a really lively mood and wants it: then they give him the cup and sing and clap their hands and stamp with their feet while he drinks.

CHAPTER III

THE FOOD OF THE TARTARS

As for their food and victuals I must tell you they eat all dead animals indiscriminately and with so many flocks and herds you can be sure a great many animals do die. However, in the summer as long as they have any cosmos, that is mare's milk, they do not care about any other food. If during that time an ox or a horse happens to die, they dry the flesh by cutting it into thin strips and hanging it in the sun and the wind, and it dries immediately without salt and without any unpleasant smell. Out of the intestines of horses they make sausages which are better than pork sausages and they eat these fresh; the rest of the meat they keep for the winter. From the hide of oxen they make large jars which they dry in a wonderful way in the smoke. From the hind part of horses' hide they make very nice shoes.

They feed fifty or a hundred men with the flesh of a single sheep, for they cut it up in little bits in a dish with salt and water, making no other sauce; then with the point of a knife or a fork especially made for this purpose—like those with which we are accustomed to eat pears and apples cooked in wine—they offer to each of those standing round one or two mouthfuls, according to the number of guests. Before the flesh of the sheep is served, the master first takes what pleases him; and also if he gives anyone a special portion then the one receiving it has to eat it himself and may give it to no one else. But if he cannot eat it all he may take it away with him or give it to his servant, if he is there, to keep for him; otherwise he may put it away in his *captargac*, that is, a square bag which they carry to put all such things in: in this they also keep bones when they have not the time to give them a good gnaw, so that later they may gnaw them and no food be wasted.

CHAPTER IV

How They Make Cosmos

Cosmos, that is mare's milk, is made in this way: they stretch along the ground a long rope attached to two stakes stuck into the earth, and at about nine o'clock they tie to this rope the foals of the mares they want to milk. Then the mothers stand near their foals and let themselves be peacefully milked; if any one of them is too restless, then a man takes the foal and, placing it under her, lets it suck a little, and he takes it away again and the milker takes its place.

And so, when they have collected a great quantity of milk, which is as sweet as cow's milk when it is fresh, they pour it into a large skin or bag and they begin churning it with a specially made stick which is as big as a man's head at its lower end, and hollowed out; and when they beat it quickly it begins to bubble like new wine and to turn sour and ferment, and they churn it until they can extract the butter. Then they taste it and when it is fairly pungent they drink it. As long as one is drinking, it bites the tongue like vinegar; when one stops, it leaves on the tongue the taste of milk of almonds and greatly delights the inner man; it even intoxicates those who have not a very good head. It also greatly provokes urine.

For use of the great lords they also make caracosmos, that is black cosmos, in this wise. Mare's milk does not curdle. Now it is a general rule that the milk of any animal, in the stomach of whose young rennet is not found, does not curdle; it is not found in the stomach of a young horse, hence the milk of a mare does not curdle. And so they churn the milk until everything that is solid in it sinks right to the bottom like the lees of wine, and what is pure remains on top and is like whey or white must. The dregs are very white and are given to the slaves and have a most soporific effect. The clear liquid the masters drink and it is certainly a very pleasant drink and really potent.

Baatu has thirty men within a day's journey of his camp, each one of whom provides him every day with such milk from a hundred mares—that is to say, the milk of three thousand mares every day, not counting the other white milk which other men bring. For, just as in Syria the peasants give a third part of their produce, so these men have to bring to the orda of their lords the mare's milk of every third day.

From cow's milk they first extract the butter and this they boil until it is completely boiled down; then they store it in sheep's paunches which they keep for this purpose; they do not put salt into the butter; however it does not go bad owing to the long boiling. They keep it against the winter. The rest of the milk which is left after the butter has been extracted they allow to turn until it is as sour as it can be, and they boil it, and in boiling, it curdles; they dry the curd in the sun and it becomes as hard as iron slag, and this they keep in bags against the winter. During the winter months when there is a scarcity of milk, they put this sour curd, which they call *grut*, into a skin and pour hot water on top of it and beat it vigorously until it melts in the water, which, as a result, becomes completely sour, and this water they drink instead of milk. They take the greatest care never to drink plain water.

CHAPTER V

THE ANIMALS THEY EAT, THEIR CLOTHES AND THEIR HUNTING

THE great lords have villages in the south from which millet and flour are brought to them for the winter; the poor provide for themselves by trading sheep and skins; and the slaves fill their bellies with dirty water and are content with this. They also catch mice, of which many kinds abound there; mice with long tails they do not eat but give to their birds; they eat dormice and all kinds of mice with short tails. There are also many marmots there which they call *sogur* and these congregate in one burrow in the winter, twenty or thirty of them together, and they sleep for six months; these they catch in great quantities.

Also to be found there are conies with a long tail like a cat and having at the tip of the tail black and white hairs. They have many other little animals as well which are good to eat, and they are very clever at knowing the difference. I saw no deer there, I saw few hares, many gazelles; wild asses I saw in great quantities and these are like mules. I also saw another kind of animal which is called *arcali*[1] and which has a body just like a ram's and horns twisted like a ram's but of such a size that I could scarce lift the two horns with one hand; and they make large cups out of these horns.

They have hawks, gerfalcons and peregrine falcons in great numbers and these they carry on their right hand, and they always put a little thong round the hawk's neck. This thong hangs down the middle of its breast and by it they pull down with the left hand the head and breast of the hawk when they cast it at its prey, so that it is not beaten back by the wind or carried upwards. They procure a large part of their food by the chase.

When they want to hunt wild animals they gather together in a great crowd and surround the district in which they know the animals to be, and gradually they close in until between them they

---

[1] This is the first mention in literature of the Argali, *Ovis Ammon*, the great wild sheep of the Altai.

shut in the animals in a circle and then they shoot at them with their arrows.

I will tell you about their garments and their clothing. From Cathay and other countries to the east, and also from Persia and other districts of the south, come cloths of silk and gold and cotton materials which they wear in the summer. From Russia, Moxel,[1] Great Bulgaria and Pascatu, which is Greater Hungary, and Kerkis,[2] which are all districts towards the north, and full of forests, and from many other regions in the north which are subject to them, valuable furs of many kinds are brought for them, such as I have never seen in our part of the world; and these they wear in winter. In the winter they always make at least two fur garments, one with the fur against the body, the other with the fur outside to the wind and snow, and these are usually of the skins of wolves or foxes or monkeys,[3] and when they are sitting in their dwelling they have another softer one. The poor make their outer ones of dog and goat.

They also make trousers out of skins. Moreover, the rich line their garments with silk stuffing which is extraordinarily soft and light and warm. The poor line their clothes with cotton material and with the softer wool which they are able to pick out from the coarser. With the coarse they make felt to cover their dwellings and coffers and also for making bedding. Also with wool mixed with a third part horse-hair they make their ropes. From felt they make saddle pads, saddle cloths and rain cloaks, which means they use a great deal of wool. You have seen the men's costume.

CHAPTER VI

How the Men Shave and the Women Adorn Themselves

THE men shave a square on the top of their heads and from the front corners of this they continue the shaving in strips along the

---

[1] Moksha, a Finnish tribe, who lived on the Moksha, a tributary of the Oka.
[2] Probably the Kirgiz, who at that time lived in Siberia north of the Altai Mountains.
[3] The text reads "papionibus", baboons: possibly it refers to some Asiatic monkey like the *Rhinopitheci* of China and Tibet.

sides of the head as far as the temples. They also shave their
temples and neck to the top of the cervical cavity and their forehead in front to the top of the frontal bone, where they leave a tuft
of hair which hangs down as far as the eyebrows. At the sides and
the back of the head they leave the hair, which they make into
plaits, and these they braid round the head to the ears.

The costume of the girls is no different from that of the men
except that it is somewhat longer. But on the day after she is
married a woman shaves from the middle of her head to her forehead, and she has a tunic as wide as a nun's cowl, and in every
respect wider and longer, and open in front, and this they tie on
the right side. Now in this matter the Tartars differ from the
Turks, for the Turks tie their tunics on the left, but the Tartars
always on the right.

They also have a head-dress which they call *bocca*, which is
made out of the bark of a tree or of any other fairly light material
which they can find; it is large and circular and as big as two
hands can span around, a cubit and more high and square at
the top like the capital of a column. This *bocca* they cover with
costly silk material, and it is hollow inside, and on the capital in
the middle or on the side they put a rod of quills or slender canes,
likewise a cubit and more in length; and they decorate this rod at
the top with peacock feathers and throughout its length all round
with little feathers from the mallard's tail and also with precious
stones. The wealthy ladies wear such an ornament on the top
of their head and fasten it down firmly with a hood which has a
hole in the top for this purpose, and in it they stuff their hair,
gathering it up from the back on to the top of the head in a kind of
knot and putting over it the *bocca* which they then tie firmly under
the chin. So when several ladies ride together and are seen from a
distance, they give the appearance of soldiers with helmets on
their heads and raised lances; for the *bocca* looks like a helmet and
the rod on top like a lance.

All the women sit on their horses like men, astride, and they tie
their cowls with a piece of sky-blue silk round the waist, and with
another strip they bind their breasts, and they fasten a piece of
white stuff below their eyes which hangs down to the breast.

The women are wondrous fat and the less nose they have the more beautiful they are considered. They disfigure themselves hideously by painting their faces. They never lie down on a bed to give birth to their children.

CHAPTER VII

THE DUTIES OF THE WOMEN AND THEIR WORK

IT is the duty of the women to drive the carts, to load the houses on to them and to unload them, to milk the cows, to make the butter and *grut*,[1] to dress the skins and to sew them, which they do with thread made out of tendons. They split the tendons into very thin threads and then twist these into one long thread. They also sew shoes and socks and other garments. They never wash their clothes, for they say that that makes God angry and that it would thunder if they hung them out to dry; they even beat those who do wash them and take them away from them. They are extraordinarily afraid of thunder. At such a time they turn all strangers out of their dwellings and wrap themselves in black felt in which they hide until it has passed over. They never wash their dishes, but when the meat is cooked, they wash out the bowl in which they are going to put it with some boiling broth from the cauldron which they afterwards pour back. The women also make the felt and cover the houses.

The men make bows and arrows, manufacture stirrups and bits and make saddles; they build the houses and carts, they look after the horses and milk the mares, churn the cosmos, that is the mares' milk, and make the skins in which it is kept, and they also look after the camels and load them. Both sexes look after the sheep and goats, and sometimes the men, sometimes the women, milk them. They dress skins with the sour milk of ewes, thickened and salted.

When they want to wash their hands or their head, they fill their mouth with water and, pouring this little by little from their

[1] Cf. *supra*, p. 99.

mouth into their hands, with it they wet their hair and wash their head.

As for their marriages, you must know that no one there has a wife unless he buys her, which means that sometimes girls are quite grown up before they marry, for their parents always keep them until they sell them. They observe the first and second degrees of consanguinity, but observe no degrees of affinity; they have two sisters at the same time or one after the other. No widow among them marries, the reason being that they believe that all those who serve them in this life will serve them in the next, and so of a widow they believe that she will always return after death to her first husband. This gives rise to a shameful custom among them whereby a son sometimes takes to wife all his father's wives, except his own mother; for the orda of a father and mother always falls to the youngest son and so he himself has to provide for all his father's wives who come to him with his father's effects; and then, if he so wishes, he uses them as wives, for he does not consider an injury has been done to him if they return to his father after death.

And so when anyone has made an agreement with another to take his daughter, the father of the girl arranges a feast and she takes flight to relations where she lies hid. Then the father declares: "Now my daughter is yours; take her wherever you find her." Then he searches for her with his friends until he finds her; then he has to take her by force and bring her, as though by violence, to his house.

CHAPTER VIII

OF THEIR JUSTICE AND JUDGMENTS, DEATH AND BURIAL

CONCERNING their penal laws I can tell you that when two men fight no one dares to interfere, even a father dare not help his son, but he who comes off the worse may appeal to the court of the lord and if the other touches him after the appeal, he is put to death. But he must go immediately without any delay and the one who has suffered the injury leads the other like a captive.

They inflict capital punishment on no one unless he has been caught in the act or confesses; but when a man is accused by a number of people, they torture him well, so that he confesses. Murder they punish by the death sentence, and also cohabiting with a woman not one's own. By one's own I mean wife or servant, for it is lawful for a man to use his slave as he will. Robbery on a grand scale they likewise punish by death. For a petty theft, such as one sheep, so long as a man has not been caught doing it often, they beat him cruelly, and if they deal him a hundred strokes, then they have to have a hundred rods. I am speaking of those who are beaten as a result of the court's sentence. Similarly they put to death false ambassadors, that is to say men who pretend they are ambassadors but are not; also sorceresses, of whom however I will tell you more later, for they consider them to be witches.

When anyone dies they mourn, wailing in a loud voice, and then they are free from paying taxes until the year is up. And if anyone is present at the death of an adult, he does not enter the dwelling of Mangu Chan for a year; if it is a child who dies he does not enter it for a month.

Near the grave of a dead man they always leave a dwelling, if he is of the nobility, that is of the family of Chingis, who was their first father and lord. The burial place of him who dies is not known; and always around those places where they bury their nobles there is a camp of men who guard the tombs. It has not come to my knowledge that they bury treasure with the dead. The Comans make a great mound over the dead man and set up a statue to him, facing the east and holding a cup in its hand in front of its navel. They also make pyramids for the rich, that is, little pointed houses; and in some places I saw large towers of baked tiles, and in others stone houses, although stones are not to be found there. I saw a man recently dead for whom they had hung up, between tall poles, the skins of sixteen horses, four facing each quarter of the earth, and they had put cosmos there for him to drink and meat for him to eat, and in spite of this they said of him that he had been baptised. Further east I saw other tombs, namely large areas strewn with stones, some round, some square and then four tall stones upright round the plot facing the four quarters of the earth.

When anyone is ill he takes to his bed and places a sign above his dwelling that there is a sick person there and that no one may enter. And so nobody visits the invalid except the one who looks after him. When anyone from one of the great ordas is sick, they place guards at a distance round the orda and they do not allow anyone to cross these bounds, for they are afraid an evil spirit or wind may come in with those entering. They summon their soothsayers as if they were their priests.

CHAPTER IX

OUR ARRIVAL AMONG THE BARBARIANS AND THEIR INGRATITUDE

WHEN we arrived among those barbarians, it seemed to me, as I have already said, as if I were stepping into another world. For after they had made us wait for a long time sitting in the shade of our carts, they surrounded us on horseback. Their first question was whether we had ever before been among them. On being told no, they began impudently to ask for some of our provisions. We gave them some of the biscuit and wine we had brought with us from the town; and when they had drunk one flagon of wine they asked for another, saying that a man does not enter a house on one foot. We gave it to them, apologising that we had but little. Then they enquired where we had come from and where we wanted to go. I spoke to them in the words I have already given, saying that we had heard of Sartach that he was a Christian and that I wished to go to him as I had your letter to deliver to him. They then diligently enquired whether I was going of my own free will or whether I was being sent. I replied that nobody forced me to go, nor would I have gone if I did not wish to, therefore I was going of my own free will and also by the will of my superior. I took great care never to say that I was your ambassador. Then they asked what was in the carts, whether it was gold or silver or precious garments that I was taking to

Sartach. I rejoined that Sartach would see well enough for himself what we were bringing him when we reached him and that it was none of their business to ask after such matters, but they ought to have me taken to their captain and he, if he would, should provide me with an escort to Sartach, otherwise I would go back.

Now there was in that province a blood-relation of Baatu, a captain by the name of Scatatai, to whom the Lord Emperor of Constantinople was sending a letter earnestly begging him to allow me to pass through his district. Then they acceded to my request, providing us with horses and oxen and two men as guides, and those who had brought us thus far went back. However, before they gave us the aforesaid things they made us wait a long time, begging for some of our bread for their little ones, and everything they saw on our attendants, knives, gloves, purses, belts, they marvelled at and wanted to have them all. I pleaded as an excuse that we still had a goodly stretch before us and ought not thus speedily to divest ourselves of things necessary for the completion of so considerable a journey. Whereupon they said I was an impostor.

It is true they take nothing away by force but they ask in a most ill-mannered and impudent fashion for whatever they see, and if a man gives to them, then he is the loser for they are ungrateful. In their own eyes they are the lords of the world and consider that nobody ought to refuse them anything; if he does not give and then afterwards stands in need of their aid, they serve him badly. They gave us some of their cows' milk to drink; the butter had been extracted from it and it was very sour, and is what they call *airan*. And so we left them and it seemed to me indeed as if I had escaped from the hands of devils. The following day we reached their captain.

During the two months which elapsed from the time we left Soldaia until we reached Sartach, we never slept in a house or tent but always under the open sky or under our carts, nor did we see any town or the remains of any building where there might have been a town—nothing but Comans' tombs and these in vast numbers. That evening the fellow who was our guide gave us cosmos to drink, and as I drank it I sweated all over from fright and the novelty of it, for I had never before drunk of it. However it struck me as being very tasty, as in truth it is.

CHAPTER X

SCATATAI'S ORDA. THE CHRISTIANS DO NOT DRINK COSMOS

THE next day we met Scatatai's carts laden with their dwellings and it seemed to me as if a large city were approaching me. I was amazed also at the great number of cattle, oxen and horses and of flocks of sheep, yet I saw few men to control them. This caused me to ask how many men Scatatai had under him and I was told not more than five hundred, and half of these we had passed in another camp.

Then the fellow who was our guide began telling me that something ought to be given to Scatatai, and he made us stop while he went ahead to announce our arrival. It was now past nine o'clock and they unloaded their houses near some water. An interpreter came to us from Scatatai, and as soon as he had learned that we had never before been among them, he asked for some of our food; we gave it to him. He also asked for a garment, seeing that he was going to act as our mouthpiece before his master. We excused ourselves. He enquired what we were taking to his master. We got a flagon of wine and filled a little basket with biscuits and a plate with apples and other fruit. He was not at all pleased that we were not taking a length of costly material.

However, we went like this with fear and embarrassment. Scatatai was sitting on his couch holding a guitar in his hand, and his wife was beside him; really I believe she had cut off her nose between the eyes so that she might be more flat-nosed, for she had no nose there at all and she had smeared the spot with black ointment, and also her eyebrows, which to us looked hideous.

Then I addressed him in the words I have given above, for we had to be careful to say the same thing everywhere. On this point we had been well warned by those who had been among the

Tartars never to change what we said. And so I asked him to condescend to accept a small gift at our hands, excusing myself on the grounds that I was a monk and it was not the custom of our Order to possess gold or silver or precious garments, which accounted for my not having any such things to offer him, but would he accept of our food for a blessing. Then he ordered it to be accepted and immediately shared it among his men who had assembled for a drink. I also handed to him the letter from the Lord Emperor of Constantinople. This was on the octave of the Ascension.[1] He at once sent it to Soldaia to be translated there, for it was in Greek and he had not anybody by him who knew Greek.

He also asked us if we were willing to drink cosmos, that is mares' milk, for the Christians—Ruthenians, Greeks and Alans[2]— who live among them, if they wish strictly to observe their law, do not drink it; they even no longer consider themselves Christians after they have drunk it and their priests reconcile them as if they had denied the faith of Christ. Whereupon I replied that we still had sufficient to drink and that when that gave out we would have to drink what was given to us. He also asked us what were the contents of the letter you were sending to Sartach. I said that your documents were private and that there was nothing in them save good and friendly words. He also enquired what we were going to say to Sartach. I replied "Words of the Christian faith." "What words?" he asked, for he would gladly hear them. Then I expounded to him the creed of the Faith as well as I could through my interpreter, who was a man of neither wit nor eloquence. When he had heard this he was silent and wagged his head.

Then he assigned to us two men to look after us and the horses and oxen, and made us drive with him until the return of the messenger whom he had sent to get the Emperor's letter translated; and we journeyed with him until the day after Pentecost.

---

[1] June 5th, 1253.
[2] Alans: a people of Sarmatian stock. Their modern descendants are the Ossetes in the northern Caucasus.

CHAPTER XI

The Alans Visit Them on the Vigil of Pentecost

On the vigil of Pentecost there came to us certain Alans, who there are called Aas. They are Christians according to the Greek rite and use the Greek language and have Greek priests; nevertheless they are not schismatics as are the Greeks, but without respect of persons they honour all Christians. They brought us cooked meat, begging us to eat of their food and to pray for one of them who had died. Then I told them it was the vigil of a great feast and that on that day we did not eat meat; and I explained to them about the feast, which greatly delighted them, for they were ignorant of everything regarding the Christian religion, with the sole exception of the name of Christ.

They also asked, as did many other Christians—Ruthenians and Hungarians—whether they could be saved, as they had to drink cosmos and to eat carrion and animals slaughtered by Saracens and other infidels, which indeed those Greek and Ruthenian priests consider the same as carrion or as sacrificed to idols; and also seeing that they did not know the times of fasting, nor could they observe them even if they did know them. Then I put them on the right path as well as I could, teaching them and comforting them in the faith.

The meat they had brought we kept until the day of the feast; for we could find nothing for sale for gold or silver, only for cotton or other materials, and we had none of these; when our servants showed them an *yperpera*, they rubbed it with their fingers and held it to their noses so that they could tell by the smell whether it was copper, and they gave us no food except cows' milk, extremely sour and evil-smelling. Our wine was now coming to an end; the water had been so much stirred up by the horses that it was not drinkable. But for the biscuit we had and the grace of God we might well have died,

CHAPTER XII

THE SARACEN WHO SAID HE WISHED TO BE BAPTISED AND THE MEN WHO LOOKED LIKE LEPERS

ON the day of Pentecost a certain Saracen came to us, and while he was talking to us we began to explain the faith to him. Hearing of the favours of God shown to the human race in the Incarnation, of the resurrection of the dead and of the Last Judgment, and hearing that sins are washed away in baptism, he said he wished to be baptised. While we were getting ready to baptise him he suddenly got on to his horse, saying he was going home to discuss the matter with his wife.

When he spoke with us on the following day, he told us that by no means dare he receive baptism, seeing that then he would not be able to drink cosmos; for the Christians of that district said that no one who was truly a Christian ought to drink it, and without that drink it would be impossible to live in this desert. By no manner of means could I shift him from this opinion. This story will prove to you that they are far removed from the faith on account of this opinion, which has flourished among them because of the Ruthenians, of whom there are very great numbers in their midst.

The same day the captain gave us one man to be our guide as far as Sartach and two to take us to the next camp, which was distant from there five days' journey at the speed the oxen could travel. They also gave us a goat for food and several skins of cows' milk and only a little cosmos, for it is precious to them. And so we set out on our journey due north and it seemed to me we had passed through one of the gates of hell. The fellows who were our guides started boldly stealing from us as they saw that we paid little heed. At last, after we had lost a lot of things, vexation made us wise.

At length we arrived at the boundary of the province which is terminated by a dyke[1] from one sea to the other, and outside it

[1] The Lines of Perekop.

was the camp of men who, when we came among them, looked to us as if they were all lepers. They were wretched creatures stationed there to receive the tax from those taking salt from the salt lakes previously mentioned. From this place, so they said, we would have to travel for a fortnight without coming across any inhabitants. We drank cosmos with them and gave them a basket full of biscuits; they gave us one goat for eight people for that long journey and I know not how many skins full of cows' milk.

So we changed our horses and oxen and set out on our journey which we completed in ten days as far as the other camp. On that route we came across no water save in holes dug in hollows, with the exception of two little streams. We directed our course due east from the time we left the aforesaid province of Gasaria, having the sea to the south, and to the north a vast wilderness, which in places is thirty days' journey wide and in it is no forest, no mountain, no stone, but the finest grass.

Here the Comans used to graze their animals. They are called Capchat [Kypchak] but by the Teutons they are called Valans and the province Valania; by Isidore, on the other hand, from the river Tanais to the Marsh of Meotis [Sea of Azov] and the Danube, it is termed Alania. This country stretches in length from the Danube to the Tanais, which is the boundary of Asia and Europe, a journey of two months' swift riding, as the Tartars ride; it all used to be inhabited by the Capchat Comans as did the country beyond the Tanais [Don] as far as the Etilia [Ityl], between which two rivers it is a good ten days' journey. To the north of this province lies Russia which has forests everywhere and stretches from Poland and Hungary as far as the Tanais; and all this was laid waste by the Tartars and is still daily being ravaged.

CHAPTER XIII

THE TRIALS THEY ENDURED, AND THE TOMBS OF THE COMANS

Now the Tartars put Saracens in charge of the Ruthenians since the latter are Christians; and when they are unable to give them any more gold or silver they drive them and their children like sheep to the wilderness to look after their animals.

Beyond Russia to the north is Prussia, the whole of which the Teutonic Knights lately reduced to subjection, and certainly they could easily take possession of Russia if they would put their hand to it, for if the Tartars heard that the great priest, that is the Pope, was preparing a crusade against them they would all take flight into their wilderness.

And so we journeyed eastward, seeing nothing but the sky and the earth and at times on our right the sea, which is called the Sea of Tanais, and also the tombs of the Comans which were visible at two leagues' distance owing to the Comans' custom of burying all the members of a family together.

As long as we were in the wilderness all went well with us, but the wretchedness I endured when we came to inhabited places I cannot express in words. Now our guide wanted me to go to each captain with a present, and our supplies were not sufficient for that. Every day we were eight persons eating our bread—not counting chance comers who all wanted to eat with us—for there were five of us and the three who were conducting us, two driving the carts, and the one who was to accompany us as far as Sartach; the meat they gave us was not sufficient and we found nothing which could be bought for money.

Furthermore, whenever we sat under our carts to get some shade, for the heat was great at that time, these men intruded upon us in such a churlish manner that they trampled on us in their wish to see all our things. If they were seized with the desire of relieving nature they did not go away from us so far as one can toss a bean; indeed they performed their filthiness by the side of us, chatting to each other; and many other things they did which were above measure trying.

But the thing which annoyed me above all else was that when I wished to speak to them some words of edification, my interpreter would say: "Don't make me preach for I don't know how to say such words." And he spoke the truth, for later when I began to understand the language somewhat, I realised that when I said one thing he would say something completely different, according to whatever came into his mind. Then, seeing the danger of speaking through him, I chose rather to keep silence.

And so we travelled with great hardship from place to place, until, a few days before the feast of St. Mary Magdalene [July 22nd, 1253], we reached the great river Tanais which separates Asia from Europe, as the river of Egypt separates Asia from Africa.

In that spot where we reached it Baatu and Sartach had established a village of Ruthenians on the east bank, and these men carried envoys and merchants across in small boats. They took us first across, and then the carts, putting one wheel in one boat and the other in another and tying the boats together, and rowing them like this they went across. At this point our guide did a very foolish thing. Under the impression that the inhabitants of the village were to supply us with horses and oxen, on the other bank he sent away the animals which had brought us so that they could return to their owners, and when we asked the villagers for animals they replied that they had this privilege from Baatu that they were under no other obligation than that of carrying across those coming and going. Moreover from merchants they received good payment.

And so we stayed on the bank of the river for three days. On the first day they gave us a large fresh barbel, on the second day some rye bread and a little meat collected by the village official from door to door at the different houses, on the third day some dried fish of which they have great quantities there.

The river there was as broad as the Seine at Paris. Before we reached that spot we passed many lovely stretches of water full of fish, but the Tartars do not know how to catch them nor do they care for fish unless it is so big that they can eat the flesh like mutton. This river is the eastern boundary of Russia and takes its rise in the Meotid Marshes,[1] which stretch as far as the ocean in the north. The river however flows southwards, forming a large sea of seven hundred miles before it reaches the Sea of Pontus [Black Sea]; and all the streams we passed flow in that direction. This same river also has a large forest on its west bank.

[1] The sources of the Don are in the neighbourhood of the town of Tula in Central Russia.

Beyond this point the Tartars go no further north, for at that season, about the beginning of August, they start going back southward, and so there is another village lower down where envoys cross in the winter.

While there, we were in great straits, for we could find neither horses nor oxen for money. At last, after I had shown to them that we were working for the common good of all Christians, they lent us oxen and men, but we ourselves were obliged to go on foot. At that time they were harvesting rye. Wheat does not thrive there; millet they have in great abundance.

The Ruthenian women adorn their heads as do ours, but their upper garment they trim on the outside with squirrel and ermine from the feet to the knees. The men wear capes like the Germans but on their heads they wear felt caps which have a long point on top.

So we walked for three days without coming across a soul, and just when we as well as the oxen were tired out and we did not know where we could find the Tartars, suddenly two horses came running up to us; we caught them with great joy and our guide and the interpreter mounted them, so that they could look and see in what direction we could find some people. When at last on the fourth day we came across some men we rejoiced like shipwrecked mariners on reaching port.

Then we got horses and oxen and went from station to station until we arrived at Sartach's camp on July 31st.

CHAPTER XIV

SARTACH'S DISTRICT AND ITS INHABITANTS

THE country beyond the Tanais is very beautiful, with rivers and woods. In the north are vast forests which are inhabited by two races of men; first the Moxel,[1] who have no laws and are pure pagans. They have no towns, only huts in the forest. Their chief and a great part of them were killed in Germany, for the Tartars

[1] See above, p. 101.

brought them as far as the borders of Germany and as a result they think highly of the Germans and hope that one day they will be freed by them from their subjection to the Tartars. If a merchant comes to them, then he at whose house he first alights has to provide for him as long as he wishes to remain among them. If anyone sleeps with the wife of another, the latter does not mind as long as he does not see it with his own eyes, which shows they are not jealous. They have great quantities of pigs, honey and wax, valuable furs, and falcons. Beyond them are the other tribe who are called Merdas and by the Latins Merdinis;[1] they are Saracens.

Beyond these is the Etilia which is the largest river I have ever seen; it comes from the north from Greater Bulgaria, and flowing in a southerly direction falls into a certain lake [Caspian] which it takes four months to go round and of which I will tell you later. In the northern districts where we crossed these two rivers, the Tanais and Etilia, they are not more than ten days' journey apart, but in the south they are far distant from each other, for the Tanais flows into the Sea of Pontus; the Etilia forms the afore-mentioned sea or lake along with many other rivers which flow into it from Persia.

Now to the south we had very high mountains inhabited, on the slopes facing this wilderness, by the Circassians and the Alans or Aas, who are Christians and to this day are fighting against the Tartars. Next to these, near the sea or lake of Etilia, are certain Saracens called Lesgi,[2] and they likewise are not subject to them. Beyond them is the Iron Gate[3] which Alexander made to keep the barbarians out of Persia; I will describe its position to you later, for I passed through it on my return. Between these two rivers in the districts through which we passed, the Capchat Comans used to live before the Tartars fell upon them.

---

[1] The Mordvins.
[2] Lesgi: Lesghians, a people who still inhabit a part of Dagestan in the N.E. Caucacus.
[3] Modern Derbent.

CHAPTER XV

SARTACH'S ORDA AND HIS MAGNIFICENCE

So we found Sartach three days' journey from the Etilia, and his orda seemed very large to us, for he has six wives, and his first-born son, who was with him, has two or three, and each wife has a large house and perhaps two hundred carts. Our guide went to a certain Nestorian, Coiac by name, who is one of the chief men of his court. The latter made us go a very long way to the house of the *Yam*. *Yam* is what they call the man whose duty it is to receive envoys.[1]

In the evening the said Coiac ordered us to come to Sartach. Then our guide began to ask what we were taking him and was much scandalised when he saw that we were not getting ready anything to take. We stood before Sartach and he sat in all his glory, having the lute played and people dance before him. Then I spoke to him the words I have mentioned before, saying why we had come to his master, and I begged him to help us so that his lord might see our letter. I also offered my excuses explaining that as I was a monk, neither possessing nor receiving nor handling gold or silver or any precious thing, with the sole exception of the books and sacred objects with which we served God, we were therefore bringing no gift to him or his lord, for I who had renounced my own possessions could not be the bearer of those belonging to others.

Then he replied kindly enough that I did well seeing that I was a monk to keep my vow, and that he had no need of our things, but rather would give to us of his if we were in want, and he made us sit down and drink of his milk. After a while he asked us to pronounce a blessing for him, which we did. He also enquired who was the greatest lord among the Franks. I said, "The Emperor, if he held his land in peace." "No," said he. "It is the

---

[1] The *yam* or post-horse service was one of the most important institutions of the Mongol empire. Marco Polo gives a long account of it as it existed under Kubilay, but it was already fully organised in the reign of Ugedey.

King." For he had heard of you from Sir Baldwin of Hainault. While I was there I also came across one of the companions of David, who had been in Cyprus, and had told Sartach of all that he had seen.

Then we returned to our lodging. The next day I sent Sartach a flagon of muscatel wine, which had survived the long journey perfectly, and a basket full of biscuits, which pleased him very much; and that evening he kept our servants with him. The next day Coiac summoned me to the court bidding me bring the King's letter, Mass equipment and books with me, as his master wished to see them. We did this, loading one cart with the books and things for Mass and another with bread, wine and fruit. Then he had all the books and vestments spread out and a crowd of Tartars, Christians and Saracens on horseback surrounded us. He examined these things, then asked if I would give them all to his lord. On hearing this I was terrified. I did not like his words; but, putting a good face on it, I replied: "Sir, we beg that your master will be so good as to receive this bread, wine and fruit, not indeed as a gift for it is little enough, but as a blessing, so that we may not come into his presence empty-handed. He himself will see my Lord the King's letter and from that will learn the reason of our coming to him; then we shall be at his command, both we and all our belongings. The vestments however are blessed, and it is not lawful for any but priests to touch them." He then bade us put them on to appear before his master, which we did.

Wearing the most precious vestments, I held before my breast a very lovely cushion, the Bible you gave me, and the most beautiful psalter presented to me by Her Majesty the Queen, in which there were some fine illuminations. My companion took the Missal and the cross. The cleric, dressed in a surplice, took the thurible. In this fashion we arrived in front of Sartach's dwelling, and they lifted up the felt hanging before the entrance so that he could see us. Then they made the cleric and the interpreter genuflect three times, but they did not demand this of us. They warned us most earnestly to be careful not to touch the threshold either on entering or leaving, and we were told to sing some blessing for him.

Then we went in singing the "Salve Regina". There was a bench standing near the entrance with cosmos and some cups on it, and all his wives had assembled, and the Mongols coming in with us thronged about us. Coiac took Sartach the thurible with some incense and this he examined carefully, holding it in his hand. Next he handed him the psalter, which he had a good look at, as did the wife who was sitting next to him; then he took the Bible. Sartach enquired if the Gospel were included. I replied, "Yes indeed, the whole of Holy Scripture." He also took the crucifix in his hand and asked if the figure were the figure of Christ. I answered that it was. The Nestorians and Armenians never put the figure of Christ on their crosses, which gives the impression that they entertain wrong ideas about the Passion or are ashamed of it. He then ordered those around us to stand back so that he could get a better view of our ornaments. At that point I handed him your letter with copies in Arabic and Syriac. I had had it written out at Acre in both those languages and scripts; and there were some Armenian priests there who knew Turkish and Arabic, and that companion of David who knew Syriac, Turkish and Arabic.

We then retired and removed our vestments, and some scribes and Coiac came and they translated the letter. When Sartach had heard it, he ordered the bread, wine and fruit to be accepted and bade us take back the vestments and books to the inn. This took place on the Feast of St. Peter's Chains [August 1st, 1253].

CHAPTER XVI

THEY ARE ORDERED TO GO TO BAATU, SARTACH'S FATHER

THE next morning a certain priest, a brother of Coiac, came and asked for the phial of chrism, as Sartach wished to see it, so he said. We gave it to him. In the evening Coiac called us and said, "The Lord King has written fair words to my master, but they contain certain difficult matters about which he dare not do anything without the advice of his father; you must therefore journey to his father. As for the two carts you brought yesterday with the vestments and books, you will hand them over to me, for my master would like to examine the things more carefully." I immediately suspected the evil designs of his greed and said to him, "Sir, not only those, but also the other two carts which we have we will leave in your care." "No," said he, "leave these, with the others do what you will." I rejoined that this could by no manner of means be done but we would hand over the whole to him. He thereupon asked if it was our wish to remain in that country. I answered, "If you have properly understood the letter of my Lord the King, you will know that that is the case." He then declared it behoved us to be exceedingly patient and humble. With that we parted from him that evening.

The following morning he sent a Nestorian priest for the carts and we took all four. We were then met by Coiac's brother, who separated all our belongings from those things which we had taken to the court on the previous day, taking them as if they were his own, namely our books and vestments. Now Coiac had ordered us to take with us the vestments we had worn for Sartach so that, if needs be, we could put them on for Baatu. These the priest took from us by force saying: "You brought these to Sartach, now you want to take them to Baatu." And when I wished to explain to him he replied: "Don't talk so much and be off with you."

Then I had need of patience for we did not enjoy free access to Sartach, nor was there anyone who would show us justice. I was also afraid that the interpreter might have said some things differently from the way I had said them to him, for he would have liked us to have made presents of everything. I had one consolation and that was that when I became aware of their covetousness I removed from among the books the Bible and Sentences and the other books I was particularly fond of. Her Majesty the Queen's psalter I did not dare to take as it had attracted too much notice on account of the gold illuminations in it.

So we went back with the two remaining carts to our lodging. Then the man, whose duty it was to conduct us to Baatu, came and wanted to set out with all speed. I told him that on no account would I take the carts. He reported this to Coiac, where-upon the latter ordered us to leave them with the *yam* together with our boy. We did this.

And so travelling due east in the direction of Baatu, on the third day we reached the Etilia and when I saw the river I wondered from what part of the north so much water flowed. Before we took our leave of Sartach, the aforesaid Coiac together with many other scribes of the court said to us, "Do not say that our master is a Christian, for he is not a Christian but a Mongol." This is because the word Christianity appears to them to be the name of a race, and they are proud to such a degree that although perhaps they believe something of Christ, nevertheless they are unwilling to be called Christians, wanting their own name, that is, Mongol, to be exalted above every other name. Nor do they wish to be called Tartars, for the Tartars were another race concerning whom I learned the following.

CHAPTER XVII

SARTACH, MANGU CHAN & KEU [GUYUK] CHAN RESPECT THE
CHRISTIANS

AT the time when the French took Antioch, the sovereignty in the districts of the north was in the hands of one called Coir Chan.[1] Coir is a proper name, Chan the name of the office, which means the same as soothsayer, for they call all soothsayers Chan.[2] The reason the chiefs are called Chan is that the government of the people by divination is in their hands. We read in the account of Antioch that the Turks sent to the king Coir Chan for help against the French, for all the Turks came from these parts. This Coir was a Caracathayan. Cara is the same as black, Cathayan the name of a race, and so Caracathayan is the same as Black Cathayan.

[1] Coir Chan is the Gur Khan, the title of the ruler of the Kara Khitayan kingdom in Turkestan.
[2] This is an error due to a confusion between Khan and Kam, the Mongol word for a shaman.

They use this name to distinguish them from the Cathayans in the east on the shores of the ocean, concerning whom I will tell you later. The Caracathayans were in certain upland pastures through which I passed.

In a certain plain among these pasture lands was a Nestorian, a mighty shepherd and lord of all the people called Naimans, who were Nestorian Christians. On the death of Coir Chan, this Nestorian set himself up as king and the Nestorians called him King John,[1] and they used to tell of him ten times more than the truth. For the Nestorians coming from these parts do this kind of thing—out of nothing they make a great rumour. This accounts for their spreading the story that Sartach was a Christian, also Mangu Chan and Keu Chan, just because they pay greater respect to Christians than to other people. And yet the truth is they are not Christians. So in the same way the great tale of this King John went abroad. Now I passed through his pasture lands and nobody knew anything about him with the exception of a few Nestorians. His pastures used to be inhabited by Keu Chan whose orda Friar Andrew visited, and I also passed by it on my return.

This John had a brother by name Unc, like him a mighty shepherd, and he was beyond the pastures of these Caracathayans, separated from his brother by a distance of three weeks' journey, and he was lord of a little town called Caracorum, having under him the people called Crit and Merkit,[2] who were Nestorian Christians. But this lord of theirs rejected the Christian religion and worshipped idols, having pagan priests by him; these all invoke evil spirits and are sorcerers.

Beyond this man's pasture lands, nine or fifteen days' journey, were the pastures of the Mongols, who were the poorest of men, without leader and without laws, except for the soothsayings and divinations to which all in these parts pay great attention. And along with the Mongols were other poor people who were called Tartars. King John died without an heir and his brother Unc grew

---

[1] Or Prester John, usually identified with the ruler of the Kerait.

[2] The Crit are the Kerait, who were the ruling people in Mongolia before the rise of Chingis Khan. Unc Chan is evidently the Wang Khan, the last Kerait ruler. See above, Introduction, p. xxiv.

rich and had himself called Chan and used to send his herds and flocks as far as the Mongol boundaries. At that time there was a certain smith, Chingis, among the Mongol people and he used to steal what he could of the animals of Unc Chan, to such an extent that Unc's shepherds complained to their master. Then he collected an army and rode into the Mongol territory to seek out Chingis himself, and the latter fled to the Tartars and went into hiding there. Whereupon Unc, having taken booty from both the Mongols and the Tartars, returned home.

Then Chingis addressed the Mongols and the Tartars saying, "Because we are without a leader our neighbours oppress us." And the Tartars and Mongols made him their leader and captain. Then secretly collecting an army he made a swift attack upon Unc and overcame him and the latter fled into Cathay. His daughter was on that occasion taken prisoner, and Chingis gave her as wife to one of his sons by whom she had that Mangu who is now in power.

Then Chingis despatched the Tartars in all directions, and as a result their name was spread abroad, for everywhere the cry was raised, "The Tartars are coming." But now on account of their frequent wars they have almost all been wiped out, and so the Mongols wish to abolish their name and bring their own to the fore. The district in which they first were and where the orda of Chingis Chan is still, is called Onankerule.[1] But since Caracorum is the part around which were their first gains, this city is considered as royal and near there they elect their Chan.

CHAPTER XVIII

OF THE RUTHENIANS, HUNGARIANS, ALANS AND THE CASPIAN SEA

As for Sartach, whether he believes in Christ or not, I do not know. But I do know that he does not wish to be called a Christian, rather indeed does he seem to me to hold Christians in derision.

---

[1] The country in Eastern Mongolia, south-east of Lake Baikal, on the rivers Onon and Kerulen, tributaries of the Amur.

Now he is on the route of the Christians, that is to say of the Russians, the Blaci,[1] the Bulgars of Lesser Bulgaria,[2] the people of Soldaia, the Circassians and the Alans, all of whom pass his way when going to his father's court, and as they bring him gifts they are in great favour with him. However, if Saracens come and bring larger gifts they are helped on their way more quickly. Also he has around him Nestorian priests who strike a board and sing their office.

There is another man called Berca, a brother of Baatu, who pastures his flocks in the direction of the Iron Gate, which is on the route of all the Saracens coming from Persia and Turkey. On their way to Baatu they pass by him and bring him gifts; and he pretends to be a Saracen and does not allow pork to be eaten in his orda. However, on our return Baatu had ordered him to remove himself from that place eastwards beyond the Etilia [Volga], as he did not wish the Saracens' envoys to go by way of him for it seemed to him to be to his loss. For the four days during which we were at Sartach's orda they never provided us with any food except once when they gave us a little cosmos.

On the road indeed between him and his father we experienced great fear. For their Ruthenian, Hungarian and Alanian slaves, of whom there is a very large number among them, band themselves together in groups of twenty or thirty and run away by night and they have bows and arrows, and whomsoever they come across by night they kill. By day they stay in hiding, and when their horses are tired they come during the night up to a large group of horses on the pasture lands and change their horses; they also take away one or two with them so that they can eat them when the need arises. And so our guide was very much afraid of meeting such men. On that journey we would have died of hunger if we had not taken a few biscuits with us.

We reached the Etilia, which is a very great river, for it is four times wider than the Seine and very deep; it comes from Great Bulgaria, which is in the north, flows in a southerly direction and empties itself into a certain lake or kind of sea, which nowadays

[1] The Vlachs or Rumanians.
[2] Modern Bulgaria on the Danube as distinguished from Great Bulgaria on the Volga.

is called the Sea of Sircan, from a city on its banks in Persia, but Isidore calls it the Caspian Sea. On its south side are the Caspian mountains and Persia, on the east the Mulidet mountains,[1] that is to say the mountains of the Assassins, which meet the Caspian mountains, while in the north there is that wilderness where the Tartars now are, but before certain Comans called Cangle[2] used to be there; and from that side it receives the Etilia which swells in the summer like the Egyptian Nile. To the west there are the mountains of the Alans and the Lesgi, also the Iron Gate and the mountains of the Georgians.

This sea consequently is shut in on three sides by mountains, but its north side is open towards a plain. Friar Andrew[3] went round two sides of it, namely the south and the east. I, on the other hand, went round the other two, the north on my way from Baatu to Mangu Chan and also on my way back; the west on returning from Baatu to Syria; it can be gone round in four months, and it is not true what Isidore says, that it is a gulf from the ocean, for at no point does it touch the ocean, but is surrounded on all sides by land.

CHAPTER XIX

BAATU'S ORDA AND HOW THEY WERE RECEIVED BY HIM

THE whole of the district from the west side of this sea, where are Alexander's Iron Gate and the mountains of the Alans, as far as the northern ocean and the Meotide marshes, where the Tanais takes its rise,[4] used to be called Albania.[5] Speaking of this country Isidore says there are dogs so big and so ferocious that they chase bulls and kill lions. What is true, as I learned from men who told me, is that there, in the direction of the northern ocean, they make

---

[1] = Mulhid or Mulahida, heretics. The headquarters of the Assassins was at Alamut in the Elburz Mountains.

[2] Kangli or Kankali, a Turkish people who lived in the Kirgiz Steppe, between the river Ural in the west up to Lake Balkash in the east, north of the Aral Sea.

[3] Andrew of Longjumeau, O.P. See Introduction, pp. xvii–xxi.

[4] Sea of Azov. The Tanais (Don) falls into this sea: it does not rise there.

[5] The ancient name of east Caucasia.

dogs draw carts as if they were oxen on account of their size and strength.

Now at that spot on the Etilia to which we had made our way, there is a new village which the Tartars have established, partly of Ruthenians, partly of Saracens, and these convey across the river the envoys going to and returning from Baatu's orda, for Baatu is on the further bank, towards the east, nor does he pass beyond that point when he goes north in the summer. He was already beginning to go south, for from January to August he and all the others go towards the cold regions, and in August they start coming back.

And so we sailed down in a boat from that village as far as his orda. From that place to the towns of Great Bulgaria in the north it is five days' journey. I wonder what devil carried the law of Mohammed there, for from the Iron Gate which leads out of Persia it is more than thirty days' journey across a wilderness following the course of the Etilia until one reaches Bulgaria, and on the way there is no city, nothing but some villages near where the Etilia flows into the sea. Yet the Bulgarians are the very worst kind of Saracens, clinging more firmly to the law of Mohammed than any others.

When I saw Baatu's orda I was overcome with fear, for his own houses seemed like a great city stretching out a long way and crowded round on every side by people to a distance of three or four leagues. Just as the people of Israel knew, each one of them, where they should pitch their tents in relation to the tabernacle, so these know on what side of the orda they are to place themselves when they unload their dwellings. In their tongue the court is called "orda", which means the middle, because it is always in the middle of his people, with the exception that no one places himself due south, for the doors of the court open in that direction. But to the right and the left they stretch out as far as they wish according to the number of sites required, so long as they do not set themselves down right in front of or opposite the court.

And so first we were taken to a Saracen who did not provide us with any food. The following day we were taken to the court. Baatu had had a large pavilion set up, as his house could not hold as many men and women as had assembled. The man who was conducting us told us that we were to say nothing until bidden by Baatu, and then we were to speak briefly. He also asked whether you had ever sent envoys to them. I told him how you had sent to Keu Chan, and I said you would have sent neither envoys to him nor a letter to Sartach, if you had not believed that they were Christians, for it was not from any fear but in order to congratulate them because you had heard that they were Christians that you sent. Then he led us in front of the pavilion and warned us not to touch the ropes of the tent, which they consider take the place of the threshold of a house. We stood there in our habits, bare-footed and heads uncovered, and we were a great gazing-stock for their eyes. Friar John of Policarp[1] had been there but he had changed out of his habit in order not to be despised, for he was an envoy of our Lord the Pope.

Then we were led in as far as the middle of the tent, and they did not require us to make any act of deference by genuflecting as envoys usually do. So we stood there before him for the space of a "Miserere mei Deus", and they all kept the deepest silence. Now he was sitting on a throne, which was long and wide like a couch, completely covered with gold, and three steps led up to it and one of his wives was next to him. On his right the men were sitting spread about, the ladies on his left, and the space which was not taken up by the women on their side—for Baatu's wives alone were there—was filled by men. At the entrance of the pavilion was a bench and on it cosmos and large goblets of gold and silver, decorated with precious stones. He eyed us attentively and we did him, and he seemed to me similar in size to Sir John of Beaumont[2] (may his soul rest in peace). His face at that time was very red.

At last he gave the command for me to speak. Whereupon the man who had brought us told us to kneel down and speak. I knelt on one knee as to a man. Then he signed me to kneel on both, which I did, not wishing to dispute about it. Then he bade me speak, and I, considering that I was praying to God since I

[1] John of Plano Carpini.
[2] The Chamberlain and companion of Louis IX in the Holy Land. See Joinville, *Life of St. Louis*, tr. R. Hague (Sheed and Ward), p. 14.

was kneeling on both knees, took my opening words from a prayer saying, "My Lord, we pray God from Whom all good things do proceed and Who has given to you your earthly possessions, that after these He will give to you the gifts of heaven, for the former without these are vain." He listened attentively and I added, "Know for certain that you will not obtain the gifts of heaven unless you are a Christian. For God says: 'He that believeth and is baptised shall be saved, but he that believeth not shall be condemned.'" At this he smiled gently and the other Mongols began to clap their hands in derision; my interpreter was struck dumb and I had to encourage him not to be afraid. Then when there was silence again I said, "I came to your son because we heard that he was a Christian, and I brought him a letter on behalf of my lord the King of the French. He sent me here to you. For what reason you ought to know."

Then he made me get up and he asked your name and mine, and that of my companion and the interpreter, and he had everything written down. He also asked against whom you were waging war, for he had learned that you had gone forth from your own land with an army. I replied, "Against the Saracens who are violating the house of God at Jerusalem." He also enquired whether you had ever sent envoys to him. "To you," I said, "never." Then he made us sit down and had some milk given to us to drink; they consider it a great honour for anyone to drink cosmos with him in his own house. And while I was sitting looking at the ground he ordered me to lift my head up, for he wished to have a further look at us, or perhaps it was because of witchcraft, for they hold it as a bad omen or sign or evil portent when anyone sits in their presence with head bent down as if he were sad, especially if he props his cheek or his chin on his hand.

Then we went out, and after a little the man who was conducting us came and, taking us to the lodging, he said to me, "The Lord King asks that you be retained in this country, and Baatu cannot do this without the knowledge of Mangu, so you and your interpreter are to go to Mangu. Your companion, however, and the other man will return to Sartach's orda and wait there until you return." Then Abdullah, the interpreter, began to wail, thinking he was lost, and my companion called to witness that they could sooner cut off his head than he would be separated from me; and I for my part said that I could not go without my companion and also that we had great need of two servants, for if one of them should happen to fall ill he could not be left alone. Then he went back to the court and repeated these words to Baatu, who gave the order: "Let the two priests and the interpreter go, and the cleric return to Sartach." The guide returned and told us the decision, and when I wanted to plead on behalf of the cleric that he should come with us, he said: "Don't say any more, for Baatu has decided and I dare not return to the court."

Out of your alms the cleric Gosset had twenty-six *yperperas*, and no more; of these he kept ten for himself and the boy, and he gave sixteen to Abdullah for us, and so we separated with tears from each other, he returning to Sartach and we staying where we were.

CHAPTER XX

THE JOURNEY TO THE COURT OF MANGU CHAN

ON the Vigil of the Assumption [August 14th, 1253] Gosset reached Sartach's orda and on the following day Nestorian priests wore our vestments in Sartach's presence.

Then we were taken to another host, who was to provide us with lodging, food and horses. But as we had nothing to give him he performed everything badly. We travelled south with Baatu, following the course of the Etilia, for five weeks, and at times my companion was so hungry that he would say to me almost in tears: "It seems to me as if I have never had anything to eat." A market always follows Baatu's orda, but it was so far away from us that we could not go to it. We also had to travel on foot owing to the lack of horses.

At last some Hungarians who had been clerics came across us. One of them still knew how to sing many things by heart and the other Hungarians considered him as a kind of priest and he used to be called upon for the funerals of their dead; another had been taught grammar quite adequately, for he understood whatever we put down for him in writing, but he could not reply. These men were a great comfort to us, bringing us cosmos to drink and sometimes meat to eat. I was much distressed when they asked us for some books and I had none that I could give them, having nothing but a Bible and breviary. Then I said to them: "Bring us some paper and I will copy for you as long as we are here." They did this and I wrote out for each of them the Hours of the Blessed Virgin and the office of the dead.

One day a Coman joined us, greeting us in Latin, saying, "Salvete Domini." Surprised, I returned his salutation and asked who had taught him that greeting, and he said he had been baptised in Hungary by our Friars who had taught it to him. He also said that Baatu had asked him a great deal about us and he had described to him the nature of our Order.

I frequently saw Baatu riding with his crowd, and all the heads of families ride with him. According to my estimation they did not number five hundred men.

At last, about the time of the feast of the Exaltation of the Holy Cross [September 14th], there came up to us a certain rich Mongol, whose father was a captain of a thousand, which is a very high rank with them, and said, "It is my duty to take you to Mangu Chan and it is a four months' journey and the cold there is so intense that the rocks and trees split from it; see whether you can stand it." I answered him: "I trust in the power of God that we shall stand what other men can stand." Then he said, "If you cannot stand it I shall leave you on the road." To this I replied, "That would not be right, for we are going not of our accord but only because we have been sent by your master, and so, since we are committed to your charge, you ought not to abandon us." At that he said, "It will be all right." He then made us show him all our clothes and what seemed to him unnecessary he made us leave in the custody of our host. The following day they brought for each of us rough goat-skin garments, trousers of the same and boots or footwear made in their style, with felt socks and fur hoods also, such as they wear.

On the day after the Exaltation of the Holy Cross we started to ride, we three having two pack horses, and we rode continuously in an easterly direction until the feast of All Saints. The whole of that territory and even more was inhabited by the Cangle who are akin to the Comans. To the north we had Great Bulgaria and to the south the aforementioned Caspian Sea.

CHAPTER XXI

The River Iagat and Various Regions and Races

AFTER we had travelled twelve days from the Etilia we came upon a large river which is called the Iagat [Ural]; flowing from the north from the country of the Pascatur it empties itself into the aforementioned sea. The language of the Pascatur is the same as that of the Hungarians, and they are shepherds without any cities and their territory adjoins Great Bulgaria on the west. From that country eastwards on the north side there is not another city, so Great Bulgaria is the last region where there are towns.

From the district of the Pascatur came the Huns, later known as Hungarians, and this is the origin of Great Hungary. Isidore says that with ferocious horses they crossed the barriers erected by Alexander among the crags of the Caucasus to keep back the savage tribes, so that as far as Egypt tribute used to be paid to them. They also laid waste all the countries as far as France and so were more powerful than the Tartars are at this present time. The Blacs, Bulgars and Vandals came with them.

For it is from Great Bulgaria that those Bulgars came who are now the other side of the Danube near Constantinople. Next to the Pascatur are the Illac,[1] which is the same as Blac, for the Tartars cannot pronounce the letter B, and from them came the people who are in the Assan territory, for they call both of them Illac, the former and the latter.

The language of the Ruthenians, Poles, Bohemians and Slavs is

---

[1] The Black Bulgars, the inhabitants of Great Bulgaria on the Volga.

the same as the Vandals' tongue; a multitude of all of these was with the Huns and nowadays, for the greater part, is with the Tartars, whom God has raised up from far distant regions to be a people which is no people and a foolish nation, according to the words of the Lord: "I will provoke them"—that is those who do not keep His law—"with that which is no people and will vex them with a foolish nation."[1] This is being fulfilled to the letter in the case of all the nations which do not keep the law of Christ.

What I have said about the land of the Pascatur I know from the Friars Preachers who went there before the arrival of the Tartars.[2] From of old they had been conquered by their Saracen neighbours the Bulgars and many of them had become Saracens. Other facts can be learned from chronicles, for it is agreed that these provinces beyond Constantinople, which are now called Bulgaria, Blakia[3] and Slavonia were provinces of Greece; Hungary was Pannonia.

And so we rode through the land of the Cangle[4] from the feast of Holy Cross until the feast of All Saints [November 1st], covering almost each day, as far as I can judge, the distance it is from Paris to Orleans,[5] and some days more, according to our supply of horses; for sometimes we changed horses twice or three times in a day. Sometimes we went for two or three days without coming across a soul, and then we were obliged to go more slowly. Of the twenty or thirty horses we always had the worst since we were foreigners, for they took the better horses before us; me they always provided with a strong horse, as I was very heavy. But as to whether it went at a steady pace or not, this was a matter about which I dared not enquire, nor did I even dare to complain if it proved a bad mount, but each one had to put up with his luck. This was the cause of one of our most difficult trials, for many a time the horses grew tired before we came across inhabitants; then

---

[1] Deut. xxxii. 21.

[2] This was the mission of Brother Julian which took place c. 1235–6. It is described in a short treatise—*Relatio Fratris Ricardi*—which is printed in *Scriptores Rerum Hungaricarum*, vol. II, pp. 538–42. Budapest 1938.

[3] Blakia: Wallachia.

[4] The land of the Kankali: the Kirgiz Steppe. The distance covered was over 1,000 miles.

[5] The distance from Paris to Orleans: over seventy-five miles.

we had to strike and lash them, even to put our clothes on to other pack animals, to change our horses for pack horses, and sometimes the two of us had to ride on one.

CHAPTER XXII

OF THE HUNGER AND THIRST AND OTHER MISERIES THEY ENDURED ON THEIR JOURNEY

OF hunger and thirst, cold and fatigue, there was no end, for they gave us no food except in the evening. In the morning they gave us something to drink or some millet to take. In the evening, however, they used to give us meat, shoulder of mutton and ribs and as much broth as we could drink. When we had our fill of meat broth we were completely refreshed and it seemed to me a most wholesome drink and extremely nourishing. On Fridays I did not break my fast until the night time, drinking nothing; then to my sorrow and grief I had to eat meat. Sometimes we had to eat meat half-cooked or almost raw, on account of the lack of fuel. This was when we were sleeping in the open and alighted at nightfall, for we could not at that time very well collect the dung of the oxen and horses. Other fuel we seldom came across, except perhaps occasionally a few briars; also at some places on the banks of some of the rivers there are woods, but this is rare.

In the beginning our guide had the greatest disdain for us, and he felt disgusted at having to conduct such insignificant men. Later, however, when he began to know us better, he took us to the ordas of wealthy Mongols and we had to pray for them. If I had had a good interpreter this would have given me an opportunity of sowing much good seed. Chingis, the first Chan, had four sons who had many descendants, all of whom now have large ordas, and these increase in number daily and are spread throughout this vast wilderness, which is like a sea. And so our guide took us to many of them. They were exceedingly surprised that we had no desire to receive gold or silver or costly garments. They also made enquiries about the great Pope, whether he was as old a man as they had heard, for they had heard that he was five hundred years old. They asked about our country, whether there were many sheep, oxen and horses there. As for the ocean they could not grasp that it had neither limit nor shore.

On the vigil of All Saints we left the route leading east, for the inhabitants had already gone a good way to the south, and we directed our course due south across some upland pastures for eight days on end. In that wilderness I saw many asses, which are called *cula* and are more like mules; these our guide and his companions chased a great deal but with no success on account of their swiftness. On the seventh day some very high mountains began to loom into sight[1] towards the south and we entered a plain which was irrigated like a garden, and we came across cultivated land.

On the octave of All Saints we entered a town of the Saracens called Kinchat,[2] and the chief man came with ale and cups to meet the leader of our party outside the town. For it is their custom that the envoys of Baatu and Mangu Chan are met with food and drink from all the towns subject to them. At that time they were walking upon ice there, and we had had frost for the first time in the wilderness on the feast of St. Michael [September 29th]. I enquired the name of the province,[3] since we were now in different territory, but they could not tell me anything except the name of that city, which was an extremely small one. A large river[1] flowed down from the mountains, which irrigated the whole region wherever they liked to conduct the water, nor did it empty itself into any sea, but was absorbed by the earth and also formed a number of marshes. There I saw vines and twice drank some wine.

[1] The Tien-Shan Mountains.
[2] Probably Chuguchat in Tarbagatai, south of Lake Zaisan.
[3] The country with no name was the territory to the N.W. of the modern town of Frunze, the capital of the Soviet Kirgiz Republic, on the border of Eastern Kazakhstan.
[4] The Chu.

CHAPTER XXIII

HOW BURI WAS PUT TO DEATH

ON the morrow we reached another village nearer the mountains, and I enquired about the latter and learned that they were the mountains of the Caucasus[1] which touch the sea on both sides from the west to the east, and I learned too that we had already passed beyond the aforementioned sea into which the Etilia flows.

I also made enquiries about the city of Talas,[2] in which the German slaves of Buri used to be, of whom Friar Andrew had made mention. I had indeed asked about them many a time at the courts of Sartach and Baatu and had succeeded in learning nothing except that Buri, their master, had been killed for the following reason: his pasture lands were not good, and one day when he was drunk he spoke these words to his men, "Am I not of the stock of Chingis Chan, the same as Baatu?" Now he was a nephew or brother of Baatu. "Why may I not go to the banks of the Etilia like Baatu to feed my flocks there?" These words were reported to Baatu, who thereupon wrote to Buri's men to bring their master to him, bound, which they did. Then Baatu asked him if he had said such a thing and he confessed that he had. However, he excused himself on the grounds that he was drunk, for it is their custom to pardon such; but Baatu gave answer, "How dared you mention my name in your drunken state?" and he ordered his head to be cut off.

As for the Germans I could find out nothing about them until I came to the court of Mangu Chan, but in this village I did learn that Talas was behind us six days' journey in the direction of the mountains. When I came to Mangu Chan's orda, I discovered

[1] The mountains were the Tien-Shan Mountains. The ancients often extended the name of the Caucasus to the whole of the great mountain barrier of Western and Central Asia.

[2] The modern town of Talas is situated on the river Talas in a valley of the Tien-Shan Mountains, some two hundred miles N.E. of Tashkent.

that Mangu had transferred them, with Baatu's permission, to the east, a month's journey from Talas, to a village called Bolac where they are digging for gold and manufacturing arms. This meant that I was not able to visit them either going or returning. And yet on my outward journey I passed near enough, perhaps three days' distance from that town. But I did not know and even if I had known I would not have been able to turn aside from my route.

From the aforementioned village we travelled eastwards following the mountains, and from that point we found ourselves among Mangu Chan's men, who everywhere came before our guide singing and clapping their hands, since he was an envoy of Baatu. For they show this honour to each other: Mangu's men receive Baatu's envoys in the manner described, and similarly Baatu's men the envoys of Mangu. However, Baatu's men are rather proud and do not carry it out with such diligence.

A few days after this we entered upon some upland pastures which used to be inhabited by the Caracathayans, and there we came to a large river[1] which we had to cross by boat. After this we entered a valley where I saw a kind of ruined fort, the walls of which were made of nothing but mud, and the land there was cultivated. Next we came across a goodly town called Equius, where there were Saracens who spoke Persian, though they were a very great distance away from Persia.

The following day, having crossed these pastures, which were in the foothills of the high mountains to the south, we entered upon a most lovely plain having lofty mountains to the right, and to the left a kind of sea or lake[2] fifteen days' journey in circumference. And the whole of this plain is well watered by the streams coming down from the mountains, which all flow into this sea. In the summer we returned by way of the north side of the sea, where there are likewise high mountains. In the plain I have mentioned there used to be large towns but they had, for the most part, all been destroyed, so that the Tartars could feed their flocks there, for it is very fine pasturage.

[1] The Chu, or perhaps the Ili, which falls into Lake Balkash.
[2] Lake Balkash.

We came across one large town there called Cailac,[1] in which there was a market, and many merchants flocked thither. We rested in this town for twelve days while awaiting one of Baatu's scribes who was to assist the leader of our party in the business to be settled at Mangu's court. That country used to be called Organum and used to have its own language and script but now it has all been seized by the Turcomans. Also the Nestorians of those parts used to perform their services and write books in that script and language; and it may be that they get their name Organa from the fact that they used to be very fine musicians or organists[2]; so I was told. It was there that I first saw pagan temples, in which connection I must tell you there are many sects in the east.

CHAPTER XXIV

HOW THE NESTORIANS AND SARACENS INTERMINGLE, AND OF THEIR TEMPLES

FIRST of all there are the Uigurs[3] whose country adjoins the Organum territory we have mentioned and is among the mountains towards the east, and in all their cities there are both Nestorians and Saracens, and the former have also spread in the direction of Persia in the Saracen towns. In the aforesaid town of Cailac they had three temples, two of which I went into in order to behold their foolishnesses. In the first I found a man who had a little cross of black pigment on his hand, which led me to believe that he was a Christian, in addition to the fact that to all the questions I put him he replied like a Christian. And so I asked him, "Why do you not have a Cross and the figure of Jesus Christ here?" He replied, "It is not our custom." From this I thought that they must be Christians but did not have them owing to a doctrinal error.

[1] Cailac: the ancient Quayaligh or Kayalig near the modern town of Kopal in Semiretchensk (Eastern Kazakhstan).
[2] The country really acquired its name from its ruler, the Khatun Organa, the widow of the successor of Jagatay.
[3] See Introduction, p. xxii.

There behind a kind of chest which they had in place of an altar and on which they put lights and their offerings, I saw a statue with wings like St. Michael and others which looked like statues of bishops holding their fingers as if in blessing. I could not find the other temple that evening for the Saracens avoid the pagans to such an extent that they are not even willing to speak about them, and so when I enquired of them about the rites of these people they were scandalised.

The next day was the first of the month and the pasch of the Saracens, and I changed my lodging so that I put up near the other temple. For they receive envoys, each one according to the room he has or the number allotted to him. Then on entering the aforesaid temple I found pagan priests, for on the first of the month they open their temples, the priests dress themselves up, offer incense, light lamps and offer up the oblations of bread and fruit made by the people.

First I will describe for you the rites common to all idolaters and afterwards those of the Uigurs who are, as it were, a sect separate from the others.

They all adore towards the north, clapping their hands together and prostrating by kneeling on the ground and placing their foreheads on their hands. Consequently the Nestorians in these parts on no account join their hands when praying but pray with their hands extended before their breast. The pagans build their temples from east to west, and on the north side they make an alcove, projecting as a choir, or sometimes if the building is square it is in the middle of the building. On the north side they shut off an alcove in place of a choir. And there they put a chest, long and wide like a table, and behind that chest they place their chief idol facing south: the one I myself saw at Caracorum was as big as St. Christopher is depicted. A certain Nestorian priest who had come from Cathay told me that in that country there is an idol so large that it can be seen two days' journey off. The other idols they set all round; they are all most beautifully gilded. On the top of the chest, which is at the same time a kind of table, they place lights and their offerings. All the doors of the temple open towards the south contrary to the custom of the Saracens.

They also have large bells like us; this I think accounts for the fact that the Christians of the east do not like to have them, though the Ruthenians and the Greeks in Gazaria do use them.

CHAPTER XXV

OF THEIR TEMPLES AND IDOLS AND HOW THEY COMPORT
THEMSELVES IN THE WORSHIP OF THEIR GODS

ALL their priests shave their heads all over and their beards, and they wear saffron garments and observe chastity from the time they shave their heads; they live together, one or two hundred in one community. The days on which they go into their temple, they bring two benches and they sit on the floor facing each other, choir to choir, holding their books in their hands and these from time to time they put down on the benches. As long as they are in the temple they keep their heads uncovered, and they read to themselves and keep silence. When I went into one of their temples in Caracorum and found them sitting like this, I tried in many ways to provoke them to speech and was in no way able to do so.

They also have in their hands wherever they go a string of one or two hundred beads, just as we carry our rosaries, and they always say these words, "On man baccam",[1] that is "O God, Thou knowest" so one of them translated it for me and they expect to be rewarded by God as many times as they make mention of Him by saying this.

Around their temple they always make a fair courtyard which is well shut in by a wall and to the south they make a large gate where they sit and talk together. Above this gate they erect a long pole which, if possible, rises above the whole town, and by means of this pole one can tell that a building is a pagan temple. These things are to be found among all idolaters.

When, therefore, I went into the aforementioned temple I found priests sitting in the outer doorway. When I caught sight of them they looked to me like Frenchmen, with their shaven

[1] "Om! Mani padme hum": "Hail to the jewel in the lotus".

beards and wearing Tartar mitres on their heads. The Uigur priests wear the following dress: wherever they go they are always in saffron coats, quite close-fitting and with a belt on top, just like Frenchmen, and they have a cloak on their left shoulder hanging down in folds over the breast and back to their right side as the deacon wears a chasuble in Lent.

The Tartars have adopted their script. They begin to write at the top and continue the line downwards, and they read it in the same way and they increase their lines from left to right. They make great use of paper and characters for their sorcery, consequently their temples are full of short sentences hanging up. Mangu Chan is sending you a letter in the Mongol language and their script.

They burn their dead after the fashion of bygone days and enclose the ashes in the top of a pyramid.

And so when I had sat down by the side of the said priests—this was after I had been inside their temple and had seen their many idols, small and large—I asked what was their belief concerning God. They replied, "We believe that there is but one God." And I asked, "Do you believe that He is a spirit or something corporeal?" They said, "We believe that He is a spirit." "Do you believe," said I, "that He has ever assumed human nature?" "No," they answered. Then I asked, "Seeing that you believe Him to be but one and a spirit, why do you make statues to Him having a body, and why do you make so many? Moreover seeing that you do not believe that He has become man, why do you make statues to Him in the form of a man rather than of another animal?" To that they replied, "We do not fashion these statues to God, but when any rich man among us dies, his son or his wife or someone dear to him has a statue of the deceased made and places it here and we venerate it in memory of him." To these words I answered, "Then you do these things for no other reason than to flatter men." "Not so," they said. "We do it in their memory."

Then they asked me, as if jeering at me, "Where is God?" In return I asked, "Where is your soul?" They said, "In our body." Whereupon I said, "Is it not everywhere in your body?

Does it not rule the whole and yet it is not seen? Similarly God is everywhere and governs all things; nevertheless He is invisible, for He is intellect and wisdom." Then when I wanted to argue more points with them, my interpreter, tired and unable to express the words, forced me to silence.

The Mongols or Tartars belong to their sect as far as their believing in only one God is concerned; they do, nevertheless, make out of felt images of their dead and they clothe these in most precious materials and place them in one or two carts; these carts nobody dares touch and they are in charge of their diviners who are their priests; I will tell you later about them.

These diviners always go before the orda of Mangu and other rich men; the poor, however, do not have them, only those of Chingis' stock. When it is time for them to move they go before them as the pillar of cloud went before the children of Israel and they inspect the place where the camp is to be measured out and first unload their dwellings and after them the orda. Then when it is a feast day or the first of the month they bring out the aforementioned images and place them in order in a circle in their dwelling. Then the Mongols come, enter the dwelling and bow to the images and venerate them. And no stranger may enter there, for I on one occasion wanted to go in and was roundly rated.

CHAPTER XXVI

OF VARIOUS TRIBES AND OF MEN WHO USED TO EAT THEIR PARENTS

THESE Uigurs who live side by side with Christians and Saracens have, as a result, I imagine, of frequent discussions, reached the point that they believe in only one God. They were the first dwellers in towns to be subject to Chingis Chan, whence it came about that he gave his daughter in marriage to their king. Caracorum itself is, as it were, in their territory and around their lands is the entire country belonging to King or Prester John and Unc his brother. But the latter have their pasture lands towards the north, while the Uigurs have theirs among the mountains towards the south. This accounts for the fact that the Mongols adopted their script, and they are their chief scribes and almost all the Nestorians can read their script.

Beyond these to the east among the mountains are the Tangut,[1] very brave men. They took Chingis prisoner in battle, and when peace was made they set him free; afterwards he conquered them. They have very strong oxen with tails all hair, like horses, and hairy bellies and backs; they are shorter in the leg than other oxen but very much stronger. They draw the large dwellings of the Mongols and they have graceful long curved horns which are so very sharp that their tips always have to be cut off. The cow will not allow herself to be milked unless she is sung to. They are of the same nature as bulls for if they see a man wearing red they rush upon him and would kill him.

Next come the Tebec,[2] men whose custom it was to eat their deceased parents so as to provide them, out of filial piety, with no other sepulchre than their own stomachs. They have stopped doing this now, however, for it made them detestable in the eyes of all men. Nevertheless they still make fine goblets out of their parents' skulls so that when drinking from these they may be mindful of them in the midst of their enjoyment. I was told this by one who had seen them. They have a good deal of gold in their country, so if anyone needs any he digs until he finds it, and he takes as much as he needs, putting the rest back into the ground, for he believes that if he were to place it among his treasures or in a box, God would take away from him all that which is in the earth.

I saw men of this tribe who were much deformed. The Tangut men I saw were tall and swarthy. The Uigurs are of medium height like us. Among the Uigurs is to be found the fount and root of the Turkish and Coman languages.

Beyond the Tebec are Longa and Solanga.[3] I saw their ambassadors at the court; they had brought more than ten large carts,

---

[1] The people of northern Tibet who at this time had extended their power over Kansu and north-west China.

[2] Tibetans.

[3] Manchuria.

each of which was drawn by six oxen. They are little men and dark like Spaniards; they wear tunics like a deacon's tunicle with sleeves a little narrower, and on their head they have mitres like bishops. The front half of these is somewhat lower than the back and they do not go to a point but are square on top; they are made out of cloth stiffened with black glue and are so highly polished that when caught by the rays of the sun they shine like a mirror or a well-burnished helmet; and at their temples there are long strips of the same material stitched on to the mitre which fly out in the wind like two horns springing from the temples; and when the wind tosses them about too much they twist them together on top of the mitre across the middle from one side to the other, and they stay like a hoop across the head, forming a most attractive head-dress.

When their chief envoy came to the court he always had an ivory tablet, a cubit long and a hand-breadth wide, and very smooth. Whenever he spoke to the Chan himself or to any other important person, he kept his eyes all the time on that tablet as if he were reading there what he was saying and he looked neither to the right nor to the left nor at the face of him to whom he was speaking. Even when coming into the presence of the Chan and when retiring he looked nowhere save at his tablet.

Beyond these tribes are men, as I learned for a fact, who are called Muc and who have towns but possess no animals of their own. There are, nevertheless, many flocks and herds in their country which no one tends, but when anyone wants anything he climbs a hill and shouts, and all the animals hearing the noise gather round him and let themselves be handled like domestic animals. If an envoy or any stranger comes to that district, they shut him up in a house, providing him with all necessities, until his business is concluded, for if a stranger were to go about that district the animals on smelling him would take flight and become wild.

Next is Grand Cathay, the inhabitants of which in ancient times, so I believe, used to be called Seres. From them came the best silken materials, which are named Seric after the people, and the latter get their name from one of their towns. I learned on good authority that in that country there is a town with walls of silver and ramparts of gold. In that land there are many provinces a number of which are still not subject to the Mongols. Between them and India lies the sea.

The inhabitants of Cathay are little men, and when they speak they breathe heavily through their noses; it is a general characteristic of all Orientals that they have a small opening for the eyes. They are very fine craftsmen in every art, and their physicians know a great deal about the power of herbs and diagnose very cleverly from the pulse; on the other hand they do not use urinals nor know anything about urine; I saw this myself, for there were many of them in Caracorum. It has always been their custom that whatever craft the father follows all the sons have to follow the same craft and that is why they pay such a large tribute, for every day they give the Mongols fifteen hundred *iascot*; a *iascot* is a piece of silver weighing ten marks, so that is fifteen thousand marks every day, not counting the silk materials and food-stuffs which they receive from them, and the other services they render them.

All these peoples dwell between the mountains of the Caucasus on the north side and the eastern ocean and the south of that part of Scythia inhabited by the Mongol nomads. They are all subject to the Tartars and are all given to idolatry; they invent numbers of gods, men who have turned into gods, and the genealogy of the gods, as do our poets.

There are Nestorians and Saracens living among them like foreigners as far as Cathay. There are Nestorians in fifteen cities of Cathay and they have a bishopric there in the city called Segin,[1] but beyond that they are pure pagans. The pagan priests of these said people all wear wide saffron cowls. There are also among them certain hermits, so I learned, in the woods and mountains, and they are of wondrous life and austerity.

The Nestorians there know nothing. They say their offices and have their sacred books in Syriac, a language of which they are ignorant, and so they sing like our monks who know no grammar, and this accounts for the fact that they are completely corrupt. In the first place they are usurers and drunkards, and some of

[1] Perhaps Hsi-chin, the pre-Mongol name for Peking.

them who are with the Tartars even have several wives like them. When they enter a church they wash their lower members like the Saracens; they eat meat on Fridays and have feasting on that day after the Saracen custom.

The bishop puts off coming into these regions; he comes per- haps scarcely once in fifty years. When he does come, they have all the little male children, even those still in their cradles, ordained priests, consequently almost all their men are priests, and after this they marry, which is clearly contrary to the decrees of the Fathers, and they are bigamists, for when their first wife dies these priests take another. They are also all of them simoniacal, administering no sacrament without payment.

They look after their wives and children well, consequently they pay more attention to gaining money than spreading the faith, whence it comes about that when any of them bring up sons of Mongol noblemen, although they teach them the Gospel and the faith, yet by their evil life and greed they rather alienate them from the Christian religion, for the lives of the Mongols them- selves and even of the *tuins*, that is the pagans, are more innocent than theirs.

CHAPTER XXVII

THE JOURNEY TO THE COURT OF MANGU CHAN

WE set out on the feast of St. Andrew [November 30th 1253] from the city I have mentioned, and three leagues from there we came across a completely Nestorian village. Entering their church with joy we sang as loudly as we could " Salve Regina ", for it was many a day since we had seen a church.

Three days' journey from there we reached the end of that province at the extremity of the lake I have spoken of [Lake Balkash], which seemed to us as tempestuous as the ocean, and we saw a large island in it. My companion went down to the shore and wetted a piece of linen in it so that he could taste the water, which was slightly salt but drinkable. A valley came down from among high mountains from a south-easterly direction, and there among the mountains was another large lake, and a river flowed through the valley from the one lake to the other,[1] and such a strong wind blows almost continuously through the valley that men cross it in great danger of being carried into the water by the wind.

We passed through that valley directing our course northwards towards some high mountains covered with deep snow which was then on the ground. This caused us to quicken our pace considerably on the feast of St. Nicholas [December 6th], for we no longer came across people, except for the *yams*, who are men placed at distances of a day's journey to receive envoys, since in many places in the mountains the road is narrow and there is little pasture. Between day and night we now took in two *yams*; this meant we made two days' journey in one and we covered more ground by night than by day. It was extremely cold there so they lent us goat-skins, the hairy side outwards.

On the second Saturday in Advent in the evening we were making our way through a place among the most dreadful rocks, when our guide sent to ask me to say some holy words which could put demons to flight, for in that pass[2] demons used suddenly to carry off men and nobody knew what became of them. Sometimes they would snatch a horse leaving the man behind, at other times they would tear out a man's entrails and leave the body on the horse, and many other such things frequently happened there. Then we sang in a loud voice "*Credo in Unum Deum*" and, by the grace of God, we reached the other side with the whole party intact. From then on they began to ask me to write out cards for them which they could bear on their heads, and I said to them: "I will teach you a word which you will bear in your hearts, by means of which both your souls and your bodies will be saved for eternity." But whenever I wanted to instruct them my interpreter let me down. However, I wrote out for them the "*Credo in Deum*" and the "*Pater noster*", saying, "Here is written down what a man ought to believe about God and a prayer in which petition is made to God for everything which is necessary for man;

[1] Probably Lake Ala-Kul.
[2] The mountains referred to are those which separate Kazakhstan from Dzungaria on the Chinese side, south of the Altai and north of the Tien-Shan Mountains.

therefore firmly believe what is written here although you cannot understand it and ask of God that He will do to you what is contained in the prayer written here, which He Himself taught His friends with His own lips; and I trust that He will save you." I could do no other, for to speak words of doctrine through such an interpreter was most dangerous; nay, it was impossible, for he did not know the words.

After this we entered upon a plain[1] where the orda of Keu Chan used to be; it used to be the country of the Naimans who were Prester John's own people. I did not see the orda on that occasion but on my return.

However, I will tell you now what happened to Keu Chan's son and wives. On the death of Keu Chan, Baatu wanted Mangu to be Chan. I was unable to learn anything definite about Keu's death. Friar Andrew said that he had died as a result of some medicine which had been given him and he suspected that Baatu was responsible, but I heard another story. Keu had summoned Baatu to come and pay homage to him and Baatu set out on his journey with great pomp. However he and his men were very much afraid, and he sent ahead one of his brothers, Stican[2] by name. When the latter reached Keu and was about to hand him a goblet, a quarrel arose and they killed each other. Stican's widow kept us throughout one day so that we could go into her house and bless her, that is to say pray for her. And so on the death of Keu, Mangu was elected by Baatu's desire, and the election had already taken place when Friar Andrew was there.

Keu had a brother called Siremon who, on the advice of Keu's wife and his vassals, set out in great state as if going to pay homage to Mangu. But in fact he intended to kill him, and to wipe out his whole court. When he was one or two days' journey from Mangu, one of his carts, which had broken down on the way, stopped behind and while the driver was working to repair it one of Mangu's men came up and helped him; and he asked so many questions about their journey that the driver let out what Siremon intended to do. Whereupon the man, turning aside as if he were

----

[1] Dzungaria.   [2] Shiban.

little concerned, went to the herd of horses and taking the strongest horse he could pick out, he rode with speed night and day and on reaching Mangu's orda he reported to him what he had heard. Then Mangu, hastily summoning all his men, had four circles of armed men drawn up round his orda so that no one could enter or leave. The rest he sent to meet Siremon. They took him, all unsuspecting that his plan had been revealed, and brought him to the orda with all his followers. When Mangu accused him of his crime he straightway confessed. He was then put to death, as was the elder son of Keu Chan and with them three hundred of the Tartar nobles. Their wives were also sent for; these were all beaten with burning brands to make them confess. When they had confessed they were put to death. Keu's little son, who was neither of an age to take part in nor aware of the plot, was left alive, and his father's orda with all that belonged to it, that is to say animals and men, became his.

We passed by the orda on our return, but my guides both on the outward and homeward journey dared not turn aside to visit it, for the "mistress of the Gentiles sat in sadness and there was none to comfort her". [Lam. i. 1–2.]

After that we again went up into mountainous country, all the time going north. At last on St. Stephen's day [December 26th] we entered upon a plain as vast as the sea and such that not even the smallest hill was to be seen, and on the following day, the feast of St. John the Evangelist, we reached the orda of the great lord. When, however, we were five days' journey distant from it, the yam at whose house we were sleeping wanted to direct us by a roundabout route, so that we would have had to toil for more than another fortnight. The reason for this, I gathered, was that we should pass through Onankerule, that is, their own country where Chingis Chan's orda is; others said they wanted us to do this so that by making the journey longer they could provide a greater display of their power; for they are in the habit of doing this to men coming from countries not subject to them. It was with great difficulty that our guide obtained leave for us to follow the direct route. They detained us on account of this matter from dawn until nine o'clock.

It was also on this part of the journey that I was told by the scribe for whom we had waited at Cailac that in the letter which Baatu was sending to Mangu Chan it said that you were asking for an army and help against the Saracens from Sartach. At that I began to wonder greatly and also to be worried for I knew the gist of your letter and knew that there was no mention of this in it, save that you admonished him to be the friend of all Christians, to exalt the Cross, and to be the enemy of all enemies of the Cross. I was also afraid that, since the interpreters were Armenians from Greater Armenia[1] with a deep hatred of the Saracens, they had, out of loathing for them and to do them harm, interpreted your letter more strongly in accordance with their own desires. I therefore kept quiet, not saying anything for or against, for I was afraid to contradict Baatu's words lest I should be falsely accused without reasonable cause.

CHAPTER XXVIII

Mangu's Court and the First Audience

And so we came on the aforementioned day to the orda. Our guide was assigned a large dwelling; we three were given a tiny hut in which we could only just put our baggage and make our beds and a little fire. Many came to visit our guide and he was brought rice wine in long-shaped flagons with narrow necks. I could not tell the difference between it and the best Auxerre wine, except that it had not the bouquet of wine.

We were summoned and closely questioned as to the business on which we had come. I replied: "We heard that Sartach was a Christian; we went to him, the French King sent him a private letter by us; Sartach sent us to his father, his father sent us here. He must have written the reason why." They asked if you wished to make peace with them. I answered: "He sent a letter to Sartach as to a Christian, and if he had known that he was not a

---

[1] Armenia in N.E. Turkey and adjacent territories of Persia and Trans-Caucasia, as distinguished from Lesser Armenia in Cilicia.

Christian, he would never have sent him a letter. As for making peace, all I can say is he has never done you any injury; if he had done anything to give you grounds for making war on him and his people, he would gladly wish, as a just man, to make amends and seek peace. If you, without cause, desire to make war on him and his people, we trust that God, Who is just, will come to their aid." They were amazed and kept on repeating, "Why have you come if you do not wish to make peace?"

For they are now so much puffed up with pride that they believe the whole world is anxious to make peace with them. But indeed, if I were given leave, I would preach war against them throughout the whole world with all my strength. As I did not wish to explain openly to them the cause of my coming for fear of saying something contrary to the message Baatu had sent, I said that the whole reason of my going there was that he had sent me.

On the following day we were taken to the court and I, thinking that I could go barefoot as in our part of the world, had removed my shoes. Those coming to the court however have to alight from their horses a long way from the dwelling in which the Chan is, about a bow-shot, and there the horses are left with the servants who look after them. When we had got off our horses and our leader had gone to the Chan's dwelling a Hungarian servant there recognised us, that is to say our Order. And when the men surrounded us and gazed at us as if we were monsters, especially because we were bare-foot, and were enquiring if we had no need of our feet since they supposed we should lose them straightway, the Hungarian explained to them the reason, telling them the rules of our Order.

Then there came to see us the chief secretary, a Nestorian Christian, whose advice is followed in almost all matters; he examined us carefully, then sending for the Hungarian he asked him many questions. Then we were told to return to our lodgings. On the way back I saw facing the orda towards the east, distant from it twice as far as one can shoot with a cross-bow, a building with a little cross on top.

Thereupon greatly rejoicing, for I presumed that it had something to do with the Christian religion, I boldly went in and found an altar most beautifully decorated. There were embroidered on cloth-of-gold figures of our Saviour, the Blessed Virgin, John the Baptist and two angels, the outlines of the bodies and the garments being picked out in pearls, and there was a large silver cross with precious stones in the angles and in the centre, and many other ornaments and a lamp with eight oil lights burning before the altar. An Armenian monk was sitting there; he was dark and thin, and wearing a very rough hair shirt which reached half-way down his legs. Over that he had a black cloak padded with bristles, and under his hair shirt he was bound with various iron chains.

Immediately we were inside, before greeting the monk, we prostrated and sang "*Ave Regina Coelorum*" and the monk stood up and prayed with us. Then having greeted him we sat down near him; he had in front of him a little fire on a dish. We told him the reason of our coming and he began to encourage us greatly, saying that we were to speak out boldly for we were the ambassadors of God, Who is greater than any man.

After that he related to us how he had come there, saying that he had preceded us by a month. He told us that he had been a hermit in the territory of Jerusalem, and that God had appeared to him three times bidding him go to the chief of the Tartars; and when he neglected to go the third time God threatened him, casting him down onto the ground and saying that if he did not go he would die; and he had told Mangu Chan that if he would become a Christian the whole world would come under his sway and the French and the mighty Pope would be subject to him; and he advised me to say the same to him. Whereupon I replied: "Brother, gladly will I urge him to become a Christian, for the reason of my coming is to preach this to all men; I will also promise him that the French and the Pope will rejoice exceedingly and will consider him as a brother and a friend, but that they should become his vassals and pay him tribute like the other nations, never will I promise, for I should be speaking against my conscience." At that he remained silent.

And so we went to our lodging which I found cold, and we had eaten nothing all day. We cooked a little of our meat and some millet in the gravy as soup. Our guide and his companions were getting drunk at the court and had little concern for us.

At that time we had as neighbours envoys from Vastacius, a fact of which we were ignorant. At dawn men from the court made us get up with all speed. I went with them bare-foot the short distance to the dwelling of the said envoys and they enquired of them if they knew us. Then a Greek soldier recognised our Order and also my companion, for he had seen him at the court of Vastacius[1] with Friar Thomas our Minister, and he together with all his companions spoke strongly in our favour. Next they asked if you were at peace or war with Vastacius. "Neither at peace," said I, "nor at war," and they enquired how that could possibly be. "The reason is," I said, "that their countries are far removed from each other and they have nothing to do with each other." At that point Vastacius' envoy said you were at peace and this put me on my guard. I then kept quiet.

That morning the tips of my toes froze so I could no longer go bare-foot. For the cold in those parts is extremely severe and from the time that it begins to freeze it does not leave off until May. Even in May it froze every morning but thawed during the day in the heat of the sun. In winter however it never thaws, but whatever the wind, the ice remains. And if there were a wind there in winter such as we have, nothing would be able to live, but the air is always still until April and then the winds get up. When we were there about Easter the cold which came with the wind killed at that time countless animals. A little snow fell in the winter but about Easter, which was at the end of April, there was such a heavy fall that all the streets of Caracorum were blocked and the snow had to be taken away in carts. It was then that they first brought us from the court sheepskin cloaks and trousers of the same and shoes. My companion and the interpreter accepted them but I did not think I needed them, for it seemed to me that the fur cloak I had brought from Baatu was enough for me.

Then on the octave of Holy Innocents [January 4th] we were taken to the court and some Nestorian priests came—I did not know they were Christians—and they asked in what direction we

---

[1] See *supra*, p. 91 n. 2.

worshipped. I said: "Towards the east." The reason they asked this was that, on the advice of our guide, we had shaved our beards so that we should appear before the Chan according to the fashion of our native land, and this led them to think that we were *tuins*[1], that is pagans. They also made us expound on the Bible. Then they asked what kind of obeisance we wished to make to the Chan, whether according to our custom or theirs. To this I replied: "We are priests dedicated to the service of God. In our part of the world noble lords, out of honour to God, do not countenance priests' bending the knee before them, nevertheless we are willing to humble ourselves to all men for God. We have come a long way; first, if it please you, we will sing praises to God Who has brought us safely from such a long distance away as far as here, and after that we will do whatever your master pleases, provided that he order us to do nothing contrary to the worship and honour of God."

Then they went into the dwelling and repeated what we had said. The Chan agreed and they placed us before the door of the dwelling, lifting up the felt which hung in front of it; and seeing that it was Christmas-time we began to sing:

A solis ortus cardine
Et usque terre limitem
Christum canamus principem
Natum Maria Virgine.

When we had sung this hymn they examined our legs, breasts and arms to see whether we had any knives on us. The interpreter they took on one side and made him leave his belt and knife outside in the care of one of the door-keepers.

Then we went in. Near the entrance was a bench with some cosmos on it, and they made the interpreter stand near this while we were made to sit on a stool in front of the ladies. The whole dwelling was completely covered inside with cloth of gold and in the middle in a little hearth was a fire of twigs and roots of worm-

---

[1] *Tuin* seems to be derived from the Chinese word "Tao jenn" or "men of the Way" or Taoists, but it was also used generally for monks and ascetics of every denomination.

wood, which grows to a great size there, and also the dung of oxen. The Chan was sitting on a couch wearing a speckled and shiny fur like seal-skin. He is a flat-nosed man of medium height, about forty-five years old; a young wife was sitting next to him and a grown-up daughter, who was very ugly, Cirina by name, was sitting on a couch behind them with some little children. For that dwelling had belonged to one of his wives, a Christian, whom he had loved deeply and by whom he had had the said daughter. Although he had introduced in addition the young wife, nevertheless the daughter was mistress of all that court which had belonged to her mother.

Then the Chan had them ask us whether we would like to drink wine or *terracina*, that is rice wine, or caracosmos, that is clear mares' milk, or *bal*, that is mead made from honey, for these are the four drinks they use in winter. I replied: " Sir, we are not men seeking our desire in drink; whatever pleases you satisfies us." Then he had some of the rice drink brought for us, it is clear and tastes like white wine; out of respect to him we sipped it for a short time. To our misfortune our interpreter was standing near the cup-bearers, who gave him a great deal to drink and he got drunk immediately.

After that the Chan ordered falcons and other birds to be brought to him and he took them on his hand and looked at them, and after a long interval he bade us speak. For that we had to kneel down. He had as interpreter a Nestorian, but I was ignorant of the fact that he was a Christian, and we had our interpreter, such as he was, for he was already drunk. Then I spoke:

"First of all we render thanks and praise to God Who has brought us from such far distant regions to see Mangu Chan to whom He has given great power on earth. And we pray Christ, under Whose dominion we all live and die, that He will grant him a good and long life."

For they always wish a blessing to be asked on their life. Then I told him:

" Sir, we heard that Sartach was a Christian and the Christians who heard this were delighted, especially my Lord the French King. And so we went to him and my Lord the King sent him a letter by us containing words of peace, and among other things he testified as to what kind of men we are and requested him to allow us to remain in his territory; for our office is to teach men to live according to the law of God. Sartach, however, sent us to his father, Baatu; Baatu sent us here to you. You are a man to whom God has given great dominion on earth, we therefore beg Your Puissance to grant us leave to stay in your country to carry out the service of God on behalf of you, your wives and your children. We have neither gold nor silver nor precious stones which we could present to you; we have but ourselves and we offer ourselves to serve God and pray to Him for you. At least give us permission to stay here until the cold has passed, for my companion is so weak that he can in no wise, without endangering his life, bear to ride any further."

My companion had spoken to me of his weakness and had entreated me to ask for permission to remain, for we strongly suspected that we would have to return to Baatu unless by a special grace we were given leave to stay.

Then the Chan began to reply: "Just as the sun spreads its rays in all directions, so my power and the power of Baatu is spread everywhere. Therefore we have no need of your gold or silver." Up to this point I understood my interpreter but beyond this I could not grasp a single complete sentence, which showed me clearly that he was drunk. And Mangu Chan himself appeared to me intoxicated. He ended however by saying, so it seemed to me, that he was not pleased that we had gone to Sartach first rather than to him. Then I, seeing my interpreter's incapacity, kept quiet, except that I begged him not to be offended at what I had said about gold and silver, for I had said it not because he had need of or desired such things, but rather because we would gladly have honoured him with both temporal and spiritual gifts.

He then told us to get up from our knees and sit down again and after a short time we took leave of him and went out, and his secretaries and his interpreter, who is bringing up one of his daughters, went with us. They began to ask a great many questions about the kingdom of France, whether there were many sheep and oxen and horses there, as if they were about to march in at once and take everything, and many other times I had to do great violence to myself to hide my indignation and anger, and I replied: "There are many good things there, which you will see if it falls to your lot to go there."

They assigned a man to us to look after us and we went to the monk. When we were coming away from him in order to return to our lodging, the aforementioned interpreter came to meet us and said: "Mangu Chan has pity on you and grants you permission to stay here for the space of two months, by which time the intense cold will be over, and he informs you that ten days' journey from here there is a fine city called Caracorum; if you wish to go there he will have you provided with all that you need; if however you wish to remain here you may and you will have what is needful; it will however be wearisome for you to ride with the orda." I replied: "May the Lord keep Mangu Chan and grant him a long and good life! We have found here this monk and we believe that he is a holy man and has come to these parts by the will of God, and so we would like to stay with him seeing that we too are monks and we could say our prayers together for the Chan's good estate." He then left us in silence.

We went to our quarters which we found cold and without any fuel and we were still fasting from food and it was already night-time. Then the man to whose charge we had been committed provided us with some fuel and a little food.

CHAPTER XXIX

THINGS DONE, SEEN AND HEARD BY FRIAR WILLIAM AT MANGU'S COURT

OUR guide returned to Baatu, first asking us for a carpet or mat which we had left at Baatu's orda at his bidding; we granted his request. He took leave of us in a peaceable manner, begging us to shake hands with him and acknowledging his fault if he had allowed us to suffer hunger and thirst on the road; we forgave him and in our turn begged his pardon and that of all his company if we had shown them any bad example.

We met with a woman from Metz in Lorraine who had been captured in Hungary and was called Paquette, and she made as big a feast for us as she could. She belonged to the court of the lady who had been a Christian whom I have mentioned before, and she told us of the unheard-of privations she had endured before she came to the court. But now things were going fairly well for her, for she had a young Russian husband by whom she had three lovely little boys, and he was skilled in making houses which is a profitable craft among them.

Moreover she told us that there was at Caracorum a certain master goldsmith called William, a Parisian by birth, whose surname is Buchier and his father's name Laurent Buchier, and he thinks he still has a brother on the Grand Pont called Roger Buchier. She also told me that he had a young man whom he had brought up, who was as a son to him and who was an excellent interpreter. But Mangu Chan had handed over to the said master three hundred *iascot*[1], that is three thousand marks, and fifty workmen to carry out special work and so she was afraid he would not be able to send his son to me. Now she had heard said to her at the court: "The men who have come from your country are good fellows and Mangu Chan would gladly speak with them but their interpreter is no use." And so she was anxious to find an interpreter.

Thereupon I wrote to the said master informing him of my arrival and asking him, if he could, to send his son to me; he wrote in reply that it would not be possible that month, but the following month his work would be finished and he would send him to me.

And so we stayed with the other envoys. They treat envoys differently in the ordas of Baatu and Mangu, for in the former there is a yam on the west side where all coming from the west are received, and similarly for the other quarters of the world; but in Mangu's orda all are together in one yam and they can visit and see one another. In Baatu's orda they remain in ignorance of each other and one does not know whether or not another is an

---

[1] " A piece of silver weighing ten marks " (p. 144).

envoy, for they are not aware of each other's lodgings, nor do they meet except at the court. And when one is invited another may not be, for they never go to the court unless they are summoned.

We came across a Christian from Damascus who said he had come on behalf of the Sultan of Mont Real and Crac[1] who wished to become a tributary and friend of the Tartars.

Also in the previous year, before my arrival, there had been a cleric from Acre there who called himself Raymond but in truth his name was Theodolus. He had started on his journey from Cyprus with Friar Andrew and accompanied him as far as Persia, and in Persia he purchased for himself some musical instruments from Armenia and he remained behind after Friar Andrew left. On the latter's return Theodolus set out with his instruments and reached Mangu Chan.

When questioned as to his reason for coming he said that he had been with a certain holy bishop, to whom God had sent a letter from heaven written in characters of gold and he had enjoined him to send it to the chief of the Tartars, for he was to be the Lord of all the earth, and also to persuade men to make peace with him. Then Mangu said to him: "If you had brought with you the letter which came from heaven and your master's letter, then you would have been welcome." Thereupon he replied that he was bringing the letters but they were with his other belongings on an untamed pack-animal which had escaped and fled through woods and over mountains so that he had lost everything. And it is certainly true that such mishaps frequently occur, and a man has to be most careful to keep hold of his horse when he is obliged to alight.

Mangu then asked the name of the bishop. Theodolus said he was called Odo; and he told the man from Damascus and Master William that he had been a clerk of the Lord Legate. The Chan next asked to whose kingdom he belonged and he replied that he was a subject of the French King called King Moles, for he had already heard about what had happened at Mansurah[2], and wanted to say

---

[1] This was the Sheik of the western Ismailians in Syria, commonly known as the Old Man of the Mountain.

[2] Where St. Louis IX of France was taken prisoner, and his forces of the Crusade destroyed by the Mamelukes in 1250.

that he was one of your men. Moreover he told the Chan that the Saracens were between the French and him and blocked the way; if only the way were clear they would send envoys and gladly make peace with him. Then Mangu Chan asked if he would take envoys to the King and the bishop. He replied that he would and also to the Pope.

Then Mangu had a very strong bow made, which two men could hardly draw, and two arrows with heads of silver, full of holes, which whistle like pipes when they are loosed. And he gave the following instructions to the Mongol he was sending with Theodolus: "You will go to that French King to whom this man will take you, and you will present him with these things on my behalf. If he wishes to be at peace with us, we will seize the territory from the Saracens as far as his kingdom and we concede to him the rest of the world westwards; but if he does not wish peace then bring back the bow and arrows to us, telling him that with such bows we shoot far and strike hard."

The Chan then dismissed Theodolus. The latter had as interpreter Master William's son and it was in his hearing that the Chan said to the Mongol: "You will go with this man; investigate the roads well and the country, the cities, fortified places, the men and their arms." The young man, thereupon, reproved Theodolus, telling him that he was making a mistake in taking envoys of the Tartars with him, for they were going for no other reason but to spy. He replied that he would put them on the sea so that they would not know where they had come from, or to what place they were returning. Mangu also gave the Mongol his golden seal, that is to say a plate of gold a handbreadth wide and half a cubit long, on which his order is engraved; whoever bears this can command whatever he will and it is carried out without delay.[1]

Theodolus got as far as Vastacius[2] and wanted to continue his journey to the Pope and deceive him as he had deceived Mangu Chan. Then Vastacius asked him if he had a letter from the Pope

---

[1] These tablets (*paitze*) were used extensively by the Mongols as marks of official status. Several of them are to be found in the Hermitage Museum at Leningrad—cf. Vernadsky, *The Mongols in Russia*, p. 128.

[2] See note *supra*, p. 91.

seeing that he was an envoy and had been given the duty of conducting envoys of the Tartars. Since he could not produce a letter, Vastacius seized him and despoiling him of all that he had acquired put him in prison. As for the Mongol he fell sick and died there.

Vastacius sent back the gold seal to Mangu Chan by the Mongol's servants; I met them at Erzerum on the borders of Turkey and they told me of Theodolus' fate. Such impostors roam about the world and the Mongols put them to death when they can catch them.

The day of the Epiphany [January 6th] was approaching and the Armenian monk, Sergius by name, told me that he was going to baptize Mangu Chan on the day of the feast. I begged him to do all in his power to enable me to be present so that I could bear witness of what I had actually seen, and he promised he would.

The day of the feast arrived and the monk did not send for me, but at midday I was summoned to the court, and I saw the monk coming away from there with some priests, and he had his cross and the priests a thurible and a Gospel-book. On that day Mangu Chan had made a great feast; and it is his custom to hold court on such days as his soothsayers tell him are feast days or the Nestorian priests say are for some reason sacred. On these days the Christian priests come first with their paraphernalia, and they pray for him and bless his cup; when they retire the Saracen priests come and do likewise; they are followed by the pagan priests who do the same. The monk told me that the Chan only believes in the Christians; however, he wishes them all to come and pray for him. But he was lying, for he does not believe in any of them as you will hear later; yet they all follow his court like flies honey, and he gives to them all and they all think they enjoy his special favour and they all prophesy good fortune for him.

We then sat before his court for a long time and they brought us meat to eat. I told them we would not eat there, but if they wished to provide us with food, they should supply it to us in our own dwelling. To this they replied: "Well then, you can go home for you were summoned for no other reason than to partake of food." We went back, therefore, by way of the monk, who was covered with confusion at the lie he had told me, and so I did not wish to oblige him to talk about the matter. Some of the Nestorians, however, wanted to assure me that the Chan had been baptised; I said to them that I would never believe it nor tell anyone else, seeing I had not witnessed it.

We arrived at our cold and empty dwelling. They provided us with some bedding and coverlets, and they also brought some fuel and gave us the meat of one thin little ram for the three of us to be our food for six days. Every day they gave us a dishful of millet and a quart of millet ale and they lent us a cauldron and a tripod for us to cook our meat; when it was cooked, we cooked the millet in the broth. This was our food and it would have been quite sufficient for us if they had allowed us to eat it in peace, but there were so many starving people who were not provided with food and who, as soon as they saw us preparing ours, bore down upon us and we had to share our meal with them. There I experienced how great a martyrdom it is to bestow bounty in one's own poverty.

The cold then began to increase greatly in intensity, and Mangu Chan sent us three cloaks of monkey skin which they wear the hairy side out, and we accepted them gratefully. They also enquired how we were faring for food and I told them we were satisfied with little but we had no building in which we could pray for Mangu Chan, for our hut is so small that we could not stand upright in it nor open our books when we lighted a fire. They took word back to him and he sent to the monk to find out if he desired our company and he replied with joy that he did. From that time onwards we were provided with a better dwelling and we took up our abode with the monk in front of the court where no one was lodged except us and their diviners; but they were nearer and facing the court of the chief wife, while we were at the far east end in front of the court of the last wife. We moved on the day before the Octave of the Epiphany.

The following day, namely the Octave of the Epiphany, all the Nestorian priests assembled before daybreak at the chapel and beat the board; and they sang solemn Matins, and put on their vestments and prepared a thurible and incense. While they were waiting in the court before the church, the chief wife, by name Cotota Caten—Caten is the same as Lady, Cotota a proper name —entered the chapel with a number of other ladies and her eldest son Baltu and her other little children; and they prostrated, placing their foreheads on the ground after the Nestorian custom, and then they touched all the statues with their right hand, always kissing the hand afterwards; and then they proffered their right hand to all present in the church, for this is the custom of Nestorians on entering church. The priests then sang many things and gave incense into the lady's hand, and she put it onto the coals and then they censed her. After this, when it was now broad daylight, she began to take off her head-dress, which is called a *bocca*, and I saw her bare head. She thereupon ordered us to leave, and as we were going out I saw a silver bowl being brought. Whether they baptised her or not I do not know; but I do know that they do not celebrate Mass in a tent but only in a permanent church. At Easter I saw them baptise and bless fonts with great solemnity, a thing they did not do on this occasion.

When we had gone back to our lodging Mangu Chan himself came and went into the church or oratory, and a golden couch was brought on which he sat with his wife, opposite the altar. Then we were summoned, still ignorant of the fact that Mangu had come, and the door-keepers searched us to see that we were not carrying any knives. I went into the oratory holding the Bible and breviary before my breast; first I bowed to the altar and then to the Chan and crossing over we took our stand between the monk and the altar. Then they made us recite a psalm in our own manner and sing, so we sang the sequence "*Veni Sancte Spiritus*". The Chan had our books, the Bible and the breviary, taken to him and he made a diligent enquiry as to the meaning of the pictures. The Nestorians answered him as well as they could, for our interpreter had not come in with us. The first time also that I had been in his presence I had carried the Bible before me, and he had had it brought to him and had had a good look at it.

He then left and his wife stayed behind and distributed gifts to all the Christians present. To the monk she gave a *iascot* and another to the archdeacon of the priests. She had placed in front of us a *nasic*, that is a piece of material as wide as a bed-cover and very long; and also a *buccaran*. As I was unwilling to accept them, they sent for the interpreter and he had them for himself. The *nasic* he took to Cyprus and sold for eighty Cyprian bezants, but it had got much spoiled on the journey.

Then the drinks were brought—rice ale, red wine, like the wine of La Rochelle, and cosmos. The lady, holding a full goblet in her hand, knelt down and asked a blessing, and all the priests sang in a loud voice and she drank it all. My companion and I were also obliged to sing another time when she wanted to drink. When they were all nearly intoxicated food was brought, the flesh of a sheep, which was immediately devoured, and after that some large fish called carp, without salt and without bread, and of this I ate a little. In this way they passed the time until evening. Then the lady, now drunk, got into a cart, while the priests sang and howled, and she went her way.

The following Sunday, which is when they read the gospel "There was a marriage in Cana", the Chan's daughter whose mother had been a Christian came and behaved in like manner though with not so much solemnity, for she did not give any presents, but she provided the priests with drink until they were drunk and gave them roasted millet to eat.

The Nestorians fast for three days before Septuagesima Sunday[1] and they call this the fast of Jonas, which he preached to the Ninevites; and the Armenians keep a fast of five days at that time which they call the fast of St. Sergius, who is their greatest saint and who, the Greeks say, was the model of what a martyr should be. The Nestorians begin their fast on Tuesday and end on Thursday, so on the Friday they eat meat.

At that time I saw the chancellor, that is the chief scribe of the court, Bulgai by name, make them allowances of meat on Friday, and they blessed them with great solemnity, just as the paschal lamb is blessed. He himself, however, did not eat of it; this is because of the teaching of Master William of Paris who is a great friend of his. The monk ordered Mangu to fast throughout the week, which he did, so I heard.

[1] In 1254 in the first week of February.

And so on Septuagesima Saturday which is, as it were, the Armenians' Easter, we went in procession to Mangu's dwelling, and the monk and the two of us, having first been searched to see if we had any knives, went into his presence with the priests. As we were entering a slave was going out, carrying away sheep's shoulder-blades which had been charred until they were as black as coal. I was greatly puzzled as to the purpose of this and when I enquired about it later I learned that the Chan does nothing in the world without first consulting these bones; consequently he does not allow anyone to enter his dwelling until he has consulted them.

This type of divination is carried out in the following manner: when the Chan wishes to do anything he has three of these bones brought to him before they have been burned, and holding them he thinks of that matter about which he wishes to find out whether he is to do it or not; then he hands the bones to a slave to be burned. Near the dwelling in which he is staying there are always two little buildings in which the bones are burned and every day these bones are diligently sought for throughout the encampment. When the bones, therefore, have been burned until they are black they are brought back to the Chan and he thereupon examines them to see if with the heat of the fire they have split lengthwise in a straight line. If they have, the way is clear for him to act; if, however, the bones have cracked horizontally or round bits have shot out, then he does not do it. The bone itself or the membrane stretched over it always cracks in the fire. If, out of the three, one is split in a straight line then he acts.

When we had come into the Chan's presence, having first been warned not to touch the threshold, the Nestorian priests took incense to him and he put it on the thurible and they censed him. Then they chanted a blessing on his drink and after them the monk gave his blessing and lastly we had to pronounce ours. When he saw us clasping the Bible he had it taken to him so that he could look at it, and he examined it most carefully. After he had drunk and the chief of the priests had handed him a goblet then they gave the priests to drink.

We then went out but my companion remained behind. When

we were already outside and he was on the point of coming out after us, he turned towards the Chan and bowed to him, then hurrying after us he stumbled against the threshold of the dwelling. While we were hastening towards the dwelling of Baatu, the Chan's son, those watching the threshold laid hands upon my companion and compelled him to stop so that he could not follow us; then, calling a man, they ordered him to take him to Bulgai, who is the chief scribe of the court and tries those guilty of capital offences. I was in ignorance of all this. When I looked round and did not see him coming I thought they had detained him so that he could be given lighter garments, for he was weak and so much weighed down by the cloaks that he could scarcely walk. They then summoned our interpreter and made him sit by him.

We made our way to the dwelling of the Chan's eldest son, who already has two wives and who lives on the right of his father's court. When he saw us coming he jumped up from the couch on which he was sitting and prostrated, striking his forehead on the ground in adoration of the cross; then rising he had it placed on a new cloth in an elevated position near him, showing it very great respect. He has as master a Nestorian priest called David, a great drunkard, who teaches him. He then made us sit down and had drinks given to the priests and he also drank after he had received their blessing.

Next we went to the court of the second wife who was called Cota and was a pagan, and we found her lying in bed sick. The monk made her get up from her couch and adore the cross, kneeling down three times and placing her forehead on the ground, and he stood with the cross on the west side of the dwelling and she on the east. This done they changed places and the monk went with the cross to the east side, she to the west; then, although she was so weak she could hardly stand on her feet, he insolently ordered her to prostrate again and adore the cross three times towards the east according to the Christian custom, and she did so. He also taught her to make the sign of the cross on herself.

She lay down on her bed again and when prayers had been said for her we next went to a third house which was that in which the Christian wife used to be. When she died she was succeeded by the young girl, who, together with the Chan's daughter, received us with joy, and all in that house reverently adored the cross, and she placed it in a prominent position on a cloth of silk, and she had food brought, that is to say, the flesh of a sheep; it was placed in front of the lady and she had it served to the priests. The monk and I, however, avoided eating and drinking.

When the meat had been eaten and a great deal of drink consumed, we had to go to the apartment of the young mistress Cirina, which was behind the large dwelling which had belonged to her mother. When the cross entered she prostrated herself on the ground and adored it with great devotion for she had been well instructed in this respect, and she placed it in a prominent position on a silken cloth; all these cloths on which the cross was placed were the monk's.

This cross had been brought by a certain Armenian who had come with the monk, so he said, from Jerusalem, and it was of silver weighing some four marks, and had four precious stones in the angles and one in the middle; it had no figure of the Saviour, for the Armenians and Nestorians are ashamed to see Christ nailed to the cross. They had presented it at the hands of the monk to Mangu Chan, who asked him what was his petition. The Armenian replied that he was the son of an Armenian priest whose church had been destroyed by the Saracens and he begged the Chan's help in the restoration of this church. The Chan then asked how much would be needed for it to be rebuilt, and he replied two hundred *iascot*, that is to say two thousand marks. The Chan ordered a letter to be given to him addressed to the official who receives the tribute in Persia and in Greater Armenia, telling him to pay him the said sum of money. The monk took this cross with him everywhere and the priests, seeing him collecting money, began to be envious of him. As I was saying, we were in the house of the young lady and she gave the priests a great deal to drink.

From here we went to the fourth dwelling, which was the last as regards both number and honour, for the Chan did not visit that wife and her house was old and she herself not at all attractive; however, after Easter he had a new dwelling made for her and new carts. She, like the second wife, knew little or nothing of the Christian religion but was a follower of the diviners and idolaters. Nevertheless when we went in she adored the cross in the way the monk and priests taught her to do. There again the priests had some drinks.

From that place we returned to our oratory which was nearby, the priests singing and shouting loudly in their drunkenness, which in that country is not considered reprehensible either in man or woman. My companion was then brought and the monk chid him very severely for having touched the threshold.

The following day Bulgai, the judge, came and made diligent enquiry as to whether we had been warned to avoid touching the threshold, and I replied: "Sir, we did not have our interpreter with us; how could we understand?" He thereupon pardoned my companion, but never afterwards was he allowed to enter any of the Chan's dwellings.

It afterwards came to pass that the lady Cota, who had been indisposed round about Sexagesima Sunday, became sick unto death and the sorceries of the pagans did her not the slightest good. Then Mangu sent to the monk to enquire of him what could be done about her and he rashly replied that if she didn't get better the Chan could cut off his head. Having given this promise the monk summoned us and, laying the whole matter before us, begged us with tears to watch with him in prayer that night, which we did.

Now he had a certain root which goes by the name of rhubarb, and he used to cut it up almost to a powder and put it into water with a little cross he had from which the figure of our Saviour had been removed. He declared that he was able to tell by means of this whether a sick man was going to get well again or going to die; for if he was going to get well it would stick to his chest as if glued to it, otherwise it would not stick. At that time I still believed that the rhubarb was some sacred thing he had brought from the Holy Land of Jerusalem. He used to give some of that water to all ailing people to drink with the inevitable result that their bowels were all disturbed by so bitter a potion. This change in their bodies they put down to a miracle. Then when he was preparing to mix some of this water, I mentioned to him the holy water which is made in the Roman Church, for it is most efficacious in driving out demons and I had understood that she was troubled with a devil. At his request we made some holy water for him, and he mixed some rhubarb with it and plunged in the cross to soak all night in the water. I also added, in case he himself were a priest, that the Order of the priesthood possesses great power for driving out devils. He replied that he was a priest; however, he lied, for he had received no Orders, nor did he know his letters, but was a weaver of cloth as I learned afterwards in his native land through which I passed on my return journey.

And so the next day the monk and I and two Nestorian priests visited the lady, who was in a little house behind her larger dwelling. When we went in she sat up in bed, and adoring the cross placed it with due honour by her side on a silken cloth, and she drank of the holy water and rhubarb and moistened her breast with it and the monk asked me to read the Gospel over her. I read the Passion of Our Lord according to John. At last feeling better she cheered up and ordered four *iascots* of silver to be brought. These she first placed at the foot of the cross and then gave one to the monk and offered one to me; I was unwilling to take it; whereupon the monk, stretching out his hand, grabbed it. She also presented one to each of the two priests, so on that occasion she bestowed forty marks. Then she had wine brought and gave the priests to drink, and even I had to drink thrice at her hand in honour of the Trinity. She also began to teach me the language, twitting me because I was silent, not having my interpreter with me.

The following day we went back again to her, and Mangu Chan, hearing that we were passing by that way, made us go in to him, for he had learned that the lady was much better. We found him with a few members of his household drinking liquid *tam*, that is a food made of paste, for comforting the head: and in front of him were lying the charred shoulder-blades of a sheep. He took the cross in his hand but I did not see him kiss it or adore it; instead he looked at it wondering I know not what. The monk then asked for leave to carry the cross on a lance raised on high, for I had previously discussed this matter with him, and Mangu replied:

"Carry it in the best way you know."

We took our leave of him and then went to the lady, whom we found well and cheerful, and she again drank of the holy water and I read the Passion over her. Those miserable priests never instructed her in the faith nor advised her to be baptized. I, for my part, sat there speechless, unable to say a word, though she did go on teaching me the language. Nor do the priests rebuke them for any kind of sorcery, for there I saw four swords drawn halfway out of their sheaths, one at the head of the lady's couch, another at the foot, and the other two one each side of the doorway. I also saw a silver chalice such as we use, which had perhaps been taken or stolen from a church in Hungary, and it was hung up on the wall full of ashes and on top of the ashes was a black stone, and the priests never teach them that such things are evil. On the contrary they themselves do and teach the like. And so we visited her for three days until she was perfectly restored to health.

At that time the monk made a banner covered with crosses and sought out a long cane like a lance and we carried the cross raised on high. I honoured him as my superior since he knew the language, but he did many things which did not meet with my approval. He had a faldstool made for himself such as it is the custom for bishops to have, and gloves and a cap made of peacocks' feathers with a little gold cross on top—this pleased me as far as the cross was concerned. He had coarse finger nails which he went to the trouble to ornament with unguents; and he also proved to be presumptuous in his speech. The Nestorians used to recite I know not what verses of a psalm, so they said, over two twigs which were joined together while being held by two men,[1] and the monk himself used to be present at such things; and many other foolishnesses came to light in him which displeased me. Nevertheless for the honour of the cross we clung to his company. We carried the cross on high throughout the whole encampment singing "*Vexilla Regis prodeunt*" and the Saracens were greatly surprised at this.

[1] This was a form of divination.

After our arrival at Mangu's orda, he only moved camp in a southerly direction twice; after that he began to return northwards, that is towards Caracorum. One thing I noticed throughout the whole journey, which Sir Baldwin of Hainault who had been there had also mentioned to me at Constantinople, and this was that the ground here gave the strange impression that as one proceeds it always slopes up-hill and never down-hill. All the rivers flowed from the east to west either directly or indirectly, that is to say turning somewhat to the south or north. I questioned some priests who had come from Cathay and they bore witness to this fact.

From the place where I found Mangu Chan as far as Cathay, it was twenty days' journey in a south-easterly direction; as far as Onankerule which is the Mongols' own territory where Chingis' orda is, it was ten days' journey due east; and as far as this eastern district there was not a town to be found. There was, however, a tribe called Su-Mongol, that is Mongols of the water, for "su" is the same as water. These men live on fish and by hunting, for they have neither flocks of sheep nor herds of cattle. Similarly towards the north there is no town, but a poor tribe who keep cattle and are called Kerkis[1]. There are also the Orengai there who bind polished bones under their feet and propel themselves over the frozen snow and ice at such a speed that they can catch birds and animals.[2]

There are several other poor tribes stretching towards the north as far as the cold permits, and in the west their boundaries touch the land of the Pascaver, that is to say Greater Hungary, concerning which I told you above. The extreme north point is unexplored on account of the great cold, for there are almost continual blizzards there. I made enquiries about the monsters or human monstrosities of which Isidore and Solinus speak. They told me they had never seen such things, which makes me wonder very much if there is any truth in the story. Since the aforementioned tribes are destitute of everything they are obliged to work for the Mongols; it was a decree of Chingis that no man should be free

---

[1] Probably the Kirgiz who at that time lived in the Minusinsk Steppe.
[2] Perhaps the Orochon or Reindeer Tungus of North-Eastern Siberia.

from service until he was so old that he could in no wise work any more.

On one occasion there sat by me a priest from Cathay, wearing a red material of a very fine hue, and when I asked him where he got such a colour from, he told me that in the eastern district of Cathay there are lofty crags in which dwell creatures having in every respect a human form except that they do not bend their knees but walk hopping I know not how; they are but a cubit high and the whole of their small bodies is covered with hairs and they live in inaccessible caves. When men go hunting them they carry with them mead which they can make very intoxicating, and they set traps among the rocks in the shape of cups which they fill with this mead (they have no wine as yet in Cathay, but are just beginning to plant vines; this drink, however, they make out of rice). And so the hunters hide themselves and these animals come out of their caves and taste the drink and they cry out "Chinchin"; from this shout they got their name, for they are called Chinchins. Then they assemble in vast numbers and drink the mead and, becoming drunk, they fall asleep on the spot. At that point the hunters approach and bind them hand and foot as they sleep. Next they open a vein in their necks and from each one extract three or four drops of blood; then they let them go free; and that blood, so I was told, is most valuable for dyeing purple.

They also told me for a truth, though I do not believe it, that beyond Cathay is a country and whatever age a man be when he enters that country he remains at that age. Cathay borders on the ocean, and Master William told me that he had seen envoys of people called Caule and Manse[1] who inhabit islands in the sea around which freezes in winter, so the Tartars can cross to them; they offered the Tartars thirty-two thousand *tumen iascot* yearly so long as they would leave them in peace. A *tumen* is a number consisting of ten thousand.

The ordinary money of Cathay is a piece of paper made out of cotton, a handbreadth in width and length, and on this they stamp lines like Mangu's seal. They write with a brush like those with

[1] Caule is Kaorli or Korea. Manse is the Sung Empire of South China which had not yet been conquered by the Mongols.

which painters paint and in a single character they make several letters which form one word. The Tebec write as we do and have letters very much like ours. The Tangut write in the same way as the Arabs, from right to left, but they increase their lines from the bottom up; the Uigurs, as has already been mentioned, start at the top and go downwards. The ordinary currency of the Ruthenians is squirrel and ermine skins.

When we went to the monk he charitably urged us to abstain from flesh meat, saying that our servants could take meat with his domestics, while he would provide us with flour and oil or butter; we did this although my companion found it a great trial on account of his weakness. And so our food was millet with butter, or paste cooked in water with butter or sour milk, and unleavened bread cooked over the dung of oxen or horses.

Then Quinquagesima came, which is the Lent of all the Easterns, and the chief wife Cotota fasted that week with all her suite; and each day she came to our oratory and gave food to the priests and other Christians, a great number of whom assembled there during that first week in order to hear the office. She presented me and my companion with a tunic and breeches of grey shot silk padded with silk wadding, for my companion had complained a great deal about the weight of the furs. I accepted them for the comfort of my companion, excusing myself however and saying that I could not wear such clothes. The things intended for me I gave to my interpreter.

The gate-keepers of the court, seeing such a great crowd streaming every day to the church, which was within the bounds watched by the orda guards, sent one of their number to the monk saying that they did not wish such a large crowd to assemble there within the confines of the orda. Whereupon the monk curtly replied that he would like to know whether they were issuing this command by Mangu's desire, and he also added threats implying that he was going to denounce them to Mangu. Then they, getting in first, accused him to Mangu of speaking too much and of assembling too large a crowd for his sermons.

As a result, on the first Sunday in Lent we were summoned to the court and after the monk had been searched for knives in a most objectionable manner, so much so that he even had to take off his shoes, we went into the presence of the Chan, who was looking at the charred shoulder-blade of a sheep which he was holding in his hand; and, as if reading from it, he began to rebuke the monk, demanding why, since he was a man whose duty it was to pray to God, he spoke so much with men. I, in the meantime, was standing in the background with head uncovered, and the Chan said to him: "Why do you not uncover your head when you come into my presence, as that Frank does?" and he had me called nearer. Then the monk, covered with confusion, took off his cap contrary to the custom of the Greeks and Armenians; and after the Chan had said many harsh things to him, we went away. The monk handed me the cross to carry to the oratory, for he himself was unable to carry it for embarrassment.

A few days later he was reconciled to the Chan, promising him that he would go to the Pope and bring all the nations of the west under his dominion. When he returned to the oratory after this conversation with the Chan, he began to ask me questions about the Pope, whether I thought he would be willing to see him if he went to him on behalf of Mangu, and if he would provide him with horses as far as St. James. He also asked about you, if you would be prepared to send your son to Mangu. I thereupon warned him not to make lying promises to Mangu, for the last error would be worst than the first, nor hath God any need of our lies that we should speak deceitfully for Him.

At that time there arose a dispute between the monk and a certain priest called Jonas, a well-educated man whose father had been an archdeacon, and he himself was regarded by the other priests as their master and archdeacon. Now the monk affirmed that man was made before Paradise and that the Gospel said this. Then I was called in to settle the argument. Not knowing that this was the point about which they were disputing, I replied that Paradise was made on the third day along with the other trees, but man on the sixth day. Then the monk started to say: "Is it not true that on the first day the devil brought earth from the four corners of the world and making slime fashioned the human body, and God breathed into it a soul?" Hearing this Manichean heresy and hearing him thus publicly and shamelessly uttering it, I sternly rebuked him, bidding him put his finger on his mouth since he did not know the Scriptures, and take care not to say things which would bring guilt upon him. Then he started scoffing at me because I did not know the language, and so I left him and went to our dwelling.

It happened afterwards that he and the priests went in procession to the court, but I was not summoned because the monk was not on speaking terms with me on account of the rebuke I had given him and he did not wish to take me along with him as had been his practice hitherto. When they came into Mangu's presence, the latter, not seeing me among them, carefully enquired where I was and why I had not come with them. The priests, frightened, made their excuses, and when they returned they told me what Mangu had said and grumbled about the monk. After this the monk was reconciled to me and I to him, and I asked him to help me with the language, saying I would help him with Holy Scripture, for "a brother that is helped by his brother is like a strong city". [Prov. xviii. 19.]

After the first week of the fast the Chan's wife stopped coming to the oratory and giving us the food and mead which we had been having. The monk would not allow it to be brought, saying that in preparing it they put in mutton fat; he also gave us oil but seldom, so we had nothing except hearth cakes and paste boiled in water to drink as soup; the only water we had was melted snow and ice, which was very bad.

Then my companion began to suffer greatly, so I told David, the master of the Chan's eldest son, of the straits we were in and he passed on the word to the Chan. The latter gave orders for us to be given wine, flour and oil. Under no circumstances do the Nestorians or Armenians eat fish during Lent. Then a bottle of wine was given to us.

The monk said he did not eat except on Sundays, when the Chan's wife sent him a dish of boiled dough with vinegar to drink. However, he had by him, under the altar, a box containing almonds, a bunch of raisins, prunes and many other kinds of fruit, which he ate all the day long whenever he was alone.

We ate once in the day and this in the greatest discomfort, for as soon as they knew that Mangu Chan had provided us with wine, the Nestorian priests, who were drinking their fill all day long in the orda, the Mongols, and the monk's servants all rushed upon us in the most impudent fashion like dogs. Also the monk himself, when anyone came to him to whom he wished to offer a drink, used to send to us for wine, so that that wine brought us more trouble than consolation, for we could not refuse without giving scandal; if we gave we had not enough for ourselves, and when it was exhausted we dared not ask for more from the court.

About mid-Lent Master William's son came, bringing with him a beautiful silver cross fashioned after the French style and having fastened onto it a silver figure of Christ. He was to present it on behalf of his master to Bulgai, the chief scribe of the court. When the monk and priests saw the figure they removed it. On hearing what they had done I was much scandalised. The young man also brought the news to Mangu Chan that the work which he had commissioned had reached completion; this work I will now describe to you.

CHAPTER XXX

MANGU'S PALACE AT CARACORUM, AND THE FEAST OF EASTER

AT Caracorum Mangu has a large orda close by the city walls; it is surrounded by a brick wall as are our priories of monks. There is a large palace there in which he holds his drinking festival twice in the year, once round about Easter when he passes by that way and once in the summer on his return. The second is the more important for on that occasion there assemble at his court all the nobles anywhere within a two months' journey; and then he bestows on them garments and presents and displays his great glory. There are many other buildings there, long like barns, and in these are stored his provisions and treasures.

At the entrance to this palace, seeing it would have been unseemly to put skins of milk and other drinks there, Master William of Paris has made for him a large silver tree, at the foot of which are four silver lions each having a pipe and all belching forth white mares' milk. Inside the trunk four pipes lead up to the top of the tree and the ends of the pipes are bent downwards and over each of them is a gilded serpent, the tail of which twines round the trunk of the tree. One of these pipes pours out wine, another caracosmos, that is the refined milk of mares, another *boal*, which is a honey drink, and another rice mead, which is called *terracina*. Each of these has its silver basin ready to receive it at the foot of the tree between the other four pipes. At the very top he fashioned an angel holding a trumpet; underneath the tree he made a crypt in which a man can be secreted, and a pipe goes up to the angel through the middle of the heart of the tree. At first he had made bellows but they did not give enough wind. Outside the palace there is a chamber in which the drinks are stored, and servants stand there ready to pour them out when they hear the angel sounding the trumpet. The tree has branches, leaves and fruit of silver.

And so when the drinks are getting low the chief butler calls out to the angel to sound his trumpet. Then, hearing this, the man who is hidden in the crypt blows the pipe going up to the angel with all his strength, and the angel, placing the trumpet to his mouth, sounds it very loudly. When the servants in the chamber hear this each one of them pours out his drink into its proper pipe, and the pipes pour them out from above and below into the basins prepared for this, and then the cup-bearers draw the drinks and carry them round the palace to the men and women.

The palace is like a church with a middle nave and two side aisles beyond two rows of pillars and there are three doors on the south side; inside before the middle door stands the tree, and the Chan himself sits at the northern end high up so that he can be seen by everyone; and there are two stairways leading up to him, and the man bringing him his cup goes up by the one and comes down by the other. The space in the middle between the tree and the steps up to him is empty, and there the cup-bearer stands and also envoys who are bringing gifts. The Chan sits up there like a god. On his right-hand side, that is to the west, are the men, on the left the women, for the palace extends from the north southwards. To the south, next to the pillars on the right, are rows of seats raised up like a balcony, on which sit his son and brothers. It is the same on the left where his wives and daughters sit. Only one wife sits up there beside him; she however is not as high up as he is.

When the Chan heard that the work was finished he gave orders to the master to place it in position and get it in working order, and he himself about Passion Sunday went ahead with the small dwellings leaving the large ones behind. The monk and we followed him and he sent us another bottle of wine. He journeyed through mountainous districts, and there was a strong wind and severe cold and a heavy fall of snow. Consequently about midnight the Chan sent to the monk and us asking us to pray to God to lessen the cold and the wind, for all the animals accompanying them were in danger, especially because at that season they were with young and bringing forth. Thereupon the monk sent him some incense, bidding him put it on the coals as an offering to God. I do not know if he did this, but the storm, which had lasted for two days and was already entering on its third, did abate.

On Palm Sunday we were near Caracorum. At dawn we blessed branches of willow, which as yet bore no sign of buds, and about three o'clock we entered the city, the cross raised on high with the banner, and passing the Saracen quarters, where the bazaar and market are, we went to the church. The Nestorians came to meet us in procession. On entering the church we found them ready to celebrate Mass; when this had been celebrated they all received Holy Communion and asked me if I wished to communicate. I replied that I had had a drink and it is not lawful to receive the Sacrament except fasting.

Mass having been said, it was now evening and Master William took us with great joy to his lodging to have supper with him. His wife, who was born in Hungary, was the daughter of a man from Lorraine and she knew French and Coman well. We also came across another man there, Basil by name, the son of an Englishman, who had been born in Hungary and knew the same languages. After supper they accompanied us with great rejoicing to our hut, which the Tartars had set up for us in a square near the church along with the monk's oratory.

The following day the Chan entered his palace and the monk and I and the priests went to him. My companion was not allowed to go because he had trodden on the threshold. I deliberated a great deal about my own case, what I ought to do, whether to go or not to go, and, fearing to give scandal by dissociating myself from the other Christians, and seeing that it pleased the Chan, and fearing lest the good I was hoping to be able to bring about might be hindered, I decided to go even though it meant that I should witness their acts of sorcery and idolatry. And there I did nothing but pray aloud for the whole Church and also for the Chan that God would direct him into the way of eternal salvation.

And so we made our entrance into that orda, which is very well laid out and in summer they convey streams of water in all directions to irrigate it. We next entered the palace, which was full of men and women, and we stood before the Chan having at our backs the tree I have mentioned which together with its basins occupied a large part of the palace; the priests brought two little blessed cakes of bread and fruit on a dish which they presented to the Chan after they had pronounced a blessing, and a butler took them to him as he sat there in a place very high and lifted up. He immediately began to eat one of the cakes and sent the other to his son and his younger brother, who is being brought up by a Nestorian and knows the Gospel, and he also sent for my Bible so that he could look at it. After the priests the monk said his prayer, and I after the monk. Then the Chan promised that the following day he would come to the church, which is quite large and beautiful, and the roof above is all covered with silk interwoven with gold. The following day he went on his way, sending a message of excuse to the priests saying he dared not come to the church for he had learned that the dead were carried there.

We however stayed behind at Caracorum with the monk and the other priests of the court to celebrate Easter there. Maundy Thursday and Easter Sunday were approaching and I had not got our vestments; I was watching closely the way the Nestorians celebrated and was much distressed as to what I should do, whether I should receive the Sacrament from them or celebrate in their vestments with their chalice and on their altar, or whether I should abstain entirely from the Sacrament. At that time there was a large crowd of Christians there—Hungarians, Alans, Ruthenians, Georgians, Armenians—all of whom had not set eyes on the Sacrament from the time they had been taken prisoner, for the Nestorians were unwilling to admit them into their church unless they were re-baptised by them, so they said. However, to us they made no mention of this, on the contrary they acknowledged to us that the Roman Church was the head of all the Churches and that they would receive a Patriarch from the Pope if only the way were open. They freely offered us their Sacrament and made me stand at the door of the choir so that I could see how they celebrated, and also on Easter Eve I stood near the font so that I could see their way of baptising.

They say they have some of the ointment with which Mary Magdalene anointed the feet of the Lord, and they always pour as much oil into it as they take away and with this they bake their bread, for all the Easterns put fat in their bread instead of yeast, either butter or sheep's-tail fat or oil. They also say they have some of the flour from which the bread was made which the Lord consecrated, and they always replace as much as they remove, and they have a room near their choir and an oven where, with great reverence, they make the bread they are to consecrate. With the above-mentioned oil they make a cake wide like the palm of a hand and this they break first into twelve pieces signifying the number of the Apostles, and these pieces they afterwards divide according to the number of people; and the priest gives the Body of Christ into each one's hand and then the man reverently receives It from his palm, and wipes his hand on the top of his head.

The Christians I have spoken of and the monk urgently begged us for the love of God to celebrate. Thereupon I made them go to confession, as well as I could by means of an interpreter enumerating the ten commandments and the seven deadly sins and other things a man ought to be sorry for and confess, all in public. They made excuses for thieving, saying that unless they stole it would be impossible to live, for their masters provided them with neither clothes nor food. Then I, deliberating as to whether they had taken goods and cattle without just cause, told them that it was lawful for them to take the necessities of life from their masters' possessions, and I was ready to tell Mangu Chan this to his face. Some of them were soldiers and excused themselves saying they were obliged to go to war, otherwise they would be put to death. I firmly forbade them to fight against Christians, or to do them any harm, rather should they let themselves be killed for then they would become martyrs. And I said if anyone wished to denounce me to Mangu Chan for teaching this, I was ready to preach the same in his hearing, for when I was teaching these things there were present the Nestorians from the orda and I suspected they might inform against us.

Then Master William had an iron made for us for making hosts, and he possessed some vestments which he had made for himself, for he had a little education and comported himself as a cleric. He had made a statue of the Blessed Virgin sculptured after the French fashion, and on the shutters enclosing it he carved the story of the Gospel most beautifully; and he made a silver pyx in which to keep the Body of Christ and relics in little compartments skilfully fashioned in the sides of the pyx. He had also made an oratory on a cart, which was very beautiful and painted with sacred stories.

I took the vestments and blessed them and we made most beautiful hosts after our fashion, and the Nestorians assigned to me their baptistery in which there was an altar. Their Patriarch has sent them from Baghdad a square piece of leather as a portable altar; it has been prepared with chrism and they use it in place of a consecrated stone. And so I said Mass on Maundy Thursday with their silver chalice and paten, which vessels were very large, and again on Easter Sunday. And I gave Holy Communion to the people with the blessing of God, so I hope. On Easter Eve the Nestorians baptised in the most correct manner more than sixty people, and there was great common joy among all the Christians.

CHAPTER XXXI

MASTER WILLIAM'S SICKNESS AND THE DEATH OF THE NESTORIAN
PRIEST

IT happened that Master William then became seriously ill. When
he was getting better the monk went to visit him and gave him
some rhubarb to drink, so that he nearly killed him. When I went
to see him and found him so very ill, I enquired what he had been
eating or drinking, and he told me how the monk had given him
the potion and he had drunk two bowlfuls, believing that it was
holy water. I thereupon accosted the monk and said to him:
"Either go about like the Apostle truly working miracles by the
power of prayer and the Holy Ghost, or act as a physician in
accordance with the science of medicine. You give men, who are
not prepared for it, a strong dose of medicine to drink as if it were
something holy; if this came to the knowledge of the public you
would incur the worst possible scandal." At that he began to be
afraid and beware of me.

It happened also at that time that the priest, who was like the
archdeacon of the others, fell ill, and his friends sent for a Saracen
soothsayer who told them: "A thin man who neither eats nor
drinks nor sleeps on a bed is angry with him. If he could obtain
his blessing he would get better." They understood this to refer
to the monk, and round about midnight the priest's wife, sister
and son came to the monk begging him to go and give him his
blessing. They also woke us up to plead with the monk. When we
asked him he said: "Leave him alone, for he with three others,
who like him will go the same evil way, formed a plot to go to the
court and obtain from Mangu Chan that you and I should be
expelled from these parts."

Now there had arisen a quarrel among them, for on Easter Eve
Mangu and his wives had sent four *iascot* and some pieces of silk
to the monk and the priests to be divided among them, and the
monk had kept one *iascot* for himself as his share, and of the

remaining three one was counterfeit, for it was of copper; consequently it seemed to the priests that the monk had kept too
large a share for himself, and it may be that they had talked about
it among themselves and this had been reported to the monk.

When day came I went to the priest, who had a very severe
pain in his side and was spitting blood, which led me to believe
that he had an abscess. I then urged him to acknowledge the
Pope as the Father of all Christians, which he did immediately,
vowing that if God gave him his health he would go and fall at the
feet of the Pope and would in all good faith see to it that the Pope
should send his blessing to Mangu Chan. I also warned him to
restore anything he might have belonging to another; he said he
had nothing. I spoke to him about the Sacrament of Extreme
Unction. He replied: "It is not our custom, nor do our priests
know how to administer it; I beseech you do for me according to
what you know ought to be done." I admonished him too concerning confession, which they do not frequent. He spoke briefly into
the ear of one of his fellow priests. After that he began to be better
and asked me to go for the monk. I went.

At first the monk did not wish to come, but when he heard that
he was better, he went with his cross; and I also went carrying in
Master William's pyx the Body of Christ which I had reserved
on Easter Sunday at Master William's request. Then the monk
began to tread on the priest and the latter most humbly embraced
his feet. Then I said to him: "It is the custom of the Roman
Church that the sick receive the Body of Christ as Viaticum and as
a defence against all the snares of the enemy; behold the Body of
Christ which I consecrated on Easter Day. You must declare your
belief in It and ask for It." Whereupon he said with great faith:
"I ask for It with all my heart." When I had taken off the cover,
with deep feeling he said: "I believe that this is my Creator and
my Saviour, Who gave to me my life and will restore it to me after
my death at the general resurrection." And thus, at my hand, he
received the Body of Christ, consecrated according to the usage of
the Roman Church.

The monk then stayed with him and gave him, in my absence, I
know not what potions. The following day he began to be in

danger of death, whereupon I took their oil, which they said was holy, and anointed him according to the form of the Roman Church as he had requested me. I had not got our own oils because Sartach's priests had kept them all. When I was saying the prayers for the dying and wanted to be present at his death, the monk sent to me telling me to leave, for if I were there when he died I would not be able to enter Mangu Chan's dwelling for a year. When I intimated this to his friends they said that it was true and begged me to go away so as not to hinder the good I might be able to promote.

After his death the monk spoke to me: "Don't worry," said he, "I killed him by my prayers. He alone was educated and was opposed to us; the others know nothing; for the rest, we shall have all of them and Mangu Chan at our feet." He then narrated to me the soothsayer's reply I have already told you; not believing it I enquired of the priest-friends of the dead man if it were true. They said that it was, but whether he had been primed beforehand or not, they did not know.

Later I discovered that the monk summoned the said soothsayer and his wife to his chapel and made them sift dust and divine for him. He also had a Ruthenian deacon with him who divined for him. When I learned this afterwards I was horrified at his foolishness and said to him: "Brother, a man full of the Holy Ghost Who teaches all things ought not to seek answers or advice from soothsayers; and all such things are forbidden and those who pursue them are excommunicated." He then began to excuse himself saying it was not true he sought such things. I was unable to part company with him for I had been put there by the Chan's command, and I could not transfer myself without his special order.

CHAPTER XXXII

CARACORUM AND THE FAMILY OF MANGU

As for the city of Caracorum I can tell you that, not counting the Chan's palace, it is not as large as the village of Saint Denis, and the monastery of Saint Denis is worth ten times more than that palace. There are two districts there: the Saracens' quarter where the markets are, and many merchants flock thither on account of the court which is always near it and on account of the number of envoys. The other district is that of the Cathayans who are all craftsmen. Apart from these districts there are the large palaces of the court scribes. There are twelve pagan temples belonging to the different nations, two mosques in which the law of Mahomet is proclaimed, and one church for the Christians at the far end of the town. The town is surrounded by a mud wall and has four gates. At the east gate are sold millet and other grain, which is however seldom brought there; at the west sheep and goats are sold; at the south oxen and carts; at the north horses.

Before the Ascension we followed the orda; catching it up on the Sunday before the Ascension.[1] The next day Bulgai, the chief scribe and judiciary, sent for us, the monk and all his household, and all the envoys and foreigners who frequented the monk's dwelling. We were summoned one by one into Bulgai's presence, the monk first and we after him; and they began to enquire closely where we were from, for what reason we had come, what was our business. This enquiry was made because it had been reported to Mangu Chan that four hundred Assassins, disguised in various costumes, had entered the country, in order to murder him. About that time the wife we have spoken about above had a relapse and sent for the monk; he, not wishing to go, replied: "She has again called pagans to her, let them cure her if they can. I will not go any more."

On the Vigil of the Lord's Ascension we went into all the dwellings belonging to Mangu Chan, and I saw how, when they were about to drink, they sprinkled their felt idols with cosmos. I then said to the monk: "What communication hath Christ with Belial? What part hath our cross with these idols?"[2]

As mentioned above Mangu Chan has eight brothers, three by the same mother and five of the same father. One of the former

---

[1] The feast of the Ascension fell on May 21st in 1254.
[2] II Cor. vi. 15–16.

he sent into the country of the Assassins, whom they call Mulibet,[1] and commanded him to kill them all; another went to attack Persia and has already entered it and is about to invade the country of Turkey, so it is believed, and from there he will send out armies against Baghdad and Vastacius; one of the others he sent into Cathay against some who are not yet subject to him; the youngest uterine brother, by name Arabuccha [Arik Buka], he has kept with him and he has the orda of their mother who was a Christian and Master William is his slave.

One of his brothers on his father's side captured Master William in Hungary in a city called Belgrade, in which there was a Norman bishop from Belleville near Rouen. At the same time he captured a nephew of the bishop and I saw him there at Caracorum. He gave Master William to Mangu's mother for she begged hard to have him; after her death Master William passed into the possession of Arabuccha along with all the other appurtenances of his mother's orda and through him he was brought to the notice of Mangu Chan, who, after the completion of the work I have described, gave this master a hundred *iascot*, that is a thousand marks.

On the Vigil of the Ascension Mangu Chan said that he wanted to go to his mother's orda and visit it, for it was not far away. The monk also said that he would like to go with him and give his blessing to his mother's soul. The Chan gave his consent. In the evening of Ascension Day, the wife we have spoken about grew very much worse and the chief of the soothsayers sent to the monk telling him not to beat the board. The following day when the whole orda moved away, the establishment of this lady stayed behind. When we came to the spot where the orda was to be set down, the monk was ordered to go further away from the court than was his custom and he did so.

Arabuccha then came to meet his brother the Chan. The monk and we, seeing that he would pass by us, went to meet him with the cross. He, recognising us, for he had on occasion been to our oratory, stretched out his hand and made the sign of the cross

---

[1] i.e. Mulahid, see note on p. 125. It was Hulagu who conquered both the Assassin strongholds and Persia. See Introduction, p. xxv.

towards us just like a bishop. Then the monk, jumping onto a horse, followed him, taking with him some fruit. Arabuccha alighted in front of his brother's orda, to wait for him until he should return from hunting. The monk thereupon alighted at the same place and offered him his fruit, which he accepted.

Sitting near him were two nobles of the Chan's court, Saracens. Arabuccha, aware of the strife which exists between Christians and Saracens, asked the monk if he knew these Saracens. He replied: "I know that they are dogs. Why do you have them in your company?" "Why," said they to him, "do you insult us when we have not insulted you?" The monk replied to them: "I speak the truth; you and your Mahomet are vile dogs." In reply they then began to utter blasphemies against Christ, and Arabuccha put a stop to them saying: "Do not say these things for we know that the Messias is God."

At that hour a mighty wind suddenly got up throughout the whole countryside so that it seemed as if demons were rushing all over it, and after a short time the report came that the wife had died.

On the morrow the Chan returned to his orda by a different route; for this is one of their superstitions that they never return by the same way as the one by which they come. Moreover when an orda has been pitched in a place, after it has been moved on no one dares to pass the site where it had been, either on horse or on foot, so long as there is any trace of a fire which had been made there.

That day some Saracens, coming up to the monk on the road, provoked him and argued with him; and when they jeered at him because he was incapable of defending himself by reasoning, he made as if to strike them with the whip he was carrying in his hand; and he made such a to-do that his words and actions were reported to the court, and the command was issued that we were to stay down with the other envoys and not in front of the court as we had done hitherto.

CHAPTER XXXIII

FRIAR WILLIAM SEEKS PERMISSION TO RETURN: THEOLOGICAL
DISCUSSIONS

I, FOR my part, was all the time cherishing the hope that the King
of Armenia[1] would come. Also a man had come about Easter from
Bolac, where those Germans are for whose sake I had largely
made my journey, and he had told me that a German priest was
about to visit the court. In consequence I did not raise the
question with Mangu of our staying or leaving; in the beginning
he had only given us permission to stay there two months, and
four months had already passed—nay rather five, for these things
happened about the end of May and we had been there throughout
the whole of January, February, March, April and May.

However, hearing no reports of the King or the said priest, and
fearing that we would have to return in the winter, the severity
of which we had experienced, I had enquiry made of Mangu Chan
what he wished to do with us, saying that we would gladly stay
there for ever if it so pleased him; if, however, we were to go back
it would be easier for us to make the return journey in the summer
than in the winter. He immediately sent a message to me telling
me not to go far away for he wished to speak with me the next day.
I, for my part, said that if he wished to talk to me, he should send
for Master William's son, as my interpreter was inadequate.

The one who spoke with me was a Saracen and had been
ambassador to Vastacius. Blinded by gifts, he had advised Vastacius to send envoys to Mangu Chan and thus play for time, for
Vastacius believed that they were on the point of invading his
territory. He sent the envoys and after he got to know the Mongols
he took little heed of them; neither has he made peace with them,
nor have they up to the present invaded his country, and they
will not be able to do so as long as he is bold enough to defend himself. They have never taken any country by force, only by guile;

[1] Hethum I (1226–70). See Introduction, p. xxi.

and when men make peace with them it is under cover of that peace that they destroy them. The man then began to ask me many questions about the Pope and the King of the French and of the routes leading to them. The monk, hearing this, secretly warned me not to answer him, saying he wished to bring it about that he should be sent as envoy. I therefore kept silence and would not reply. The man uttered I know not what insult against me which made the Nestorian priests want to denounce him, and he would have been killed or beaten to within an inch of his life, but I would not allow it.

The next day, that is to say the Sunday before Pentecost, they took me to the court and the chief scribes of the court came to me—one a Mongol, who is the Chan's cup-bearer, the others Saracens, and they enquired on behalf of the Chan the reason for my coming. Then I gave them an account in the words I have already given, how I had come to Sartach and from Sartach to Baatu and how Baatu had sent me here; after that I added: "I have nothing to say on behalf of any man. The Chan must know what Baatu has written to him; I have but the words of God to utter if he is prepared to hear them." They fastened on to this and enquired what were the words of God I wanted to say, for they imagined I would prophesy some good fortune as many others do.

I gave them answer: "If you wish me to speak the words of God, provide me with an interpreter." They said: "We have sent for him; however, do your best to speak through this one, we shall understand you well enough." And they put much pressure on me to speak. Then I said: "This is the Word of God—'To whom more is committed, from him more will be required'. Likewise in another place: 'He to whom more is given ought to love more.' Starting with these words of God I say to Mangu that God has given him much. For the power and riches he possesses were not given to him by the idols of the *tuins* but by God Almighty, Who made heaven and earth and in Whose hand are all kingdoms, which He transfers from nation to nation on account of the sins of men. Wherefore if he love Him, all will go well with him; but if not, let him know that God will require of him an account of everything down to the last farthing."

Then one of the Saracens spoke: "Is there any man who does not love God?" I replied: "God says, 'If any one love Me, he will keep My commandments; and he that loveth Me not keepeth not My commandments.' Therefore he who does not keep the commandments of God does not love God." Then said he: "Have you been in heaven that you know the commandments of God?" "No," I replied, "but He gave them from heaven to holy men and finally He Himself came down from heaven to teach us and we have them written down and we see by a man's works whether he keeps them or not." Then he said: "By this you mean that Mangu Chan does not observe God's commandments." To which I rejoined, "The interpreter will come, so you say, and I will recite the commandments of God in the presence of Mangu Chan, if he allow me, and then let him judge of his own case whether he observe them or not." At that point they retired and they told him I had said he was an idolater or *tuin* and that he did not keep the commandments of God.

The next day he sent his scribes to me, who said: "Our master sends us to you and he says: 'Here you are, Christians, Saracens and *tuins*, and each one of you declares that his law is the best and his literature, that is his books, the truest.' He therefore wishes you all to meet together and hold a conference and each one is to write down what he says so that he can know the truth." I answered: "Blessed be God Who has put this into the heart of the Chan. But it says in our Scriptures: 'The servant of God ought not to wrangle, but be mild towards all men',[1] and so I am prepared to give an account, without strife and contention, of the faith and hope of Christians to all who ask." They wrote down what I said and took it to him. It was then enjoined on the Nestorians that they should provide their own representatives and write down what they wanted to say, likewise on the Saracens and even the *tuins* in the same way.

On the morrow he again sent the scribes, who said: "Mangu Chan wishes to know what is the reason of your coming to these parts." I answered them, "He must know this from Baatu's letter." Then they said: "Baatu's letter has been lost and he has

[1] II Tim. ii. 24.

forgotten what Baatu wrote to him, so he wants to know from you." Being thus reassured I said to them: "It is the duty of our religion to preach the Gospel to all men. Therefore when the fame of the Mongol race came to my ears, I was filled with the desire of coming to them; and while I was cherishing this desire I heard that Sartach was a Christian. I thereupon directed my course to him; and my Lord the King of the French sent a letter to him containing good words, and among other things he vouched for us to him, saying what kind of men we are, and asking him to allow us to pass some time among the Mongol people. Then Sartach sent us to Baatu, and Baatu sent us to Mangu Chan; we have therefore asked him and we still ask that he allow us to stay." They wrote down all this and took it to him.

The next day he again sent them to me saying: "The Chan well understands that you have no mission to him, but have come to pray for him like many another priest; but he wants to know if ever any of your envoys have been to us or any of ours to you." I then told them all about David and Friar Andrew[1] and they put everything down in writing and took it to him. Again he sent them to me saying "The Lord Chan says you have been here a long time; he wants you to return to your country and asks if you are willing to take with you an envoy from him." I replied to them: "I would not dare to take his envoys with me outside his territory, for between you and us there is a land of war, and sea and mountains, and I am a poor monk, wherefore I would not dare to take them under my leadership." Writing all this down they went back.

The Vigil of Pentecost [May 30th 1254] arrived. The Nestorians wrote out a chronicle from the creation of the world up to the Passion of Christ; and passing over the Passion they touched on the Ascension, resurrection of the dead and the coming in Judgment; in the course of this there were some points on which they were at fault and I informed them about them. We, on the other hand, simply wrote out the creed of the Mass—"*Credo in Unum Deum.*"

I then enquired of them how they wanted to proceed. They

---

[1] See Introduction, p. xix.

said they would like first to have a debate with the Saracens. I
pointed out that this was not a good idea, for the Saracens agree
with us in that they say there is one God; they would therefore be
on our side against the *tuins*. They assented. I then asked them
if they knew how idolatry had come into being in the world, and
they did not know. I thereupon gave them an account, and they
said: "You will tell us these things and then let us do the talking,
for it is difficult to speak with an interpreter." I answered: "Let
us try how you will get on against them. I will take the part of
the *tuins*, do you uphold the Christian side. Suppose I am a follower
of their religion; they say there is no God, prove that God exists."
(For there is one sect there which says that any soul and any power
in anything is the god of that thing, and that otherwise there is no
God.) The Nestorians did not know how to prove anything, they
could only repeat what the Scriptures tell. I said: "These people
do not believe in the Scriptures; if you tell them one story, they
will tell you another." I thereupon advised them to let me have the
first encounter with them, for if I were worsted, there would still
be the opportunity for them to speak; if they were worsted, I would
get no hearing afterwards. They agreed to this.

And so on the Vigil of Pentecost we assembled at our oratory,
and Mangu Chan sent three scribes to act as judges—one a
Christian, one a Saracen and one a *tuin*; and the proclamation
was made: "This is the decree of Mangu and let none dare to say
that the decree of God is otherwise. He decrees that no one shall
dare to speak words of contention or abuse to another, and no one
is to cause a disturbance such as would hinder these proceedings,
on pain of death." Then all were silent. There were many people
there, for each party had collected the wisest of its men, and many
others had assembled.

The Christians then placed me in the middle, telling the *tuins*
to discuss with me. The *tuins*, of whom there was a great
gathering there, began to murmur against Mangu Chan, saying
that never before had any Chan attempted to find out about their
secrets. They then chose as my opponent one who had come from
Cathay and he had an interpreter with him. I had Master William's
son. He opened by saying to me: "Friend, if you are brought to a

standstill, seek one wiser than yourself." I held my peace. Next he asked what I wanted to discuss first, how the world had been made or what happens to souls after death. I replied: "Friend, that ought not to be the beginning of our disputation. All things are from God and He is the source and head of all things; therefore we ought first to speak of God, concerning Whom you have different beliefs from us and Mangu wishes to know whose are the best." The judges decided that this was right.

They wanted to begin with the points mentioned above, because they consider them the most important, for they are all followers of the Manichean heresy that half of creation is evil and the other half good, and that there are at least two principles; and concerning souls they believe that all migrate from one body to another.

Even the wisest priest among the Nestorians asked me if the souls of dumb animals could escape anywhere after death where they would not be compelled to work. As a proof of this false doctrine, so Master William told me, a boy was brought from Cathay, who, judging by his size, was not yet three years old, nevertheless his reasoning powers were fully developed, and he himself said that he had had three reincarnations; he knew also how to read and write.

So I said to the *tuin*: "We firmly believe in our hearts and profess with our lips that God exists and that there is but one God and that He is one with a perfect unity. What do you believe?" He answered: "Fools say that there is but one God, but wise men say that there are many. In your country are there not mighty lords, and here is not the chief lord Mangu Chan? So it is with the gods; in the different regions there are different gods." To this I gave answer: "That is a bad illustration or simile you put forward, arguing from men to God; for, according to this, any powerful man could be called a god in his own territory."

When I wanted to refute the comparison, he prevented me by inquiring "What is your God like, of Whom you say there is but one?" I replied: "Our God, besides Whom there is none other, is omnipotent, and therefore He has no need of anyone's help, rather do we all need His help. It is not so with men. No man can do all things, consequently there have to be many lords on the earth, for no single man can bear everything. Also He knows everything, and therefore has no need of a councillor; but rather all wisdom is from Him. Again, He is the supreme good and has no need of our goods, but in Him we live and move and have our being. Such is our God and therefore no other ought to be considered." "It is not so," said he. "On the contrary there is one supreme god in heaven, of whose origin we are still ignorant, below him are ten, and under them is one lower. On earth there is an infinite number."

When he wanted to weave other fairy tales, I questioned him about this supreme god, whether he believed he was omnipotent or dependent on another god. He, fearing to reply, asked: "If your God is such as you say, why did He make half of creation evil?" "It is untrue," said I, "it is not God Who made evil; and all things that are, are good." All the *tuins* were astonished at this saying and put it down in writing as something untrue and impossible. Then he began to ask, "That being so, where does evil come from?" "You ask the wrong thing," I replied. "First you ought to ask what evil is, before asking where it comes from; but go back to the first question, whether you believe that any god is omnipotent, and afterwards I will answer all the questions you wish to put."

He sat for a long time unwilling to reply, so that the scribes who were listening on behalf of the Chan had to order him to give an answer. At length he said that no god was omnipotent. At that all the Saracens burst into loud laughter.

When there was silence again I said: "And so not one of your gods can save you in every danger, for a mishap may occur over which he has no power; moreover 'no man can serve two masters', how therefore can you serve so many gods in heaven and on earth?" The audience told him to reply, but he remained silent. When I wanted to put forward the arguments for the Unity of the divine essence and the Trinity in the hearing of all, the Nestorians belonging to the country told me I had said enough, for they wished to speak.

I then gave place to them and when they wanted to dispute with the Saracens the latter replied: "We grant that your faith is true and that whatever is in the Gospel is true, therefore we do not wish to argue on any point with you." They admitted that in all their prayers they beseech God to grant that they may die a Christian death.

There was an old man there, a priest of the sect of the Uigurs, who say that there is one God and yet make idols, and the Nestorians spoke a great deal with him, giving him an account of everything from the coming of Christ to the Judgment, and also by means of comparisons explaining the Trinity to him and the Saracens. They all listened without a word of contradiction, yet not one of them said, "I believe, I wish to become a Christian."

When this was finished the Nestorians and Saracens alike sang loudly while the *tuins* kept silence, and afterwards they all drank their fill.

CHAPTER XXXIV

FRIAR WILLIAM'S LAST AUDIENCE WITH MANGU

ON the day of Pentecost Mangu Chan summoned me and the *tuin* with whom I had debated to his presence; before I went in the interpreter, Master William's son, told me we would have to return to our own country and that I was not to offer any objection for he had learned this was settled. When I came before the Chan I had to kneel down with the *tuin* beside me together with his interpreter. Then the Chan said to me: "Tell me if it is true that the other day when I sent my scribes to you, you said I was a *tuin*." I replied: "My lord, I did not say that, but, if you allow me, I will tell you the words I used." I then repeated to him what I had said and he answered: "I well thought you had not said it, for that was not the sort of thing you ought to say, but your interpreter translated badly." And he stretched out towards me the staff on which he was leaning, saying "Fear not". I smiled and said quietly: "If I were afraid I would not have come here." He enquired of the interpreter what I had said and he repeated it to him.

He then began to make a profession of his faith to me. "We Mongols," said he, "believe that there is but one God, by Whom we live and by Whom we die and towards Him we have an upright heart." I said, "God Himself will grant this for it cannot come about but by His gift." He asked what I had said and the interpreter told him. Afterwards the Chan continued: "But just as God gave different fingers to the hand so has He given different ways to men. To you God has given the Scriptures and you Christians do not observe them. You do not find in the Scriptures that a man ought to disparage another, now do you?" he said. "No," I replied, "but from the beginning I made it clear to you that I had no wish to wrangle with anyone." "My words do not apply to you," said he. "Similarly you do not find that a man ought to turn aside from justice for the sake of money." "No, my Lord," I said, "and for a truth I have not come to these parts in order to gain money, rather have I refused that which was offered to me." There was a scribe present, who bore witness to the fact that I had refused a *iascot* and some pieces of silk. "My words do not apply to you," he said. "As I was saying, God has given you the Scriptures and you do not keep them; to us, on the other hand, He has given soothsayers, and we do what they tell us, and live in peace." He drank four times, I believe, before he finished saying these things.

And while I was listening closely to hear if there was still more he wished to declare concerning his faith, he began to speak of my return saying: "You have stayed here a long time, it is my wish that you go back. You have said that you dare not take my envoys with you; are you willing to take a message and letter from me?"

From then onwards I had neither the opportunity nor the time to put the Catholic Faith before him, for a man may not say more in his presence than he desires, unless he be an envoy; an envoy can say whatever he will, and they always enquire whether he wishes to say still more. I, however, was not allowed to continue speaking, but had to listen to him and reply to the questions he put.

I then answered him that if he would have his message explained to me and put down in writing, I would gladly take it to the best of my ability. He next asked if I desired gold or silver or costly garments. I said: "Such things we do not accept, but we have no provisions and without your aid cannot leave your country." He answered: "I will arrange for you to have all that you need as far as my territory stretches, do you wish for more?" I replied, "That is sufficient for me." He then enquired: "How far do you wish to be conducted?" I said: "We can manage for ourselves when we reach the land of the King of Armenia. If I were given a guide as far as that I would be satisfied." He answered: "I will have you accompanied thus far, after that you can fend for yourselves." And he added, "There are two eyes in a head, yet although they are two, nevertheless they have but one sight, and whither the vision of one is directed so is that of the other; you came from Baatu, it therefore behoves you to return by way of him."

When he had said this I asked his leave to say a few words. "You may speak," he answered. Then I said: "My Lord, we are not warlike men, we would like to see those holding dominion over the world who would govern it most justly according to the will of God. Our duty is to teach men to live according to the will of God; for this reason did we come to these parts and we would gladly have remained here if you had allowed it. Since it is your good pleasure that we return, it must needs be; I will go back and carry your letter to the best of my ability in accordance with your commands. I would like to ask of your Eminence that, when I have taken your letter, I may be granted your permission to return to you, especially as you have some poor serfs at Bolac who speak our language and need a priest to teach them and their children their faith, and I would gladly abide with them." He replied: "Provided your masters send you back to me." I then said: "My Lord, I do not know what my masters have in mind, but I have permission from them to go wherever I will, where there is need to preach the word of God; and it seems to me that it is most necessary in these parts, therefore whether he send back an envoy to you or not, given your permission I would return."

He kept silent and sat for a long time as if turning things over in his mind, and the interpreter told me not to speak any more. However, I anxiously awaited his reply. At last he spoke: "You have a long journey ahead of you, fortify yourself with food so that you may be strong enough to reach your own country." And he had me given something to drink. I then left his presence, and never afterwards returned. If I had had the power of working miracles like Moses, he might have humbled himself.

CHAPTER XXXV

THE SOOTHSAYERS

THEIR soothsayers,[1] as the Chan admitted, are their priests, and whatever they order to be done is carried out without delay. Their function I will describe to you as I was able to learn it from Master William and others who gave me a plausible account of them. There are many of them and they always have a chief like a pontiff and he always sets his house in front of Mangu Chan's chief dwelling, about a stone's throw away. All the carts carrying their idols are in his care, as I said above. The others are behind the court in the places assigned to them, and there come to them men from different parts of the world who put their trust in their art.

Some of them are skilled in astronomy, especially their chief, and they foretell the eclipse of the sun and moon; when this is going to take place all the people lay in stores of food so there will be no need for them to go out of the door of their dwelling. During the eclipse they beat their timbrels and sound their musical instruments and make a great din and mighty noise. When the eclipse is over, then they spend their time in eating and drinking and they make a great feast. The soothsayers declare which days are favourable or unfavourable for carrying on any kind of business; consequently the Mongols never perform military exercises or go to war unless they have given the word; and they would long since have returned to Hungary, but the soothsayers do not allow it.

[1] William's account of the influence of the diviners or *Kams* at the Mongol court is very important and shows how the enlightened views of the Great Khans, which aroused Gibbon's admiration, were associated with a very primitive type of Shamanism and magical practices.

Everything that is sent to the court they pass between fires, and they get their due share out of this. They also purify all the bedding of the dead by taking it between fires; for when anyone dies everything belonging to him is set on one side and is not mixed with the other things in the orda until they have all been purified by fire; I saw this carried out in the case of the orda of the wife who died while we were there. There was therefore a two-fold reason why Friar Andrew and his companions had to pass through fires, both because they were bearing gifts and because these were intended for one who had already died, I mean Keu Chan. No such things were demanded of me for I was carrying nothing. If any animal or anything else falls to the ground while they are thus taking them through the fires, this belongs to the soothsayers.

On the ninth day of the month of May the soothsayers collect all the white mares of the herd and consecrate them. The Christian priests are also obliged to assemble there with their thurible. Then they cast new cosmos on the ground and they make a great feast on that day, for that is when they count on drinking fresh cosmos for the first time, just as with us in some places they do with the wine on the feast of Bartholomew or Sixtus and with fruit on the feast of James and Christopher.

The soothsayers are also called in when any male child is born, in order to foretell his fate; likewise when anyone is ill they are summoned and they recite their incantations and pronounce whether the sickness is natural or the result of sorcery. In this connection the woman from Metz, of whom I have already spoken, told me a remarkable story.

On a certain occasion a presentation was made of some very valuable furs, which were placed in the court of her mistress who, as I have already said, was a Christian. The soothsayers carried them between the fires and took of them more than was their due, and the woman in charge of this lady's treasure accused them of this to her mistress who, consequently, reprimanded them. After this it happened that the mistress fell ill and began to suffer from sudden pains in various parts of her body. The soothsayers were called in and, sitting some distance away, they ordered one of the

maids to put her hand on the place of the pain and draw out whatever she might find. The girl, getting up, did this and discovered
in her hand a piece of felt or some other kind of material. They
then ordered her to put it on the ground; placed there it began to
crawl like a live animal. It was then put into water and it turned,
as it were, into a leech, and they said: "My lady, some witch has
injured you with her sorcery." And they accused the woman who
had brought the accusation against them concerning the furs.
She was led outside the camp to the fields and for seven days was
beaten and tortured in other ways to make her confess. In the
meantime the mistress died. The woman hearing this said to
them: "I know that my mistress is dead; kill me so that I can
follow her, for I have never done her any harm." As she would
confess nothing Mangu gave orders that she was to be allowed
to live.

The soothsayers thereupon accused the nurse of the daughter
of the lady I have mentioned; she was a Christian and her husband
was the most esteemed of all the Nestorian priests. She was led
to the torture along with one of her handmaids to make her confess;
and the maid confessed that her mistress had sent her to speak
with a horse to ask for an oracle from it. The woman herself
confessed that she had done certain things to make herself loved
by her mistress and to do good to her, but she had done nothing
which could possibly harm her. She was then questioned as to
whether her husband was aware of this. She made excuses for
him saying that she had burned the characters and writing she had
done herself. Then she was put to death, and Mangu sent her
husband, the priest, to his bishop in Cathay for sentence, although
he had not been found guilty.

In the meantime it came to pass that Mangu Chan's chief wife
gave birth to a son. The soothsayers were called in to foretell the
child's fate, and they all prophesied good fortune, saying that he
would have a long life and would be a mighty lord. A few days
later it turned out that the child died. Then the mother, in a fury,
summoned the soothsayers and said to them: "You said that my
son would live, and see, he is dead." Then they replied: "My
lady, we now see the witch, Cirina's nurse, who was put to death

the other day. She has killed your son, and now we see she is carrying him off." A full-grown son and daughter of that woman had remained in the camp, and the Chan's wife, mad with rage, immediately sent for them, and she had the young man put to death by a man and the girl by a woman in revenge for her son, who, the soothsayers had said, had been killed by their mother.

A few days after this the Chan dreamed about these children and in the morning asked what had become of them. His servants were afraid to tell him and he, more anxious, asked where they were, for they had appeared to him in a vision by night. Then they told him. Straightway he sent to his wife, demanding where she had got the idea from that a woman could pass sentence of death without her husband's knowledge, and he had her shut up for seven days and ordered that no food was to be given to her. The man who had put the youth to death he had beheaded and his head hung round the neck of the woman who had murdered the girl, and he ordered her to be beaten with burning brands through the camp and afterwards put to death. The wife also he would have put to death but for the fact that he had children by her; and he left his orda and did not return for a month.

The soothsayers also disturb the weather with their incantations and when in the natural course of things the cold is so intense that they are unable to apply any remedy, then they search out men in the camp whom they accuse of being responsible for the cold and, without any delay, these are put to death.

Shortly before I left, one of the concubines had been sick and ailing for some time and the soothsayers chanted incantations over one of her slaves, a German, who slept for three days. When she returned to herself they asked her what she had seen; she had seen many people all of whom, they declared, would soon die; and since she had not seen her mistress there they pronounced that she would not die of this illness. I saw the girl still suffering from a severe headache as the result of her sleep.

Some of the soothsayers also invoke demons and they assemble in their dwelling by night those who wish to consult the demon and they place cooked meat in the middle. The *Kam* who is performing the invocation begins to chant his incantations, and, holding a tympanum, strikes it heavily on the ground. At length he begins to rage and has himself bound. Then the devil comes in the darkness and gives him meat to eat and he utters oracles.

On one occasion, so Master William told me, a Hungarian hid among them and the demon stayed on top of the dwelling saying that he could not come in because there was a Christian with them. Upon hearing this the Hungarian made his escape with all speed, for they were beginning to search for him. These and many other things they do which it would be tedious to tell of.

CHAPTER XXXVI

OF THE CHAN'S FESTIVALS, THE LETTER TO BE SENT TO KING LOUIS AND FRIAR WILLIAM'S RETURN

AFTER the feast of Pentecost they began to compose the letter which the Chan was to send to you. In the meantime he returned to Caracorum and held his great reception just on the octave of Pentecost, and he wanted all the envoys to be present on the last day. He also sent for us but I had gone to the church to baptise the three children of a poor German I had come across there. For that feast Master William was the chief cup-bearer because he had made the tree which pours forth drink; and all, rich and poor, sang and danced and clapped their hands in front of the Chan. He then began to address them, saying: "I have parted with my brothers and have sent them into danger against foreign nations. Now we shall see what you will do when I wish to send you to extend our empire." On each of the four days they changed their clothes, which they gave to them on each day all of one colour, from the shoes to the headdress.

At that time I saw the envoy of the Caliph of Baghdad there; he had himself conveyed to the court in a litter between two mules, which led some to say that the Chan had made peace with them, the condition being that they should provide him with an army of ten thousand horsemen. Others were saying that Mangu had declared he would not make peace with them unless they destroyed all their fortifications, and the envoy had replied: "When you take all the hooves off your horses, we will destroy all our fortifications."

I also saw there the envoys of a Sultan of India who had brought eight leopards and ten greyhounds trained to sit on the back of a horse like leopards. When I asked about India, in what direction it was from that spot, they pointed towards the west, and the envoys accompanied me on our return journey for about three weeks, travelling all the time westwards. I saw, too, envoys of the Sultan of Turkey[1], who brought costly presents for the Chan; he replied, so I heard, that he had need of neither gold nor silver but of men; by this he meant he wanted them to provide him with an army.

On the feast of St. John [June 24th] the Chan held a great drinking festival and I counted a hundred and five carts laden with mares' milk, and ninety horses; and the same on the feast of the Apostles Peter and Paul [June 29th].

The letter he is sending to you being at length finished, I was summoned and they translated it. I have written down the gist of it as well as I could grasp it by means of an interpreter and it is as follows:

"This is the decree of the eternal God. In heaven there is but one eternal God, on earth there is but one lord Chingis Chan, the son of God, Demugin Cingei, that is the sound of iron." (They call Chingis the sound of iron because he was a smith; and puffed up with pride they now call him the son of God.[2])

"This is the message which is spoken to you: whosoever there be Mongol, or Naiman, or Merkit, or Mussulman, wherever ears can hear and whithersoever a horse can go, there make it heard and understood: from the time they hear my decree and understand, and will not to believe, but wish to make war against us, you will hear and will see that they will have eyes, but will not see, and when they wish to hold anything they will be without hands, and when they wish to walk they will be without feet. This is the decree of the eternal God. By the power of the eternal

---

[1] Kilij Arslan IV, the ruler of the Seljuk kingdom of Rum or Iconium.
[2] Temuchin, the original name of Chingis, means "smith". He was named after a Tartar chief who had been slain by his father.

God throughout the great realm of the Mongols, let the decree of Mangu Chan be known to the lord of the Franks, King Louis and to all the other lords and priests and to all the world of the Franks so that they may understand our message. The decree of the eternal God was made by Chingis Chan, but this decree has not reached you from Chingis Chan or from others after him.

"A certain man, David by name, came to you as if he were an envoy of the Mongols but he was a liar, and you sent your envoys with him to Keu Chan. It was after the death of Keu Chan that your envoys arrived at his orda. Chamus his wife sent you cloths of *nasic* and a letter. But how could that wicked woman, more vile than a dog, know about matters of war and affairs of peace, and how to pacify a great race and see how to act for good?"

(Mangu told me with his own lips that Chamus[1] was the worst kind of witch and that by her sorcery she had destroyed her whole family.)

"The two monks, who came from you to Sartach, Sartach sent to Baatu; Baatu however, seeing that Mangu Chan is chief over the Mongol people, sent them to us.

"Now, in order that the great world and the priests and the monks might all live in peace and rejoice in the good things of life and in order that the decree of God might be heard among them, we wished to appoint Mongol envoys to accompany your afore-mentioned priests. The priests however gave answer that between us and you there was a land of war and many evil men and difficult going, and therefore they were afraid they would be unable to bring our envoys to you safe and sound, but they said that if we gave them our letter containing our decree they would take it to King Louis. This is the reason why we have not sent our envoys with them, but by the hands of these your priests we have sent to you the decree of the eternal God in writing.

"It is the decree of the eternal God which we have made known to you. When you have heard and believed it, if you wish to obey us, send your envoys to us; in this way we shall know for sure whether you wish to be at peace or war with us. When by the

[1] "Chamus" is Ogul Gamish, widow of Guyuk and regent of the empire from 1249–51. She was executed with most of Guyuk's ministers in the palace revolution that followed the election of Mongka.

power of the eternal God the whole world from the rising of the sun to the going down thereof shall be at one in joy and peace, then it will be made clear what we are going to do; if, when you hear and understand the decree of the eternal God, you are unwilling to pay attention and believe it, saying 'Our country is far away, our mountains are mighty, our sea is vast', and in this confidence you bring an army against us—we know what we can do: He who made what was difficult easy and what was far away near, the eternal God, He knows."

At first they called us your envoys in this letter. Then I said to them, "Do not call us by the name of envoys, for I have told the Chan clearly that we are not envoys of King Louis." They went to him and told him; on their return they said he had taken it in good part and had ordered them to write what I should say to them. So I told them to remove the title of envoy and to call us monks or priests.

In the meantime, while this was being done, my companion heard that we were to return through the wilderness to Baatu and that a Mongol was to be our guide, so, unknown to me, he ran to Bulgai the chief scribe and intimated to him by means of signs that he would die if he were to go on that journey. When the day arrived on which we were to be given our leave to depart, that is to say a fortnight after the feast of St. John [July 9th or 10th], when we were summoned to the court, the scribes said to my companion: "See, Mangu wishes your companion to return by way of Baatu, and you say you are a sick man and it is clear you are. Mangu therefore says, if you wish to go with your companion you may go, but on your own head be it, for perhaps you will stay at the house of some *yam*, and he will not make provision for you and you will be a hindrance to your companion; if, on the other hand, you wish to remain here, the Chan will provide you with what you need until some envoys arrive with whom you can make the return journey more slowly and by a route along which there are towns." The Friar replied: "God grant the Chan good fortune! I will remain." I however said to the Friar, "Brother, take heed to what you are doing. It is not I who am forsaking you." "You," said he, "are not forsaking me, but I am leaving you, for if I go with you, I shall see both my body and soul in danger, for I cannot endure such intolerable hardship."

The scribes were holding three garments or tunics and they said to us: "You do not wish to receive gold or silver and you have been here a long time praying for the Chan; he begs you at least to accept, each one of you, a simple tunic, so that you may not leave him empty-handed." We then had to accept them out of respect to him, for they take it ill when their gifts are disdained. He had frequently before sent to ask us what we wanted and we always gave the same answer, so much so that the Christians there scoffed at the pagans, who look for nothing but presents. The pagans used to reply that we were fools, for if he wished to give them his whole orda, they would gladly accept it and they would be acting prudently. When we had received the garments they asked us to say a prayer for the Chan, which we did. And so having obtained our leave we went to Caracorum.

It happened one day while we were with the monk some distance away from the court along with the other envoys that the monk sounded the board so loudly, that Mangu Chan heard it and enquired what it was. They told him and he asked why the monk was so far removed from the orda. They explained that it was troublesome to bring him horses and oxen every day to the orda, and added that it would be better for him to stay at Caracorum near the church and pray there. Then the Chan sent to him saying that if he wished to go to Caracorum and stay there near the church he would give him all he needed. The monk however replied: "I came here from the Holy Land of Jerusalem by the command of God, and I left a city in which there are a thousand churches better than the one in Caracorum; if he wishes me to stay here and pray for him, as God commanded me, I will stay; otherwise I will go back to the place I came from." That evening oxen harnessed to carts were brought for him, and the following morning he was taken back to the site he used to occupy in front of the court.

Shortly before our departure a Nestorian monk arrived, who seemed a prudent man. Bulgai, the chief scribe, placed him before his own orda and the Chan sent his children to receive his blessing. And so we came to Caracorum, and while we were in Master William's house, my guide arrived bearing ten *iascot*, five of which he put into Master William's hand, saying that he was to spend them on behalf of the Chan for the needs of the Friar; the other five he placed in the hand of Abdullah, my interpreter, ordering him to spend them on the journey for my needs. Unknown to us Master William had put them up to this.

I immediately sold one of the *iascot* and distributed it among the poor Christians there who all looked to us for help; another we spent in purchasing necessary clothes and other things of which we stood in need; with the third Abdullah made some purchases by means of which he earned a little profit for himself. The rest we also spent there, for nowhere from the time we entered Persia were we given a sufficient supply of necessities, not even among the Tartars, and there we seldom came across anything for sale.

Master William, at one time your subject, sends you a leather strap ornamented with a precious stone which they carry as a protection against thunder and lightning, and he sends you countless greetings and prays for you; for him I could never render sufficient thanks to God or to you.

There we baptised in all six souls.

And so we parted from each other with tears, my companion remaining with Master William while I returned alone with my interpreter, with my guide and a servant who had an order that he would receive a sheep in four days' time for the four of us.

CHAPTER XXXVII

FRIAR WILLIAM'S JOURNEY TO THE COURT OF BAATU IN HIRCANIA

IN two months and ten days we reached Baatu, during which time I never saw a town or the trace of any building other than tombs, with the exception of a village in which we did not eat bread; nor did we ever rest during these two months and ten days except for one single day when we could not obtain horses. We returned through altogether different regions, though for the most part coming across the same people, for we went in the winter and returned in the summer by far more northerly districts, except that for fifteen days both on the way there and on the way back we had to follow a river among the mountains, where there is no grass except near it. We went for two days and sometimes three taking no food except cosmos. At times we were in great peril, unable to find any inhabitants and with our food supplies getting low and our horses tired out.

After I had ridden for twenty days I heard news of the King of Armenia; he had passed by at the end of August on his way to meet Sartach, who was going to Mangu Chan with his flocks and herds, his wives and children, although his large dwellings had been left behind, between the Etilia and the Tanais. I paid my respects to Sartach, saying that I would gladly have remained in his country, but Mangu Chan wanted me to return and take his letter. He replied that Mangu Chan's wishes must be carried out.

I then enquired of Coiac about our servants. He replied that they were being carefully looked after in Baatu's orda. I also asked to have our vestments and books back, whereupon he replied, "Did you not bring them to Sartach?" I said, "I brought them to Sartach, but I did not give them to him as you know," and I repeated the reply I had given when he had asked whether I wished to present them to Sartach. Then he answered: "You speak the truth, and no one can withstand the truth. I deposited your possessions with my father, who is staying near Sarai[1], the new town Baatu has built on the Etilia; but our priests have some of your vestments here with them." I said, "You may keep such of the vestments as you wish, provided the books are returned to me." Then he replied he would tell Sartach what I had said. I continued: "I must have a letter to your father, telling him to restore everything to me." They were all ready to continue their

[1] Sarai: there were two towns of that name, successive capitals of the Golden Horde. One of these, Sarai-Berka, was situated on the Akhtube, a tributary of the Volga, near the town of Tsarev, some thirty-five miles east of Stalingrad. The other Sarai, Sarai-Batu, founded in about 1241 by Batu, was situated on the Volga further down the river, near the village of Selitrennoe. Ruins of what in all probability was Batu's palace have been found there.

journey and he said to me, "The women's orda is following close behind us; you will put up there and I will send you Sartach's reply by this man."

I was anxious not to be deceived by him; however, I was not in a position to argue with him. In the evening the man he had pointed out to me came, bringing with him two tunics, which, I had the impression, were made entirely of one piece of uncut silk, and he said to me: "Here are two tunics; Sartach sends one for you and the other, if it seems good to you, you will present to the King on his behalf." I replied, "I do not wear such garments; I will present them both to the King in honour of your master." "No," said he, "do with them whatever you please." It has pleased me to send them both to you and I am sending them by the bearer of this letter. He also gave me a letter to Coiac's father, telling him to restore to me all my belongings for he did not need anything of mine.

We reached Baatu's orda on the very same day on which I had quitted it a year back, the day after the Exaltation of the Holy Cross [September 14th], and to my joy I found our servants safe but, according to what Gosset told me, suffering from the most dire poverty; and if it had not been for the King of Armenia, who afforded them great relief and recommended them to Sartach, they would have been lost, for they believed that I was dead, and the Tartars had already started asking them if they knew how to look after oxen and milk mares. If I had not returned, they would have been reduced to being their slaves.

Then Baatu made me come before him and he had the letter which Mangu Chan is sending to you translated for me. Mangu had written to him saying that if he wanted to add or remove or change anything he was to do so. Then he said to me, "You will take this letter and translate it." He also asked what route I wanted to take, whether by sea or land. I said that since the sea would be closed, for it was winter, I would have to go by land. I also believed that you were still in Syria and directed my journey towards Persia. If I had thought you had proceeded to France, I would have gone to Hungary and would have reached France more quickly and by a route less toilsome than that to Syria.

We journeyed for a month with Baatu before we were able to obtain a guide. At last he assigned to me a Uigur who, realising that I would give him nothing, had a letter made out telling him to bring me to the Sultan of Turkey, although I had told him I wanted to go straight to Armenia, for he hoped that he would receive gifts from the Sultan and gain more by going that way.

Fifteen days before the feast of All Saints [October 17th] I started on the journey to Sarai, travelling due south, following the Etilia, which there in its lower reaches divides into three large branches each of which is almost twice as large as the river of Damietta;[1] it forms four other smaller branches, so that we crossed that river by boat seven times. On the middle branch is the town called Summerkent,[2] which has no walls, but when the river is in flood it is surrounded by water; the Tartars besieged it for eight years before they captured it. In it were Alans and Saracens. There we found a German with his wife, a very good fellow, with whom Gosset had stayed, for Sartach had sent him there to relieve his orda of the burden.

In these regions about Christmas time Baatu is on one side of the river and Sartach on the other, and they go no further south. Then the whole river freezes and they make their way between the streams where there is an excellent supply of grass and there they lurk among the reeds until the ice begins to melt.

On the receipt of Sartach's letter Coiac's father restored to me the vestments with the exception of three albs, an amice embroidered in silk, a stole, a girdle, an altar-cloth adorned with gold embroidery, and a surplice; he also gave me back the silver vessels except the thurible and the phial containing the chrism, which were in the possession of the priests who were with Sartach. He restored my books, except for my Lady the Queen's psalter, which he kept with my permission since I could not refuse it to him, for he said that it had greatly pleased Sartach.

He also begged me, should I happen to return to these parts again, to bring for them a man skilled in the making of parchment. He was building a large church on the west bank of the river by Sartach's command, and a new village, and he wanted to make

[1] The Lower Nile.   [2] Probably Astrakhan.

books for Sartach's use, so he said. However I know that Sartach's interests do not lie in that direction.

Sarai, with Baatu's palace, is on the east bank, and the valley through which the branches of the river spread is more than seven leagues across and there is a plentiful supply of fish there.

I did not recover a Bible in verse and a book in Arabic, worth thirty besants, and several other things.

So we left him on the feast of All Saints and travelling all the time south, we reached the mountains of the Alans on the feast of St. Martin [November 11th, 1254].

During the fifteen days between Baatu and Sarai we did not come across any human beings, except one of his sons who was going ahead of him with his many falcons and falconers; and one very small village. During the fortnight after the feast of All Saints we did not meet a soul and we almost died of thirst for throughout a whole day and night until about nine the next morning we did not come across any water.

The Alans in these mountains are still offering resistance, consequently out of ten of Sartach's men two had to come to guard the entrance to the passes in case they should emerge from the mountains to plunder their animals in the plain between them and the Alans and the Iron Gate, which is two days' journey from there, where the Aracci plain begins between the sea and the mountains.

Among the mountains there are some Saracens called Lesgi, who are likewise holding out, so the Tartars at the foot of the mountains of the Alans had to give us twenty men to escort us to beyond the Iron Gate. I was delighted, for I was hoping I should see their armed men, for I had never managed to have a look at their weapons although I had been most anxious to do so. When we reached this dangerous stretch, of the twenty there were two who had habergeons. I asked how they had come by these; they said they had procured them from the aforementioned Alans, who are fine artificers of such things and excellent smiths. This makes me think they have few arms apart from their bows and arrows and leather garments. I saw them being presented with iron plates and helmets from Persia, and I also saw two men who appeared before Mangu armed with tunics made of curved pieces of stiff leather, which were very clumsy and cumbersome. Before we reached the Iron Gate we came to a town of Alans, which belonged to Mangu Chan, for he had conquered that territory. It was there we first came across vines and drank wine.

The following day we arrived at the Iron Gate, which Alexander, King of Macedon, made; it is a city the east end of which is on the shore of the sea, and between the sea and the mountains there is a small plain across which the city extends as far as the top of the mountain adjoining it on the west, so that there is no route above it on account of the ruggedness of the mountains nor below by the sea, only straight across through the middle of the city, where there is the Iron Gate from which the city takes its name.[1] The city is more than a mile long and at the top of the mountain there is a strong fortress; in width however it is but as far as one could throw a large stone. It has very strong walls, without moats and towers, made of large polished stones, but the Tartars have destroyed the tops of the towers and the ramparts of the walls, rasing the towers to the level of the wall.

Inside that city the land used to be like paradise. Two days from here we came across another city called Samaron, where there were many Jews; and when we had passed by it we saw that it had walls running from the mountains right down to the sea. Leaving the road by the sea along the walls, since it turned off eastwards, we climbed up the mountains towards the south.

The following day we passed through a valley where there were to be seen foundations of walls from one mountain to another and there was no route across the tops of the mountains. These used to be Alexander's barriers for keeping back the barbarians, that is to say the nomads of the wilderness, so that they could not encroach upon cultivated territory and cities. There are other enclosures in which there are Jews, but I was unable to learn anything definite about them; however there are many Jews throughout all the cities of Persia.

The next day we reached a large city called Samag, and the day after we entered a vast plain, known as Moan,[2] through which the

---

[1] Derbent, the Persian name of the Iron Gate.
[2] The Mugan steppe, south of the river Kura.

Cur flows, which gives their name to the Curgi whom we call
Georgians. It flows through the middle of Tiflis, which is the
capital of the Georgians, and coming straight from the west it
goes east to the sea of which we have spoken, and contains the
finest salmon. In that plain we again came across Tartars. It is
also through this plain that the Araxes flows, coming from
Greater Armenia from due south-west, and it is after this that
the land of Ararat is named, which is the same as Armenia.
That is why in the Book of Kings it says that when the sons
of Sennacherib had slain their father they fled into the land of
the Armenians, whereas in Isaias it says they fled into the land
of Ararat.

To the west therefore of this very fair plain is Georgia. At
one time the Crosminians [Khorezmians] were in this plain. At
the foot of the mountains there is a large city called Ganges,[1]
which was their capital and prevented the Georgians from des-
cending into the plain. We came to a bridge of boats which were
held together by a large iron chain stretched across the river at
the point where the Cur and Araxes join each other. The Araxes
however loses its name at that spot.

From then on we climbed ever upwards, following the Araxes of
which it is said *pontem dedignatur Araxes* [Aen. VII, 728], and
leaving on the left, towards the south, Persia and the Caspian
mountains, and on the right towards the west the sea and Georgia,
we made our way south-west in the direction of Africa. Our
journey led us through the encampment of Baachu, the chief of
the army stationed near the Araxes, who conquered the Georgians,
the Turks and the Persians. At Tabriz in Persia there is another
man, Argon by name, who is in charge of the tribute; both these
men have been recalled by Mangu Chan to give place to his brother
who is coming to that region. The country I have described to
you is not Persia proper, but it used to be called Hircania. I was
in Baachu's house and he gave us wine to drink; he himself however drank cosmos, which I would have preferred to have, if he
had given it to me. The wine was new and special, but cosmos is
a more satisfying drink for a hungry man.

---

[1] Gandja.

We followed the course of the Araxes from the feast of St. Clement [November 23rd] to the second Sunday of Lent [February 21st], until we reached the source of the river. Beyond the mountain on which it rises there is a large city called Erzerum, which belongs to the Sultan of Turkey, and near there towards the north at the foot of the mountains of Georgia the Euphrates takes its rise. I would have gone to its source, but there was so much snow that no one could leave the beaten track. On the other side of the mountains of the Caucasus towards the south the Tigris takes its rise.

CHAPTER XXXVIII

THE JOURNEY FROM HIRCANIA TO TRIPOLI

WHEN we left Baachu my guide went to Tabriz to speak with Argon, taking with him my interpreter. Baachu had me taken to a city called Naxua[1] which was at one time the capital of a great kingdom and a very large and beautiful city, but the Tartars have reduced it almost to a wilderness. The Armenians used to have eight hundred churches there; now there are but two little ones, for the Saracens destroyed them. In one of these I celebrated the feast of the Nativity as well as I could, with our cleric.

The following day a priest of that church died, and a bishop, along with twelve monks, came down from the mountains for his funeral. All the Armenian bishops are monks, as are for the most part the Greek bishops. The bishop told me that near there was the church in which St. Bartholomew and also St. Jude Thaddeus were martyred, but the way was closed because of the snow.

He told me also that they have two prophets: the first is the martyr Methodius, who belonged to their race and clearly prophesied about the Ismaelites, which prophecy has been fulfilled in the Saracens. The other prophet is called Acacron, who on his deathbed prophesied about a race of archers who are to come from the north; he said they would get possession of all the lands of the east, and they would spare the eastern kingdom so that it might

[1] Nakhichevan.

deliver the kingdom of the west to them—but our brethren, he says, the Catholic Franks, will not trust them—and they will seize the countries from the north to the south, and they will reach as far as Constantinople and seize the harbour of Constantinople, and one of them, who will be called the Wise Man, will enter the city and seeing the churches and services of the Franks will have himself baptised, and he will advise the Franks how they may kill the chief of the Tartars and there the Tartars will be thrown into confusion. On hearing this the Franks from the centre of the world, that is Jerusalem, will attack the Tartars in their territory and with the aid of our people, that is, the Armenians, will pursue them so that the King of the Franks will set up his royal throne at Tabriz in Persia. Then all the orientals and all the races of un-believers will be converted to the faith of Christ, and there will be such peace in the world that the living will say to the dead, "Woe to you who have not lived to see these days." I had read this prophecy, brought to Constantinople by Armenians who live there, but I had not taken much notice of it; when however I spoke with the said Bishop, I remembered and paid more attention; and throughout the whole of Armenia they consider this prophecy as true as the Gospel. The Bishop also said to us: "Just as the souls in Limbo were awaiting the coming of Christ to be set free, so we are awaiting your coming to be liberated from this servitude in which we have been so long."

Near this city are mountains on which, they say, Noah's ark rested; there are two, one bigger than the other, and the river Araxes flows at the foot of them. There is a town there called Cemanium, which means "eight", and they say it is so called from the eight people who came out of the ark and built it on the higher mountain. Many have tried to climb the mountain and have failed. The Bishop told me that a certain monk was most anxious to do so, and an angel appeared to him bringing him a piece of the wood of the ark, telling him not to exert himself any more. That wood they have in their church, so they told me. To look at, the mountain is not so high that it would not be quite possible for men to climb it. An old man gave me a good enough reason why no one ought to climb it. They call the mountain Massis and it is of the feminine gender in their language. "No man," he said, "ought to climb the Massis, for she is the mother of the world."

In that city Friar Bernard the Catalan of the Order of Friars Preachers met me; he had stayed in Georgia with a prior of the Sepulchre, who has great possessions in land there; and he had learned a little Tartar and had been with a Friar from Hungary to Argon at Tabriz to ask for transit to Sartach. When they arrived there they were unable to obtain an audience, and the Hungarian Friar returned by my arrangement to Tiflis with a servant, but Friar Bernard remained at Tabriz with a German lay-brother, whose language he did not understand.

We left the afore-mentioned city on the octave of the Epiphany [January 13th]; we had stayed there a long time on account of the snow. In four days we came to the territory of Sahensa, a Georgian, at one time most powerful but now a tributary of the Tartars, who have destroyed all his fortifications. His father, by name Zacharias, acquired that land of the Armenians, rescuing them from the hands of the Saracens. And there are some very fine villages there composed entirely of Christians who have churches just like the Franks; and every Armenian has in his house in an honourable position a wooden hand holding a cross, and he places a lighted lamp in front of it; and as we sprinkle with holy water in order to put the demon to flight, so they do with incense, for every evening they burn incense and take it to every corner of the house to rout out any kind of evil thing.

I had a meal with Sahensa and was shown great respect by him, his wife and his son who is called Zacharias, a very good-looking and sensible young man, who enquired of me whether you would be willing to keep him if he came to you, for he finds the domination of the Tartars so irksome that, although he is well supplied with this world's goods, nevertheless he would prefer to be a pilgrim in a strange land rather than bear their yoke. Moreover they said they were sons of the Roman Church and, if the Lord Pope would send them help, they would bring all the neighbouring nations into subjection to the Church.

On the first Sunday in Lent, fifteen days after leaving that country, we entered upon the territory of the Sultan of Turkey, and the first place we came across is called Marsengen.[1] All in the town were Christians—Armenians, Georgians and Greeks—but the Saracens have the mastery. The governor there said that he had received an order that they were not to give provisions to any Frank or envoy of the King of Armenia or of Vastacius; consequently from that place where we were on the first Sunday in Lent, as far as Cyprus, where I landed eight days before the feast of St. John the Baptist, we had to buy our food. The man who was acting as my guide forced me to have horses, he was given the money for the food and put it into his purse; when he came to a field anywhere and saw a flock of sheep, he used to steal a sheep by force and give it to his company to eat, and he was surprised that I was unwilling to eat of the plunder.

On the feast of the Purification I was in a city called Aini,[2] which belongs to Sahensa and is in a very strong position. In this city there are a thousand Armenian churches and two Saracen synagogues. The Tartars have put a bailiff there.

There five Friars Preachers came to see me, four of whom came from the French province and the fifth had joined them in Syria. They had but one sickly servant, who knew Turkish and a little French. They had letters from the Lord Pope to Sartach, Mangu Chan and Buri, like the one you gave to me, begging that they be allowed to stay in their country and preach the word of God, etc. However, when I had related to them what I had seen and how the Tartars were sending me back, they directed their course towards Tiflis where there are some of their Friars, in order to have advice as to what they were to do. I made it clear to them that by means of those letters they would be able to make the journey if they wished, but they should be well prepared both to endure hardship and to give a reason for their coming, for if their mission had no other object than the duty of preaching, the Tartars would make little account of them and particularly since they had no interpreter. What they did afterwards I do not know.

On the second Sunday in Lent we reached the source of the Araxes, and crossing the summit of the mountains we came to the

---

[1] Manzikert. The modern Turkish village on that site is Malazkirt, about fifteen miles N.W. of Lake Van.

[2] Ani, the ancient Armenian capital between Erivan and Kars.

Euphrates, which we followed down for eight days, always going towards the west, until we arrived at a fortress called Camath.[1] There the Euphrates changes its course towards the south in the direction of Aleppo. We, however, crossing the river, kept on journeying westwards across very high mountains and very deep snow. There had been such a big earthquake there that year that in one city, called Arsengen, there had perished ten thousand persons known by name, not counting the poor of whom there was no knowledge. For three days as we rode along we saw a chasm, just as it had been cleft by the earthquake, and mounds of earth which had slipped down from the mountains and filled the valleys, so that if the earth had been shaken but a little more that saying of Isaias would have been fulfilled to the letter: "Every valley shall be filled and every mountain and hill shall be made low."

We passed through the valley in which the Sultan of Turkey was defeated by the Tartars. It would take too long to write down how he was defeated, but one of my guide's servants, who had been with the Tartars, said that the Tartars were not more than ten thousand in all, and a Georgian slave of the Sultan said that the Sultan had two hundred thousand men with him, all on horseback. On the stretch of level ground where this battle,[2] or rather rout, took place, a large lake had gushed out in the earthquake; and I reflected within myself that all that earth had opened her mouth to receive the blood of the Saracens.

During Holy Week we were in Sebaste[3] in Lesser Armenia. There we visited the burial-place of the Forty Martyrs. The church of St. Blaise is there, but I could not go to it as it was up in the fort. On the octave of Easter we arrived at Caesarea in Cappadocia, where there is the church of St. Basil the Great.

Fifteen days later we reached Iconium,[4] travelling short stages each day and resting in many places, for we were not able to

---

[1] Camath: probably the modern Keban, or Kamakh.
[2] The battle mentioned was fought in 1243 at Közädagh (Kuza-Dagh), between Erzingan and Sivas. The defeated Sultan of Rum was Ghiyas ed-din Kaikhosrau II.
[3] The modern Sivas. Lesser Armenia is not the medieval kingdom of Lesser Armenia in Cilicia, but the old Roman province of the same name, or *Armenia Prima*.
[4] Konya, at that time the capital of the Seljuk Kingdom of Rum.

obtain horses so quickly. My guide did this on purpose, taking lodging for three days in each place. I was much distressed at this, but dared not say anything for he could have sold or murdered me and our servants. There would have been none to say him nay.

At Iconium I came across several Frenchmen and a Genoese merchant from Acre, by name Nicholas of Santo Siro, who, together with his partner, a Venetian called Boniface of Molendino, has the monopoly of the alum from Turkey, so that the Sultan cannot sell any to anyone except these two, and they have rendered it so dear that what used to be sold for fifteen besants is now sold for fifty.

My guide presented me to the Sultan, who said he would gladly have me conducted as far as the sea of Armenia or Cilicia. Then the merchant I have mentioned, knowing that the Saracens were not much interested in me and that I was vexed beyond measure by the presence of my guide, who pestered me every day to give him presents, had me taken to Curca,[1] a port belonging to the King of Armenia. I arrived there the day before the Ascension and stayed until the day after Pentecost.

Then I heard that messengers had come from the King to his father. I put our belongings in a ship to be taken to Acre. Having got rid of these I went to the King's father[2] to find out if he had heard any news of his son; I found him at Sis together with all his sons, except one called Barunusin, who was building a fort. He had received messengers from his son saying that he was returning and that Mangu Chan had greatly reduced the tribute for him and had granted him the privilege that no envoy should set foot on his territory. On account of this the old man was holding a great festival along with all his sons and the whole people.

He had me taken as far as the sea to the port called Ayas,[3] and from there I crossed to Cyprus. At Nicosia I found our Minister, who took me with him that very day to Antioch; he is in a very poor state of health. We were there on the feast of the Apostles Peter and Paul. From there we came to Tripoli, where our Chapter was held on the Assumption of the Blessed Virgin [August 15th, 1255].

[1] Corycas, west of Mersin.
[2] Constantine of Lambron, the father of King Hethum.
[3] Lajazzo: the chief port of Cilicia at this time.

Epilogue

The Minister decided that I was to lecture at Acre and would not allow me to come to you but bade me write to you what I wished by the bearer of this letter. I, not daring to refuse the obedience, have done as well as I could and knew how, and I beg you of your persistent kindness to pardon anything which is unnecessary or inadequate, or said in an unwise or even foolish fashion, seeing that it is done by a man of little wisdom and unaccustomed to dictating such long accounts. The peace of God, which surpasseth all understanding, keep your heart and mind! I would like to see you and those spiritual friends I have in your kingdom; therefore, if it would not be displeasing to your Majesty, I would beg you to write to the Minister and ask him to release me to come to you, and I would go back to the Holy Land after a short time.

As for Turkey, I can inform you that not one man in ten there is a Saracen; rather are they all Armenians and Greeks and the power is in the hands of boys. For the Sultan, who was conquered by the Tartars, had an Iberian[1] as a legitimate wife and by her he had a son who was a cripple and he gave the command that he was to be Sultan; he had another son by a Greek concubine, her he gave to a powerful emir; a third he had by a Turk, and many Turks and Turcomans collected round this son and wanted to kill the sons of the Christians.

They also arranged, so I understood, that, once victory was theirs, they would destroy all the churches and put to death as many as were unwilling to become Saracens; but he was defeated and many of his men were killed. He patched up his army again but next he was taken prisoner and is still kept in chains. Pacaster, the son of the Greek, obtained of his half-brother that he should be Sultan, for the other was a cripple, and they sent the latter to the Tartars; his relations on his mother's side, that is to say the Iberians and Georgians, were indignant about this. As a result of all this a boy rules in Turkey, having no money, few soldiers and

---

[1] The daughter of Queen Rusudan of Georgia.

many enemies. The son of Vastacius[1] is weakly and is at war with the son of Assan,[2] who likewise is a boy and worn out by servitude to the Tartars.

Consequently if an army of the Church were to come to the Holy Land it would be a very easy thing to subjugate all these countries, or pass through them. The King of Hungary has at the most not more than thirty thousand fighting men. From Cologne to Constantinople it is but forty days' journey by cart. From Constantinople it does not take so many days to reach the land of the King of Armenia. Of old, brave men made their way through these regions and all went well with them, although they had very brave men resisting them, whom God has now wiped off the face of the earth. They did not have to be in peril of the sea or at the mercy of a crew of mariners, and the price they would have had to give as passage money, was sufficient for the expenses of going by land. I say to you with confidence, if your peasants, I will not say Kings and knights, were willing to go as do the Kings of the Tartars and to be content with the same kind of food, they could take possession of the whole world.

It does not seem to me expedient that any other Friar should again go to the Tartars as I went and as the Friars Preachers are going; but if the Lord Pope, who is head of all Christendom, would send a bishop with marks of honour, and would reply to the foolishnesses which they have three times written to the Franks—once to Pope Innocent IV of happy memory and twice to you—once by David who deceived you, and now by me—he would be able to say to them whatever he wished and also to make them put it down in writing. For they always listen to what an envoy has to say and always enquire whether he wishes to say more, but he would have to have a good interpreter, nay, several interpreters, and abundant supplies.

[1] Theodore Lascaris II.   [2] Michael Assan of Bulgaria.

THE LETTERS OF JOHN OF MONTE CORVINO,
BROTHER PEREGRINE AND ANDREW OF PERUGIA

The following letters are very inferior in literary and historical value to the two great narratives of John of Plano Carpini and William of Rubruck. But they are of very great importance for the history of Christendom since they record the beginnings of Catholic missionary activity in China, and thus form a link between the Mongol mission of William of Rubruck and the greater achievements of Matteo Ricci and the Jesuit missionaries of the sixteenth and seventeenth centuries who were the founders of the Christian Church in China in modern times. However, they form an essential part of the present volume, since these later missionaries were the direct successors of the earlier travellers and reaped in China the harvest that had been sown years before in Mongolia.

John of Monte Corvino, at least, is well worthy to stand beside John of Plano Carpini and William of Rubruck. He was a true disciple of St. Francis, a man of great simplicity of character but also of heroic constancy and apostolic spirit, and the story of his solitary mission for twelve years at the court of the Mongol Emperors of China is one of the most outstanding episodes in missionary history.

John of Monte Corvino was born in southern Italy in 1247. He took part in the Franciscan mission to Armenia and Persia about 1279–83 and returned to Italy in 1289 bringing a letter from King Hethum II of Armenia to the Pope. He was sent back to the East with letters from Pope Nicholas IV to all the patriarchs and princes of the East. He finally left Tabriz, the capital of the Il Khans, in 1291, on the great journey from which he never returned. His first letter, which is not included here, since it does not deal with the Mongols, was written in India and has survived only in an Italian translation. The two letters from China exist in three MSS., one at Paris and two at Rome. They were first printed by Luke Wadding in his *Annals* and consequently have been well known to ecclesiastical historians for the last three hundred years.

Wadding also edited the letter of Andrew of Perugia from a MS. at Assisi.

But the letter of Brother Peregrine is less well known and doubts have been expressed about its authenticity, since it survived only in a MS. which belonged to the notorious forger Alfonso Ceccarelli who was executed at Rome in 1583. But whatever Ceccarelli's misdeeds, I do not think that he can have forged this particular document, and most scholars now regard it as genuine.

We know from the letter of Andrew of Perugia that Peregrine succeeded Brother Gerard as second Bishop of Zaytun and died a few years later on July 7th, 1323. He was succeeded by Brother Andrew, who wrote the following letter during his episcopate. But these letters are not the only evidence of Brother Andrew's presence in China. During the last war, the medieval walls of Ch'uan-chou-fu, or Zaytun, were demolished and a Chinese schoolmaster discovered a number of carved stones and inscriptions among the debris, a large number of which were Muslim and Christian grave stones. Among the latter which have been fully described with illustrations by the Rev. Professor John Foster, D.D., of Glasgow University, in the *Journal of the Royal Asiatic Society*, and also in a talk for the Third Programme of the B.B.C. on May 10th, 1954, there is one with a Latin inscription. Though it is in an extremely bad state Professor Foster has been able to decipher:

Hic . . . . . sepultus
Andreas Peruginus
Ordinis . . . . . .
. . . . apostolus
M XII

Here lies buried Andrew of Perugia of the Order (of Friars Minor). . . . And the date must presumably be 1332, MCCCXXXII, since we know that he was alive in 1322.

THE LETTERS OF JOHN OF MONTE CORVINO, BROTHER PEREGRINE AND ANDREW OF PERUGIA

THE SECOND LETTER OF JOHN OF MONTE CORVINO

I, BROTHER JOHN of the Order of Friars Minor, departed from Tauris [Tabriz] a city of Persia, in the year of Our Lord 1291 and entered India and I was in the country of India and in the Church of St. Thomas the Apostle for 13 months. And there I baptized about one hundred persons in different places. And my fellow traveller was Brother Nicholas of Pistoia of the Order of the Friars Preachers, who died there and was buried in the same church. And going on further, I reached Cathay, the kingdom of the Emperor of the Tartars, who is called the Great Chan. Indeed I summoned the Emperor himself to receive the Catholic faith of Our Lord Jesus Christ with the letters of the Lord Pope, but he was too far gone in idolatry. Nevertheless he behaves very generously to the Christians and it is now the twelfth year that I have been with him. However the Nestorians, who call themselves Christians, but behave in a very unchristian manner, have grown so strong in these parts that they did not allow any Christian of another rite to have any place of worship, however small, nor to preach any doctrine but their own. For these lands have never been reached by any apostle or disciple of the apostles and so the aforesaid Nestorians both directly and by the bribery of others have brought most grievous persecutions upon me, declaring that I was not sent by the Lord Pope, but that I was a spy, a magician and a deceiver of men. And after some time they produced more false witnesses, saying that another messenger had been sent with a great treasure to the Emperor and that I had murdered him in India and made away with his gifts. And this intrigue lasted above five years, so that I was often brought to judgment, and in danger of a shameful death. But at last, by God's ordering, the Emperor came to know my innocence and the nature of my accusers, by the confession of some of them, and he sent them into exile with their wives and children.

Now I have been alone in this journeying without a confessor for eleven years, until there came to me Brother Arnold, a German of the Cologne province, more than a year ago. I have built a church in the city of Cambaliech [Khanbalik or Peking] where the chief residence of the king is, and this I completed six years ago and I also made a tower and put three bells in it. Moreover I have baptized about 6,000 persons there up to the present, according to my reckoning. And if it had not been for the aforesaid slanders I might have baptized 30,000 more, for I am constantly baptizing.

Also I have purchased by degrees forty boys of the sons of the pagans, between seven and eleven years old, who as yet knew no religion. Here I baptized them and taught them Latin and our rite, and I wrote for them about thirty psalters and hymnaries and two breviaries by which eleven boys now know the office. And they keep choir and say office as in a convent whether I am there or not. And several of them write psalters and other suitable things. And the Lord Emperor takes much delight in their singing. And I ring the bells for all the Hours and sing the divine office with a choir of "sucklings and infants". But we sing by rote because we have no books with the notes.

Of Good King George[1]

A certain king of these parts, of the sect of the Nestorian Christians, who was of the family of that great king who was called Prester John of India, attached himself to me in the first year that I came here. And was converted by me to the truth of the true Catholic faith. And he took minor orders and served my Mass wearing the sacred vestments, so that the other Nestorians accused him of apostasy. Nevertheless he brought a great part

[1] John of Monte Corvino in no way exaggerates the importance of this conversion. The princes of the Ongut, who were Nestorian Christians and lived on the frontiers of China by the northern loop of the Yellow River, held an exceptionally influential position in the Mongol Empire owing to their intermarriages with the descendants of Chingis Khan.

of his people to the true Catholic faith, and he built a fine church
with royal generosity in honour of God, the Holy Trinity and the
Lord Pope, and called it according to my name "the Roman
church". This King George departed to the Lord a true Christian,
leaving a son and heir in the cradle, who is now nine years old.
But his brothers who were perverse in the errors of Nestorius
perverted all those whom King George had converted and brought
them back to their former state of schism. And because I was
alone and unable to leave the Emperor the Chaan, I could not
visit that church, which is distant twenty days' journey. Nevertheless if a few helpers and fellow workers were to come, I hope in
God that all could be restored for I still hold the grant of the late
King George.

Again I say that had it not been for the aforesaid slanders great
results might have followed. If I had even two or three fellow
coadjutors, perhaps the Emperor the Chan might have been
baptized. I beg for some brethren to come, if any are willing to
do so, so being as they are such as are anxious to offer themselves
as an example and not to gain notoriety[1].

As to the road: I report that the way by the land of Cothay[2], the
emperor of the Northern Tartars, is safer and more secure, so that,
travelling with envoys, they might be able to arrive within five or
six months. But the other route is the most long and perilous since
it involves two sea voyages, the first of which is about the distance
of Acre from the province of Provence, but the second is like the
distance between Acre and England, and it may happen that the
journey is scarcely completed in two years. But the first was not
safe for a long time on account of the wars, and for twelve years I
have not received news of the Roman Curia, and of our Order and
of the state of the West. Two years ago there came a certain
physician, a surgeon from Lombardy, who infected these parts with
incredible blasphemies about the Roman Curia and our Order and
the state of the West, whereupon I greatly desire to know the truth[3].

---

[1] Literally, " to enlarge their fringes " (Matt. xxiii. 5).
[2] An error for Toctay or Tokhta, who was Khan of Kypchak 1291–1313 and
controlled the western end of the land route to the east.
[3] No doubt this was an echo of the great controversy between Boniface VIII
and Philip the Fair. The effectiveness of Nogaret's propaganda campaign is

I ask the brethren who shall receive this letter that they should do their best to bring its contents to the notice of the Lord Pope and Cardinals and the Procurator of our Order in the Curia. I beg the Minister General of our Order for an antiphonary, and the legends of the saints, a gradual and a noted psalter as an example, for I have nothing but a small breviary with shortened lessons and a small missal.

If only I had an example, the aforesaid boys could make copies from it.

Now I am in the act of building another church, so that the boys can be divided among several places.

I have already grown old, and my hair is white from labours and tribulations rather than years, for I am fifty-eight years old. I have an adequate knowledge of the Tartar language and script, which is the usual language of the Tartars[1], and now I have translated into that language and script the whole of the New Testament and the Psalter and have had it written in beautiful characters. And I bear witness to the Law of Christ and read and preach openly and in public. And I planned with the aforesaid King George, if he had lived, to translate the whole of the Latin Office so that it might be sung through the whole land under his dominion. And while he lived Mass was celebrated in his church according to the Latin rite in their own script and language, both the words of the Canon and the Preface. And the son of the said king is called John after my own name and I hope in God that he will follow in the footsteps of his father.

Now from what I have seen and heard, I believe that there is no king or prince in the world who can equal the Lord Chan in the extent of his land, and the greatness of the population and wealth.

FINIS

Given in the city of Cambaliech of the kingdom of Cathay, in the Year of Our Lord 1305, the 8th day of January.

---

notorious, but one would hardly have expected to find traces of its influence as far away as China!

[1] It is not clear whether he means the Mongol language and the Uighur script or the Uighur language also. I think he means the latter.

THE THIRD LETTER OF JOHN OF MONTE CORVINO

To the Reverend Father in Christ . . . . . to Brother . . . . . to Brother . . . . . to the Vicar . . . . . of the Minister General of the Order of Friars Minor, to the Vicar of the Master of the Order of Preachers and to the brethren of both Orders who are residing in the province of Persia: Brother John of Monte Corvino, an unprofitable servant of Christ, a preacher of the Christian faith, and legate and envoy of the Roman Apostolic See—greeting and love in Him who is the true love and health of all.

The order of charity demands that those far away and above all those who travel for the law of Christ should at least be consoled by words and letters, when they cannot see one another face to face. I have thought that you may well wonder why you have never received letters from me who have dwelt so long in such a distant land. But I have wondered no less that never until this year have I received letters or good wishes from any Brother or friend, so that it seemed to me that no one remembered me, especially as I heard that rumours of my death had reached you. Wherefore I now notify you that last year at the beginning of January, I sent letters by a friend of ours who was among the companions of the Lord Cothay Chaan who came to the Lord Chaan of Cathay, to the Father Vicar and the brethren of the province of Gazaria [Crimea], informing them briefly of my present situation and circumstances. In this letter I asked the Vicar to send on copies of it to you, and now I find from reliable men who have come to the Lord Chaan of Cathay with the envoys of the aforesaid Lord Cothay that my letter has reached you and that the same messenger who carried it afterwards came from the city of Sarai to Tauris [Tabriz]. Wherefore I did not intend to mention the matter and contents of this letter further, so as not to repeat myself: firstly about the persecution [I suffered] from the Nestorians: secondly about the church and houses that have been completed. I have had six pictures made of the Old and New Testaments for the instruction of the ignorant, and they have inscriptions in Latin, Turkish and Persian, so that all tongues may be able to read them. The third thing is that of the boys whom I bought, some have departed to the Lord. And fourthly, from the time I have been in Tartary, in Cathay, I have baptized several thousand people.

Now in this year of our Lord 1305, I have begun a new house before the gate of the Lord Chaan, and the distance between his court and our house is only a stone's throw from the gateway of the Lord Chaan. Master Peter of Lucalongo, a faithful Christian and a great merchant, who was my companion from Tauris, bought the land for the house of which I have spoken and gave it me for the love of God and by the inspiration of grace, for one could not find a more suitable place for building a Catholic church in the whole empire of the Lord Chaan. I received the site at the beginning of August and with the aid of my benefactors and helpers it was completed by the feast of St. Francis, with a surrounding wall and buildings and simple offices and a chapel which can hold two hundred people. But I could not finish this church on account of the winter. However, I have collected timber in the house and by God's mercy I will complete it in the summer. I assure you it seems a marvel to all who come from the city and elsewhere, when they see the place newly made and a red cross set aloft above it, since they had not yet heard a word of it from here. And we sing office solemnly in our chapel in the common chant, because we have not got noted psalters[1]. The Lord Chaan can hear our voices in his chamber, and this is told as a wonder far and wide among the nations, and will count for much according to the disposition and fulfilment of God's mercy.

From our first church and house to the second church, which I built afterwards, it is about two and a half miles' distance inside the city, which is very large. And I have divided the boys and placed some in the first church and some in the second and they sing office by themselves. But I celebrate Mass in each in alternate weeks as the chaplain, for the boys are not priests.

---

[1] *Secundum usum quia notas non habemus.*

Of the Great Tartar Empire

Concerning the lands of the Orientals and especially the empire of the Lord Chaan, I declare that there is none greater in the world. And I have a place in his court and the right of access to it as legate of the Lord Pope, and he honours me above the other prelates, whatever their titles. And although the Lord Chaan has heard much of the Roman Curia and the state of the Latins, yet he greatly desires to see envoys come from those parts.

In this country there are many sects of idolators who have different beliefs, and there are many kinds of monks with different habits, and they are much more austere and strict in their observance than are the Latin religious.

Concerning India, I have seen a great part myself and have made enquiries about the rest, and it would be of great profit to preach the Christian faith to them if Friars would come. But none save thoroughly reliable men should be sent, for these countries are most beautiful, abounding in spices and precious stones, though they have few of our fruits. And owing to the high temperature and the warmth of the climate of this country they go naked with nothing but a small loin cloth and therefore they have no needs of the arts and products of our tailors and shoemakers. There it is always summer and never winter. I baptized there about a hundred persons.

In the same letter Brother John himself says that a stately embassy came to him from Ethiopia, requesting that he should go there to preach or should send good preachers, for from the time of St. Matthew and his disciples they have had no preachers to instruct them in the Christian faith and they greatly desired to come to the true faith of Christ. And if Friars were sent there, they would convert them all to Christ and they would become true Christians. For there are very many in the East who are Christians only in name and believe in Christ, but know nothing of the Scriptures and the doctrines of the Saints, living in simplicity because they have no preachers and teachers.

Brother John also says that since the Feast of All Saints he has baptized more than four hundred people. And because he has heard that a number of Friars of the two Orders have reached Gazzaria and Persia, he exhorts them to preach the faith of our Lord Jesus Christ fervently and to gain fruit of souls.

This letter was written in the city of Cambaliech [Peking] of the Kingdom of Cathay in the year of Our Lord 1306 in the month of February, on Quinquagesima Sunday.

THE LETTER OF BROTHER PEREGRINE, BISHOP OF ZAYTUN

To the Reverend Father in Christ, to Brother . . . Vicar of the Minister General, and to the other brethren of the Vicariate of the East, Brother Peregrine, made bishop of poverty in another world, sends homage and greeting, desiring to hear news from the world of the faithful.

For though I and my companions had acted like the prodigal son in flying to distant lands, as others have done, yet the Order like a good mother ought at least to remember the sons whom it has consigned to a strange exile. For a mother's heart does not treat a son with the rigour of justice. *And below*: and I am a bishop, however unworthy. *And below*: and I reached Ca[m]baliech [Peking] with our father, Brother Andrew of Perugia the Bishop.

First of all I will speak of the Archbishop, Brother John. His outward life is good and hard and difficult. For as to that King George, it is certain that he converted him completely and worthily to the true faith, though previously he had mingled with the Nestorians. And the king himself in one day converted several thousands of his people. And had he lived, we should indeed have subdued his whole people and kingdom to Christ, and a change might even have been wrought with the Great Chan. For before the said Archbishop came to the empire of the Great Chan, no Christian of whatever nation or class could erect an oratory however small it might be, or a cross, on account of the power of the Nestorians, who prevented it. And so they were compelled either to follow a schismatic and erroneous rite or to take the way of the unbelievers. But after Brother John came, with the help of God he has erected a number of churches, in spite of the Nestorians. And the other Christian peoples who hate the schismatic Nestorians have followed Brother John, especially the Armenians who are now building for themselves a remarkable church and intend to give it to him. Wherefore he is constantly with them and has left the Latin Church to the other brethren. Likewise there are good Christians, called Alans, 30,000 of whom are in the great king's pay, and these men with their families come to Brother John; and he preaches to them and encourages them.

Nor do we see . . . . . and we can preach to them and administer the Sacraments of the Church. But among the infidel we can preach freely and in the mosque [*moscheta*] of the Saracens we have preached often that they might be converted, and to the idolators likewise in their great cities by means of two interpreters. Many come together and wonder greatly and enquire diligently about these things. And now it is begun, we have good hopes, seeing the crowds eager to hear and running to where we preach. Truly we believe that if only we possessed their languages, God would show forth His wonders. Truly the harvest is great and the labourers are few and they have no sickle. For we brethren are few and quite aged and unskilled in the learning of languages. May God forgive those who hinder the brethren from coming. Of a truth I believe the enemy has done this for fear that we should invade his kingdom of which he holds undisputed possession.

In Cambaliech there are the Archbishop and Brother Andrew of Perugia and Brother Peter of Florence, the Bishop, and they lack nothing in temporal things. But in spiritual things they have never been so rich. For the Holy Spirit has fallen upon them and come on these two bishops, and they are so constant in prayer and in holy meditation and the Spirit so visits and consoles and animates them that they seem to forget all else, waiting day and night in holy vigils on the Lord.

Now I have been made Bishop of Cayton,[1] and there I am free to serve God in peace and quiet with three devout brethren. And these servants of God are Brother John of Grimaldi, Brother Emmanuel of Monticulo and Brother Ventura of Sarezana who has become a Friar in this country, and since they are well established in all virtues, God is honoured by them. Would that we had a hundred like them with us! In the city of Cayton we have a good church which an Armenian lady left us, with a house, and she provided the necessaries of life for ourselves and for others if they come. And outside the city we have a fair place with a wood

[1] Zaytun or Ch'uan-chou-fu: the great medieval port in Fukien province near Amoy.

where we want to make cells and a chapel. We stand in need of nothing so much as brethren, whom we long for. For Brother Gerard the Bishop is dead, and we other Friars cannot live long, and no others have come. The church will be left without baptism and without inhabitants.

If I were to write an account of the state of this mighty empire —the greatness of its power, the size of its armies, the extent of its territory, the amount of its revenue and its expenditure of charitable relief—it would not be believed. The Latins here have compared it in these respects to all the other kings of the world, but I do not write how it surpasses them. The great city of Cayton, where we are, is on the sea and is distant about three months' journey from Cambaliech the great.

Given at Cayton the 3rd of the Kalends of January in the Year of Our Lord 1318.

The Letter of Andrew of Perugia

Brother Andrew of Perugia of the Order of Friars Minor, called by divine permission to be a bishop, to the reverend father Brother Guardian of the Convent of Perugia: greeting and everlasting peace in the Lord.

And below he continues:

For on account of the vast distance of lands and seas that lies between you and me, I can scarcely hope that the letters I have sent can reach your hands.

And below he goes on:

You should know that I with Brother Peregrine of good memory, my fellow bishop and the inseparable companion of my pilgrimage, with much labour and weariness, fasting and hardship and danger by land and by sea, in which we were robbed of everything, even our tunics and habits, came at last with the help of God to the city of Cambaliech, the imperial residence of the Great Chan, in the year of Our Lord's Incarnation 1318, as I suppose.[1] Here we consecrated the Archbishop according to the mandate given us by the Apostolic See, and stayed there almost five years. Throughout this time we received *alafa* from the noble Emperor for the food and dress of eight persons. For *alafa* is a grant which the Emperor makes to the envoys of great men, to ambassadors, soldiers, artificers in different crafts, minstrels, poor men and persons of every sort and kind; and the sum of these grants exceeds the income and expenditure of many Western kings.

I forbear to speak of the wealth and magnificence and glory of this great Emperor, of the vastness of the empire and the number of its cities and their size; and of the government of the empire, in which no man dares to draw sword against another; for it would be too long to write and would seem unbelievable to my hearers. For even I who am on the spot hear such things that I can hardly believe them.

---

[1] There is an error in the date; from what he says later in the letter it seems he must have arrived in China about 1313.

There is a certain large city by the ocean called Zayton in the Persian tongue. In this city a rich Armenian lady has built a church, fair and large enough, which she has given and bequeathed with suitable endowment to Brother Gerard the Bishop and our brethren that were with him, after it had by her will been made a cathedral by the Archbishop.

Now after the said Bishop, who was the first to hold the see, had died and been buried there, the Archbishop wished to make me his successor. But as I did not consent to this appointment and succession, he conferred it on Brother Peregrine, the Bishop I have already mentioned, who betook himself there, when he had an opportunity, and after he had ruled it for a few years ended his life there in the year of Our Lord 1322, the day after the Octave of the Apostles Peter and Paul. And since for various reasons I was not contented in Cambaliech, almost four years before the death of the Bishop I got leave that the aforesaid *alafa*, or imperial alms, should be paid to me at this city of Zayton which as I said is almost three months' journey from Cambaliech. I travelled there very honourably with a train of eight horses allowed me by the Emperor, and arrived while Brother Peregrine was still alive. There is a wood near the city, a quarter of a mile away, and here I caused a fair and fitting church to be built with buildings to house twenty brethren, and with four chambers, any of which is good enough for a bishop.

Here then I have taken up my abode, and I live on the bounty of the Emperor which I have already referred to and which, according to the estimate of the Genoese merchants, may amount to the value of a hundred gold florins or thereabouts. And a great part of this alms I have spent in this house and I think there is not a heritage among all those in our province to be compared with it for beauty and convenience.

At last, not long after the death of Brother Peregrine, I received the Archbishop's decree appointing me to the above cathedral church, to which appointment I gave my assent as seemed reasonable. And now I live either at the residence or church in the city or at the hermitage, according as I will. And I am healthy in body and vigorous and active, so far as my age allows: in fact I have none of the natural defects and characteristics of old age except my white hairs.

In this vast empire there are verily men of every nation under heaven and of every sect; and each and all are allowed to live according to their own sect. For this is their opinion, or I should say their error, that every man is saved in his own sect. And we can preach freely and securely, but of the Jews and the Saracens none is converted. Of the idolaters, exceedingly many are baptized: but when they are baptized they do not adhere strictly to Christian ways.

Concerning the Holy Brethren[1]

Four of our brethren were martyred by the Saracens in India: one of whom was thrown twice over into a great fire and came out unhurt. Yet none of them was converted from his unbelief by such a stupendous miracle.

I have taken care to send a brief account of all these things to your Paternity that through you they may be brought to the notice of others. I do not write to my spiritual brethren and my chief friends because I know not who has died and who still live. So I pray that they hold me excused. But I greet them all and commend myself to all as closely as I can. And do you, Father Guardian, commend me to the Minister and the Guardian at Perugia and to all the brethren in general. All the suffragan bishops appointed by the Lord Pope Clement for the see of Kambalik have departed to the Lord in peace. I alone remain. Brother Nicholas of Banthra [Banzia] and Brother Andrutius of Assisi and another bishop died on their entry into Lower India in an exceedingly hot country where many other brethren have died and been buried.

May your Paternity fare well in the Lord now and for ever.

Given at Zayton in the year of Our Lord 1326 in the month of January.

[1] The martyrdom of the Franciscans at Tana near Bombay took place in 1321.

INDEX